M000202102

To my reasons why...
my husband, Evan,
and my children, Brayden, Chase, and Parker

ON THE
EDGE OF
SHATTERED

A Mother's Experience of
Discovering Freedom
Through Sobriety

KIMBERLY KEARNS

Copyright ©2022 Kimberly Kearns

ISBN: 978-1-957917-10-8 (paperback edition)
ISBN: 978-1-957917-11-5 (e-book edition)

Library of Congress Control Number: 2022915315

All rights reserved. No part of this book may be reproduced, stored in a retrieval system, or transmitted in any form or by any means without prior written permission from
the author, except for the use of brief quotations in a book review.

Cover design by Judith S. Design & Creativity
www.judithsdesign.com
Published by Glass Spider Publishing
www.glassspiderpublishing.com
Author photo by Erica Pezente

GLASSSPIDERPUBLISHING

You can't really know where you are going until
you know where you have been.
—Maya Angelou

PART I

November 27, 2020

My first line of defense is always our dog, and tending to him is the perfect excuse to be alone in the house. A smart move on my part.

"I need to put Bunker in the crate," I say to my children and husband. "I'll be out in a minute."

Managing the dog falls under my daily job description, among practically every other household chore. Getting Bunker was a family decision, but after only a few months, I am now in charge of all things canine. I deal with the feeding. The walking. And everything in between. Now this Covid puppy has become my fourth baby.

I'm often complaining about the lack of help from my family when it comes to the stinky little guy, but at times like this I won't complain. Dealing with Bunker allows me to stay behind. To linger. It's a nice way to secretly do what I need to do without anyone questioning my behavior.

"Let's go, kids! We want to pick out the best Christmas tree on the lot before they're all gone!" I announce, my voice slightly shrill. I wipe my sweaty palms on my jeans.

It's almost nine o'clock in the morning. It is completely gray out on this November day in New England, but thankfully, it's unseasonably warm. We have a babysitter for the kids coming later in the afternoon to give us a break, which is rare. It's hard to find someone these days. No one wants to go into other people's houses for fear of getting exposed to the virus.

Bunker looks up at me with an accusing stare, as if he can tell what's on my mind. I scowl at him. My neck and shoulders ache, and my fingers start to fidget with the house keys. I hold my slender hands out in front of me briefly and stare at them, quivering ever so slightly. I stuff my fists into the back pockets of my jeans. Only I know why my body feels this way.

"Now, people!" I yell again at my kids. "Are you trying to move this slowly on purpose?"

"I don't want a coat," Brayden says.

"You need one. You don't have a choice," I tell him.

Chase looks up at me, smiles, and zips his fleece jacket. I attempt to help my children by fetching their boots. I stand by while my youngest, Parker, struggles to zip her faux-fur jacket. All three of my kids are at the age where they should be more self-sufficient. They're in elementary school and shouldn't need my help getting out the door like this anymore. They aren't babies, for goodness' sake. But they like their mom's attention, and I can't help but smile at my daughter when she finally figures out her fancy leopard-print coat.

"Okay, go get in the car! I'll be right out!" I say, frantically ushering them along.

I know I should just follow them out the door, but I can't do it. There's a need. This force pulls me. It's something I can't control; a want deep within that directs my movements, my thoughts, my hands, as I gently guide my children by the shoulders out the door.

"Geez, Mom, why are you being so pushy?" Brayden demands, kicking a soccer cleat out of his way.

The comment and the irritated look in his blue eyes sting, and it causes a sadness deep within my belly. I feel torn for a moment. But I'm power-less. These are "unprecedented times," they keep saying. But I don't even care. It's the weekend. I'm technically off the clock.

My husband, Evan, oblivious to the inner turmoil I feel, walks to the driver's side of the Expedition. He is consumed by his own thoughts—like usual. He's immune to the arguing and couldn't care less about who has a coat on and who doesn't. I've been the one homeschooling these kids non-stop while Evan gets to shower and dress and go to work every day. At this point in the week, I am so done. I need everyone out of this house right now so I can just be alone for one minute before we leave.

I show the kids out the door of our disheveled mudroom and scoop up Bunker. I press my back against the heavy door, hearing it click behind me. The silence envelops me and I sigh. I feel giddy now. The drastic change in emotion makes my heart race, and my head throbs a tiny bit less. I wait a moment before I walk down the narrow hallway, tucking the wiggling dog under my arm.

I pull open the bathroom door and position it so that it blocks any direct view from the hallway. My second line of defense. If anyone were to run back in from the garage, the door would block them from seeing me in the midst of my indiscretions.

I need to keep this ritual completely private. What I'm about to do will stay secret, known only to me. My husband doesn't ever need to see this. My kids must never know.

I shuffle past three large canvas photos on the wall of our children from years ago, avoiding the leering eyes of their baby faces. It's been a long week. It's a holiday weekend. We're in a global pandemic. I deserve this, even if it's only nine o'clock in the morning.

When I get to the hutch that functions as our bar top, I feel like I'm floating. I'm on autopilot now. I've done this a hundred times.

My hands tremble with anticipation, and I plop the dog down on the floor. I avoid thinking about my kids in the car. Or my husband, anxiously waiting. Are they wondering what I'm doing? I don't care. I need this to survive the day and to nourish my present hangover. Mama deserves this.

A wave of nausea washes over me as I look at the dirty shot glasses lining the bar top. My stomach heaves just seeing the filmy residue of alcohol left at the bottom of each glass. I contemplate the many times I've stood here. I remember the lies I've told, and the memories hit me out of nowhere. If only these dirty shot glasses could speak.

I reach for one now. I can't even bring myself to touch it. But I need it to make it through the day ahead.

I take a deep breath and grab the bottle of Tito's vodka. The bottles clink together, sending a gentle ringing through the cavernous house, down the hallway and into the mudroom.

I turn my back to my dog. I don't need to see Bunker's judgmental eyes on me now.

I am a robot. A machine, unable to fight it. I am a character inside a video game.

My heart pounds. The veins inside my head and down my neck throb. It's as if there's a screaming inside my ears.

I just need one sip to ignite my body. To soothe my insides. To feel something. Because lately . . . I feel nothing.

I know exactly what I'm doing because I've perfected this routine.

With my left hand, I twist the gold top off and watch as it falls to the wooden bar top. It moves almost in slow motion, and I hold my breath as it spins in a circle on the counter and makes a tiny clicking sound.

I listen for the sounds of my children or husband as Bunker rubs his face against my ankles curiously. I hear nothing. I am alone. Finally.

The scream inside begins to gently subside as I wrap my fingers around the Tito's bottle. For a split second, I consider the shot glasses in front of me again, as that is my usual ritual, but I've waited too damn long now. I can feel every muscle in my body begin to relax as I raise the bottle to my mouth. And as the cool, clear liquid finally burns my tongue, the thumping inside begins to quiet. I take another large gulp while my family waits patiently for me in the car.

I deserve this.

I'm fine. This isn't a big deal.

November 28, 2020

I open my left eye and see darkness all around me. There's a pulsating inside my head. A heaviness within. A stabbing pain deep in my brain sends a jolt through my body. I open my other eye and breathe in the stale air. My mouth is dry, and I try to clear my throat.

I'm totally naked except for my right sock, which is starting to slip off from around my heel. A feeling strikes deep inside my belly. I immediately wonder: *Did I screw up again?* But I know the answer. It's the same damn thing as it always is on mornings like this.

I lay still, slowly absorbing the muted colors of the room, allowing my surroundings to come into focus. I recognize the duvet that we took so painstakingly long to choose one Saturday morning at Pottery Barn when picking out our bedroom decor many years ago. I sit up a bit more and recognize the coordinated ivory rug and cornflower-blue throw pillows. We argued over the color of that rug, but I won.

I try to think back to last night. What time did we get home? Why do I have one sock on? I rewind the tape to the car. The mudroom. The night goes dark after that.

I close my eyes again.

At thirty-eight years old, I always pictured our life just as it is. A husband. Three kids. A house in the 'burbs. Living outside of Boston. A bright, neatly decorated home with elegant New England style. Lots of light blues and whites in every room. I had told Evan exactly what I wanted life to look like over brunch and mimosas before we ever had kids. Now here we are.

I lie in bed and gaze at the long, black shadows cast across the gray wall in the early-morning light. There's a slight comfort in knowing that I wound up in my bedroom last night instead of on the mudroom or kitchen floor. It's happened before.

I wonder if the kids are okay. I remember coming home and relieving the babysitter early, but I don't remember putting the kids to bed. My heart thumps wildly deep within my chest. But when I glance over and see Evan sleeping peacefully beside me, snoring, I know the kids are fine. Ever the responsible one, he probably tucked them all in last night, me included. He's always so blissfully content at this time of the day. Unlike me, he never wakes up frantic and confused.

A small sliver of moonlight shines in from the window across the room.

Without checking the clock, I know what time it is. Four o'clock in the morning. The fog of booze always lifts at around this hour. This is usually when I emerge from my blackout.

I lie still another few minutes and squeeze my eyes shut as the room spins. I don't want the day to begin. But at the same time, I want the painful loneliness of this shameful routine to end.

I stare up at the artwork above our headboard, which was meant to complement the hues of the rest of the bedroom. This was the final piece when designing the space that made it feel complete. The Bermuda beach scene appears distorted in the morning light. No longer picturesque and bright, the painting has grown dark and gruesome. The beautiful coastal cliffs look threatening in the pale shadows. Maybe it's just the hangover, but it appears as if the sea is angry, about to swallow me whole. The sky—a mass of dark rain clouds—is ready to open up and storm down on me.

The familiarity of my situation dawns on me as I try to piece together the events of yesterday. We decorated our Christmas tree in the morning; that I do remember. I fumble around and search for my phone on the bedside table, unwilling to shift the hair off my face. If I don't move anything else, maybe then I'll fall back asleep.

Why do I always do this to myself?

A few moments pass, and I prop myself up on my elbow in hopes of spotting my phone somewhere on the sheets.

I need water.

A throbbing pain jabs at my skull.

Where is my cell phone?

I look over the edge of the bed and see the damn thing lodged between the nightstand and the edge of the mattress in one of its usual hiding places. How the hell does my phone always end up down there? I manage to grab it without my insides exploding and brace myself for the dreaded game of *who did I text last night?* But I can't deal with that shame game yet, so I toss the phone aside.

I lie back down and think through yesterday evening some more, attempting to piece together one fragmented memory after the next. I vaguely remember staring at the lights on the Christmas tree last night. Did Evan and I have an argument? Likely. Anything is possible on a night when the curtains have come down.

I want to vomit, and I lean over the side of the bed looking for a trash can. There is a realization that I'm shaking. Full-body tremors accompanied by sweat.

Why did I start sneaking drinks so early in the day yesterday? I begin to cry.

I check to make sure Evan is still asleep. I can't risk him waking and wondering what's wrong. I bury my face in the pillow and heave a few deep sobs.

Rolling out of bed, I manage to land on my feet and stumble into the bathroom. I can't let him hear me. I need to get away from this room. I need to make these feelings stop.

In the bathroom, I close my eyes and sit on the floor. Curling into a ball on the tile, I begin to shiver. A few moments pass, and a darkness presses down on me. A heaviness.

I imagine that I'm in the ocean, inside the painting of Bermuda, the one from above our bed. I'm alone at the bottom of the steep cliffs standing ankle-deep in the turquoise blue water. The saltwater bubbles around my feet, anchoring me. I am by myself at the base of the rocks, and I can hear the distant calls of the Bermuda Longtails flying above and children's laughter nearby. But the roar of the ocean is deafening and all around me. The clouds are dark, and I can feel the rain begin to pelt my naked body.

Looking over my shoulder, I envision a massive wave charging toward me, the churning white cap careening high above. I look up at the face of the rocks in search of help. Is there someone who can guide me up and out of the water? Desperately, I study the cliff for a passage to the light above, out of the murkiness and away from the danger below.

How can I get to my children? My husband? I hear their voices, but I cannot see them.

I hear them calling for me.

"Mom!"

The waves crash, and thunder rumbles on the distant horizon.

"Kim!"

"Mommy!"

Can I climb up the sides out of this dark chasm?

My hands slip on the wet rocks. I try to yell, but my words can't be heard over the roar. My fingernails dig into the crumbling rock as pieces of it fall away beneath me. I picture the wave as it crashes into my body, pinning me against the jagged pillar.

I hear my children crying now.

I see my husband's hands over the side, and I reach for them.

I want to climb up and out of this lonely abyss. I am drowning.

Grabbing at the rocks, I see myself start to climb, my feet slipping and bleeding.

All at once, the dark clouds are no longer, and I see sunshine. My children's faces peer over the edge. My husband smiles down at me.

I truly believed I loved the ocean. I really thought I wanted to live by the sea. I tried to make a home beneath the rocks, but I didn't realize the strength of this world. The pull of the waves. The tide came in without me realizing, and I've grown weak.

It's too dangerous and cold by this ocean. Too lonely down here. And I can no longer live in the shadows of my secrets.

There is always a choice in this world, I realize as I open my eyes, drawing myself away from the dark images in my mind. I sit on the floor of the bathroom and pull my robe up around my naked body, shivering on the freezing tile. Slowly, I drag myself up, using the counter to stand on my feet. Hesitantly, I look at the person in the mirror.

Pale-faced with mascara smeared in deep, black circles beneath my hollow green eyes, I look at myself. My long brown hair hangs loosely around my pale, freckled cheeks.

I manage to find my way back to bed and look over at Evan, still asleep. I look at the bit of stubble on his cheek and chin that never fully manages to grow in. I contemplate the Bermuda cliffs and ocean scene above our bed, listening to his heavy breathing.

In that moment, I am overcome with feeling. An unbearable thought that I need to share with my husband.

Unable to fully trust that I can do what needs to be done, I reach over and gently poke his shoulder. He doesn't move.

I sigh and consider just curling back up into a ball. Let the waves wash over me. But instead, there is a flash of light through the roaring, murky gray. I feel something strong. Slowly, a brightness begins to pull me from the shadows, and a force pushes me forward. I breathe deeply.

I can't keep putting myself through this shameful cycle anymore. I can't keep waking up feeling this way every day. It has to stop.

Something guides my hands, a tiny force within, and I surprise myself with my sudden courage. I find myself putting my hand on Evan's muscular back. His balding forehead catches the moonlight.

Using both hands, I try to wake him again. He doesn't move. I shake him. Nothing. Then, before I know it, with a rush of adrenaline I grab him with all of my strength.

"Evan! Evan, wake up!"

"What?" he asks, suddenly alert.

"I need you."

"What? What are you doing?"

"I need to talk to you."

"What's wrong?"

"I think . . . I need to talk to you about something."

I wait a moment. We sit in silence, and he attempts to pull me close to him. He knows there's something wrong. But I sit back and take a deep breath. Does he know what I'm about to say? Maybe he's been waiting for this.

"I think . . . I think I need your help. What would you say if I asked you to help me stop drinking? Would you help me?"

He wraps himself around me, squeezes me tightly, and kisses the top of my head. "I would say absolutely. If that's what you need."

"Really?"

"Yes. I'll help you. I'll do whatever you need me to do."

"I don't know how," I say, crying into the sheets.

"It's okay, we can do this."

"Will you stop drinking too?"

"If you want me to, I can."

"How do I do this?"

"We'll figure this out, Kim."

As I lay there crying, I feel a lightness. A deep, dark heaviness seems to subside, and a pressure slowly begins to release.

I don't know what I'm doing, and I'm scared. But I've finally said the words out loud that I've been ignoring for far too long, and there's no taking them back now. I feel relieved to have finally told my husband what I've been wanting to say.

I've been going full speed, unable to control myself, wondering when I'm going to crash. Finally, it's as if someone has hit the brakes and I'm coming to a halt. I wipe my tears. My racing thoughts ease to a crawl, and the blurred images come into focus.

Little do I know that this moment will mark the beginning of a long road that will force me to confront parts of my life that I worked hard to forget—unlocking a door I'd once sealed shut, and finally setting myself free.

Growing up in Greenwich (1988): Six Years Old

Growing up with my family in Greenwich, Connecticut, in the eighties, life felt simple. I was born in 1982—a true eighties child. Our yellow house sat on the corner of Winterset Road in a quiet neighborhood of wide, meandering roads. Set back behind a row of trees but still visible from the street, the long driveway was perfect for bike riding. The front yard dipped down toward a small creek in front where we spent many childhood winters sledding.

Our house was situated on a hill with mature oak trees. Acres of woods stretched out behind our grassy backyard, providing endless space to explore. Winding brooks led to ponds buried deep within the hills of the forest. Fallen trees of thick brush provided spaces for make-believe and hide-and-go-seek. I imagined living there forever.

The house was special, and it existed as more than just a home to me. It gave me a safe world where I could explore, create, and learn. Later, I would unknowingly spend much of my life searching to recreate the spirit and emotion I felt there as a child, for my own family.

Having two older sisters, I was fortunate. Jen was four years older than me, and Laura was born only eighteen months before me. Mom stayed home full time, and her job was to take care of us, and I was grateful for that. Dad worked hard starting his own insurance brokerage company, and he focused on giving us all the extravagance he felt we deserved. He wanted to provide all the things he never had growing up underprivileged in rural New Hampshire. He wanted a different life for us, and we were lucky.

"Girls, dinnertime in a half hour!" Mom called as I ran out the door into the backyard carrying her best Tupperware to make mud pies. "And bring back my dishes, Kimmy!"

"I promise I will. Be back later!" I yelled, chasing after my sisters. I was the type of six-year-old who didn't mind getting messy. I preferred being outdoors exploring, catching frogs, and climbing trees.

The woods behind our home were dark and deep. They stretched far back for what felt like miles, blanketed in rolling hills of thick maples, oaks, and evergreens. My sisters and I explored these jungly woods but never ventured too far, always keeping the house in view. Although I sometimes had visions of getting lost back there and never finding my way back home, the monsters stealing me away for good, the quiet whistle of the wind through the leaves in the trees always comforted me, and I craved the adventure that awaited every afternoon when I climbed off the school bus.

My sisters and I played make-believe at the top of a steep hill by a massive tree stump at the edge of our yard. We spent hours pretending to be "the Wilderness family" surviving alone in the rural mountains of Canada. We made our little home on the wet leaves and cold rocks beneath the branches of the trees. The three of us played there until the sun began to set behind the tall woods in the distance and the spring peepers began their evening calls.

From a very early age, I knew I was fortunate to grow up in such a safe neighborhood in a town like Greenwich. It was ingrained in me; in all of us. I learned for myself and eventually saw firsthand that the rest of the world was not afforded the same opportunities I was given as a child.

My mother, Gay, worked hard to maintain a modest image, having grown up in Orange, Massachusetts, and attended college in Keene, New Hampshire. She didn't shop at the fancy stores like Saks on Greenwich Avenue like the other moms I knew. She enjoyed sewing, crafting, and baking.

My dad, John, took us on extravagant vacations and gave us memberships to country clubs—always a point of contention between him and Mom. Dad grew up in Keene, New Hampshire, and spent his childhood summers on a farm in Whitefield. He wanted us to thrive and find success in life, and I guess he hoped that living in Greenwich would provide us with endless opportunities to do so.

I grew to understand that the rest of the country didn't look like the pristine, perfectly manicured, tree-lined streets of Greenwich. I knew it wasn't normal that some of my friends' families had private chefs or a full staff at their disposal to shop, clean, cook, and chauffeur them around town, to school, or into "the city," as we called it. As I got older, I discovered not everyone in this world belonged to a separate yacht club and country club. Eventually, I came to the realization that not every family in the United States had the ability to "summer" on Nantucket and spend their Christmas vacations on a private yacht in the British Virgin Islands. We didn't vacation that way, but it seemed that everyone I knew did.

While Dad worked hard trying to give us a privileged life, Mom would have been happy without any of it. She appreciated the simple things and often talked about moving back to New Hampshire. Still, it seemed my parents compromised. We vacationed often, spending summers at our modest lake house in New Hampshire near our extended family. We skied in Vermont and took yearly trips to the island of Bermuda.

Because money breeds opportunity, the people in the town of Greenwich pursued overly ostentatious lifestyles that oozed materialism and greed. And much like the sprawling homes that stood ominously behind the protective gates that lined the backcountry roads of Greenwich, my parents put up their own shields to protect our family, as well. Mom and Dad each had secrets they kept from themselves and from the people around them.

For a long time, I was led to believe that the town I loved and the place that I called home played a delicate role in the demise of my parent's marriage. But sadly, Mom and Dad each struggled in ways far deeper than I realized. It is true that my family tried to conform to the wealthy lifestyle around them, but privilege doesn't make you immune to pain. Eventually, I was forced to recognize this. I had no choice but to one day confront my family's painful, secretive past, as well as my own.

Day 1: November 28, 2020

It smells like Saturday nights, friends, and laughter. But I feel none of the sensations that normally accompany these things. I squeeze my body tight to keep from shivering, and I watch the light-pink liquid flow out of the bottle of my favorite rosé, Whispering Angel, as Evan tips it toward the drain. It trickles into the sink, and the sweet, tart smell fills the air.

I plug my nose, close my eyes, and take a deep breath to calm down. As much as I will myself not to, I can't help it—I allow my hand to drop and breathe deeply through my nose. The smell washes over me as energy surges down my spine. A need. A want. A yearning.

I am disgusted by this part of me.

I sit numbly in the kitchen, cold, hugging my knees to my chest. I balance on the Serena & Lily counter stool at our oversized island. Evan lines up the empty wine bottles on the marble countertop beside the sink, and I roll my eyes at his organization. Typical of his type A personality to create nice rows of bottles from smallest to largest. I wonder why he bothers with such precision when they're just going to be tossed into the recycling.

Next, I watch Evan pour out the bottle of Tito's vodka, the very same bottle I drank from yesterday. I close my eyes again. I can't watch this part.

In the upstairs playroom, the boys argue over Xbox as their sister yells at them to stop fighting. I squeeze the bridge of my nose, mustering up strength from within not to scream back at them.

"How are you doing?" Evan asks me. He finishes emptying the bottles into the sink and stares intently at me, eyebrows furrowed. He narrows one eye at me in a playful way but smiles at the same time, a gesture I usually find charming and sweet. He leans into the countertop, his favorite faded green t-shirt from high school looking slightly tight across his belly. I don't want to smile at him or anyone else right now. I just want to cry.

"I have no idea," I say to him, resting my head on my knees.

"I'm proud of you," he tells me.

"Thanks," I sigh.

"You know how many times I've told you how worried your drinking makes me. I'm proud of you for wanting to do something about it." He sits on the stool beside me, attempting to get closer.

I stare back blankly and shrug. My body is weak. I pick up my phone and begin reading an article I found earlier when I Googled "How to stop drinking alcohol." The search results brought up a scary list of links, but I chose one that seemed a bit less frightening than the rest. It's a brief article that offers "six tips on how to quit." I start skimming.

"What are you looking at?" Evan asks.

"I'm reading an article."

"Okay." He stares at me, waiting for me to say more.

"Do you think I should join a support group?" I look at my husband.

He sits back and crosses his arms over his chest. "Do you think you need it?" he asks, looking worried. He has no idea that as he was emptying the bottle of Tito's, I was seriously contemplating snatching it away and chugging from it. One last hurrah. He doesn't even realize that I'm still thinking about the translucent blush wine, crisp and refreshing, and that it took every bit of strength in me not to steal one last taste.

"Yeah, it might be nice to get a little help from someone who knows what they're doing. Francy mentioned something called The Luckiest Club."

"Okay, what's that? You aren't going to, like, go to AA, right?"

"So what if I did? I talked to Jen and told her that I need her help. She said her brother has been going to AA." I've slowly been texting certain friends over the last hour, quietly firing my flare gun. I feel the need to sound an alarm for some reason. To strategically alert certain people of this life-altering moment because I'm not quite sure if I believe it's happening. I need to hold myself accountable, I guess.

"Oh, I don't know," Evan says. "That's fine, I guess. You do whatever you need to do. I'm here for you with whatever you decide."

He looks away from me, and I feel embarrassed by this conversation. I feel judged by my husband, the one person I thought wouldn't be judgmental. How am I going to do this when even Evan is ashamed of me? Neither of us ever imagined ourselves at this point.

I fold my arms onto the counter, balling my hands into fists. I lay my head down and close my eyes, refusing to look at him, exhausted all at once by the conversation unfolding.

Then the doorbell rings. Evan sighs at the realization that we won't be finishing this talk after all. I rise from the stool and make my way to the front door. Standing before me is the one person I was able to reach this morning that may understand what I'm going through. Francy smiles widely, holding a huge box of Dunkin' Donuts and two coffee cups.

"I come bearing gifts!" Francy announces, marching into the house, disregarding any and all Covid protocol, and I couldn't care less. "Donuts for the kids! Coffee for you and Evan!" She wraps me in her arms. Francy stopped drinking almost five years ago, and she's one of the only people I know who is sober. It's barely seven o'clock in the morning, and this friend is at my doorstep. With presents! And I don't even know her all that well. We see each other at school drop-offs and our kids' soccer games. I texted her at five o'clock in the morning, asking her if she might have some advice for me. Her response was immediate. I have never felt so much love than

I do at this moment.

Francy's hair looks perfectly blown out. Her long brown ponytail hangs loosely over her shoulders, and her sparkling blue eyes prove she's more awake than anyone in my house. This lady is certainly ready for the challenge in front of her.

I stand there shifting my weight and shaking my head. "Thank you," I say, and my lip begins to quiver, but for some reason I don't feel all that embarrassed to be crying in front of her. I glance over my shoulder to make sure my kids haven't unexpectedly appeared.

"You've made the choice, and that's the hardest part. We've got this," Francy says.

"How did this become my fucking life?" I say, unable to control the tears.

I hate you. Love, Kimmy (1988): Six Years Old

"You go into the family room and watch TV, now, Kimmy," Dad said, turning me around gently and ushering me out of the kitchen.

"Are you going for a drive?" I asked.

Dad sometimes stormed out of the house in a quiet fury after dinner and got in his car. Upon his return, he told me he'd just needed a break. Wanted some time to think. All adults needed a time out too, just like kids. I wasn't supposed to ask why or I wasn't allowed to question the adults in the room, but sometimes I couldn't help myself.

"No, not tonight," Dad replied.

"Why were you yelling at each other?" I asked, looking at Mom for answers.

"No reason. Everything is fine," she said, staring at me over the rim of her wine glass as she sat perched on the counter barstool.

Some nights I heard them speaking in hushed voices after dinner while they cleared the table, scraping crusty spaghetti off the blue-and-white plates into the trash, and talking about things I couldn't understand.

Mom sometimes yelled, Dad often urging her to calm down. Jen always took on the role of wise caretaker, usually turning up the TV so that Laura and I didn't hear the arguing. Some nights, she turned on the stereo and we danced across the beige shag carpet, creating our own choreographed moves to *The Phantom of the Opera*.

"Everything is going to be okay," Jen always told me when I asked why Mom and Dad were having one of their fights.

On nights like these, I wondered why they were always so mad at each other. Why wasn't I allowed to stay in the kitchen and finish my dessert?

Laura was kind, caring, and often more oblivious than me. She lost herself in the music, unaware of what was happening at the other end of the house.

On this particular evening, I stood next to the swinging kitchen door, listening, hiding from my parents. I wanted to understand. I was curious, and I needed to know more that night. First I heard whispers. Then soft shouting. I peeked around the corner.

"Kimmy is listening again," Mom said, slurring her words. She stood and walked over to me. Taking my hand, she whispered, "Go on. Everything is fine, I promise. Bedtime soon, and we can have extra cookies tomorrow night."

I stood waiting for more and allowed her to kiss the top of my head. The smell of wine on her breath was sweet and pungent. Then she shut the kitchen door firmly. Again, I did not move. I stood alone, unable to leave.

I sat down in the darkness of the hallway. I pulled my legs up against my body, listening to the familiar sounds of the evening's argument coming to an end. It comforted me to imagine that all normalcy had resumed behind the kitchen door. Dad wiped down the counters with his blue bottle of Windex. This was his favorite part of the day, as tidying up and cleaning made him happy. I listened to the spray of the bottle and the squeak of the paper towels across the granite. He always covered every inch of the countertop at least twice.

I listened to the glug, glug, glug of wine as it poured into Mom's glass while she stood at the kitchen counter, mapping out the schedule for tomorrow in her planner. My sister's ballet practice. Softball for me.

I waited. Still. For what, I didn't know.

Then came the comforting sound of plates clanging together. More ice cubes hitting the bottom of her glass.

I stayed motionless in the quiet outside the kitchen, caught between the safety of the unknown and wanting to understand more about the adult world on the other side. I curled up in the shadowy light that spilled out beneath the door, feeling solace in the smell of my mother's pot roast and the familiar sound of the vacuum cleaner as it glided across the kitchen tile.

I snuggled into the light, listening for more conversation. Longing for more of something. For a hint. A clue. Maybe laughter. Perhaps the return of jovial conversation. I lay there waiting, but there were no more words that evening.

When I was a little girl, my world revolved around my family. Nothing could shake that. I loved my mom, dad, and sisters more than anything. That was the scope of my concern. That was all I worried about, and my parents did a good job of keeping it that way.

Occasionally, Dad forced me outside my comfort zone. He was the parent that encouraged me to try new things, and it was Mom who often suggested we take it easy.

"It's time you learn how to ski!" Dad said to us one winter morning.

"Really? Are they old enough, John?" Mom asked, wringing her hands. She was always questioning every decision, nervous about her children injuring themselves.

"Sure, of course," he stated, composed and calm. "They need to learn at some point, Gay."

I wasn't much older than six or seven when Dad dropped me off at the Little Cubs ski school with my sisters at Stratton Mountain that Saturday morning. It was one of the first weekends we traveled up to Vermont for winter break, and all of the children were separated into groups based on their abilities. I was in the beginner's group, and I hated every part of it.

There were too many excited children, and the cacophony of loud voices frightened me. I wanted nothing more than to stay back at the condo by the fire with Mom.

Everything about ski school made me feel small. I was always separated from my sisters, and I didn't know any of the other children. The day was long and tiring, and I was scared of getting lost alone on the mountain or falling and hurting myself. Most of all, I was terrified of the ski lift. The process of getting in line, getting on the chair, getting off the chair, and then skiing down the mountain just seemed too much. I was ready to quit before I began.

"I want to stay with Mom," I told Dad.

"No," Dad said, "you need to learn how to ski just like your sisters. It's a lifelong skill. You'll learn to love it. You'll see."

"John, please," Mom pleaded, "don't make her if she doesn't want to. Let her stay with me."

But Dad insisted. "No, she's doing it."

"What's the point of forcing her?"

"Because it's good for her, and she should learn to challenge herself."

So off I went, begrudgingly. I wanted to make Dad happy, so I let him drop me off to fend for myself in that foreign, arctic land. A few days into ski school, it was time for my Little Cubs group to take the final exam on the bunny hill to determine if we were ready for the chairlift.

I had a choice. I knew my sisters had both already passed the test, skiing down from the top of the mountain through the green trails with Dad. I listened to them tell me about the frozen, snow-covered trees at the top of the mountain and the beautiful view from the summit. But I insisted that I had no interest in doing or seeing any of it. I crossed my arms over my chest and stared at the ground.

"I don't care. I don't want to do it," I told them.

"You're missing out," Laura said.

"It's so fun!" Jen told me.

There was a part of me that wondered how far you could see from the mountaintop. Did it really feel like being in the clouds? But the sheer height of the peak, and having to ride the chairlift, paralyzed me with fear. When it came time to ride the magic carpet up the bunny slope to perform the three small pie turns for my ski instructors, I knew what I had to do.

I had made a friend in my group named Mikey. He was in the same boat, equally terrified and spiteful of his parents for forcing him into ski school all week. He went first, showing me exactly what to do to fail the test. As he purposefully tumbled head over heels, skis and poles flying every which way, I giggled to myself. When it was my turn, I did exactly as Mikey had done. I crossed my skis and landed in a heap on top of him at the bottom of the bunny hill. Mikey and I high-fived.

I had succeeded. There would be no way the instructors would force me onto the ski lift. And I was right. That morning, for once, my determination prevailed, and I didn't have to continue onto the top of the mountain with the rest of my ski class.

That afternoon, though, when Dad found out what I'd done, he gave me no choice and told me it was time to face my fears. I couldn't hide. I felt a little braver with him beside me on the chairlift, but not much. I was also annoyed that my plan had backfired. After all my conniving, Dad still found a way to get me up on the mountain. I felt completely defeated and terrified when he gave me a small nudge and sent me flying down the hill.

"I hate you!" I screamed at him, terror filling my tiny body.

But once I got going and felt the wind in my face, something switched. I began to move my body, practicing the pizza pie like my instructors had shown me in class. Before I realized it, I was turning, and I made a large swoop across the mountain, the snow gliding beneath me.

The thrill was incredible. Feeling the ice crunch under my skis and the trees whizzing by was something I had never experienced before, and I realized I was having fun. I found myself going back and forth, back and forth, finishing at the bottom of the run with a huge smile.

"That was so cool!" I said. "Let's go again!"

"I knew you could do it!" Dad said, laughing, pulling up behind me.

We did it again and again, all afternoon. From that point on, I was a skier. My parents couldn't get me off the mountain, and I lived on the double black diamonds from morning until night.

"Scotland's burning, Scotland's burning!" I sang on the chairlift.

"Look out! Look out!" Laura chimed in.

"Fire! Fire! Fire! Fire!" Jen shouted.

"Pour on water! Pour on water!" Dad sang along.

These were the ways we kept warm on the ski lift as kids with my dad, singing old folk tunes we'd learned in music class at school. As soon as we stepped off the chairlift, we chased one another to the bottom of the hill. We continued this routine until the sun began to set late into the day, and I was content to come home to find Mom welcoming me with hot cocoa and a warm dinner every evening.

Skiing became part of who I was. It defined me. I spent weekends perfecting my form, only stopping once or twice to thaw my frozen toes in the warming hut at the bottom of the mountain.

On the weekends when we weren't skiing in Vermont, we were back home in Greenwich, where Mom and Dad were strict about us going to church every Sunday. We were raised Protestant and expected to attend the congregational church up off Stanwich Road. Every Sunday morning was a battle of wills that ended in ripped tights and the silent treatment.

"I hate church!" I yelled from the back seat of the car, arms crossed against my chest, yanking at the lacy trim on the dress Mom had picked out for me. "It's so stupid. And it's boring. And it smells funny!"

"It's good for every one of us to go to church. You need to learn about Jesus," Mom said. "Don't you want to be a nice little girl? This is how we're reminded to be kind to one another, Kimmy."

"You can pray and talk to God. You can ask for your forgiveness there," Dad said.

"I don't need forgiveness. I *am* a nice little girl!" I screamed, sticking my tongue out at them when they weren't looking. I pulled the pink bow out of my hair and pushed my thick brown bangs out of my eyes. Mom insisted on keeping our hair short, trimming it every few weeks on the stool at the kitchen counter. My sisters and I all had brown hair and bowl cuts, mine being the largest and roundest of all.

Mom and Dad seemed hopeful and determined, week after week, as if attending those church services would provide the answers to all of their questions. I despised sitting in the cold pews and listening to the painfully long sermons, though. I wanted nothing more than to tear off the flowered dress Mom always picked out for me and to hop onto my bike or dig up worms in the backyard at home.

I never found the relief that Mom and Dad experienced behind those sterile church walls. I never experienced the peace and joy that my parents seemed to feel after listening to the pastor. I only ever felt agitated, confined, and confused.

Sometimes after I got home from church I'd write small notes to my family members and stuff them into Mom's expensive vases or hide them under couch cushions. I think I secretly hoped that my parents would find these messages someday, or perhaps it was my way of rebelling against their rules. I don't know if I was acting out to get attention, but I felt the need to write my feelings down and release my frustrations. I wanted to have secrets of my own, because whether I knew it or not, my parents kept things from me.

The messages I left said things like "You're so mean, Mommy," or "I hate you, Daddy—love, Kimmy." It made me feel better about being forced to do the things I hated.

What does Jesus think of that? I wondered.

Day 2: November 29, 2020

I hear a crash in the family room and the sounds of what might be the beginning of a scuffle between Brayden and Chase.

"Can you keep the peace downstairs, please?" I ask Evan, sighing with frustration.

"Yes," he says. "How long will the meeting last?"

"It's an hour, but who knows if I'll stay that long. I have no idea what to expect. Wish me luck."

Evan wraps his arms around me and presses his body against mine. His warmth is reassuring. I rest my head on his shoulder for a moment. I turn around and reach to shut the door, but he stops me.

"You got this," he says. "I'm so proud of you. Seriously. You going to these meetings. This is amazing. Incredible, actually. I mean it. You can do this. Don't worry about the kids, okay? Take your time."

"Thanks." I know he's trying to be extra supportive after coming across judgmental and noncommittal yesterday. It's just all so new to both of us.

"Good luck," he says and kisses me.

I close the bedroom door and walk into my closet. It feels quiet and warm, away from the chaos. Being in this enclosed space feels safe. But when I contemplate the number of times I hid in here with a glass of wine or a bottle of vodka, I feel sick.

This closet is my private retreat. Row after row of neatly folded pants and sweaters line the wall to my right. All my things are placed in cubbies, color coded and organized by season. I have a section for dresses, skirts, and an extra-long rack for my shirts and blouses. The wall to my right contains dozens of neatly folded yoga pants and workout clothing in a variety of material and patterns. There are drawers, shelves, and shoe racks as well as a small stool to sit on. This orderly hideaway is my sanctuary. I settle down onto the floor, placing my laptop on the fabric covered stool.

I just spent the last two hours researching online recovery support groups. There are quite a few now. Francy read about this one. It was started by a woman from Marblehead, Massachusetts. Knowing she lived close to Boston felt like a sign.

The Luckiest Club began in early Covid, and all meetings are on Zoom. There are no in-person meetings, which is a good thing and a bad thing. It's good because I don't need to leave the house. But some say it is a bad thing. Apparently, human contact during sobriety is important. But these days, we don't have much of a choice.

I login into Zoom two minutes early and park in the virtual waiting room. My heart beats uncontrollably, and even though I know I don't need to turn my camera on and no one even needs to see me, I'm terrified.

What if I recognize someone in the meeting? What if I get called on to talk because there are only a few people? It feels like I'm back in third grade and the teacher is asking us to introduce ourselves and our favorite flavor of ice cream, the words "let's go around the room" sending anxious shock waves through my body. How is this my goddamn life?

I hear the kids beginning to argue and fight downstairs, but Evan's job is to keep them quiet and out of my room for the next sixty minutes.

Let's see if we can do this.

My laptop screen lights up. The meeting begins, and I see hundreds of tiny faces on my computer screen staring back at me.

"Welcome to The Luckiest Club!" the moderator announces.

I am overwhelmed. Tears well up in my eyes when she begins to speak. She has such kind eyes. Her name is Louise, and she has an English accent. She explains the rules of the group. You can't take pictures. You can't share personal information. It is a safe space. I don't have to talk or turn my camera on, she reminds me. I double-check that there's a black box on the screen where my face should be. I feel my body relax slightly. I listen to Louise's soft, soothing voice.

"Here is a poem by Charles C. Finn. The poem describes the many different masks we all wear, as we all put up a facade. Everyone is in disguise, just trying to survive," she says. "Get comfy, sit back, and chill. It's a long one. Close your eyes, and let the words wash over you."

I do as I'm told. Like an obedient student, I close my eyes and feel a release. This isn't so scary.

Louise's words trail off, and I realize for the first time that there are others out there who feel just like me. I can't help but watch the people on the screen. The woman in the bottom right corner, she looks like someone I would be friends with.

I flip through and see a few more women about my age, and I begin to relax a bit. Maybe I'm not so alone after all. I lean back, gazing at the hundreds of tiny eyes spread across my computer screen. I feel as if I'm full of a million cracks, waiting to shatter into pieces. I'm hanging onto the edge. But it's time for me to heal. To remove my mask. To start remembering.

Wolves in People's Skins (1989): Seven Years Old

As a little girl, I liked to walk the country club golf course near our house with my family. One fall afternoon, skipping along after my sisters through the orange and yellow leaves decorating the fairway, I looked up at the large houses that sat on the hilltops looming over us.

"Where are the people that live there?" I asked Dad. "Why is it always so dark up in those houses?"

We all stopped walking and peered up at the blackened windows, searching for movement in the towering, stately homes. Some afternoons you'd see a light or two on, but for the most part, the homes always looked uninhabited. Vacant and frigid. Occasionally, a figure passed through, a shadow behind a window, suggesting some life that existed beyond the darkness.

"I think I see someone!" Laura whispered, pointing at one especially large brick home.

"Ah, yes. But those are wolves," Dad said with a smirk. "They're wearing people's skins. They're just pretending to be human."

"What? How do you know that?" I asked incredulously, a shiver creeping down my spine.

"I saw one once, a long time ago, when I was out here walking by myself," Dad replied matter-of-factly.

"No way! Liar!" I snapped and quickened my pace.

"I did. They hide up there in those enormous homes and come out only at night."

"I know that's not true," I retorted, trying not to look directly at the houses for fear the wolves would spot me watching them.

"Well, someday, you'll learn. You'll see," Dad said wistfully, tipping his baseball cap down low over his face.

"Oh, John, don't scare them," Mom said, scolding him like a child.

I turned back around one last time to stare into the windows on the hills. "It's a joke, right?" I asked Dad, chasing after him, but I couldn't help shake the feeling we were being watched by someone or something.

I often thought about the wolves when I went to sleep at night. I envisioned them sneaking into my bedroom and capturing me, bloody human masks covering their large, hairy faces. I hid under my blankets, certain I'd never see my family again. For many years after, I wondered why Dad told me such stories.

But was it possible? Could it be? Maybe there were people out there moving through the world disguised as something else. Maybe I could be deceived by what was right in front of me. Did everyone have something to hide? What was Dad not telling me?

Day 3: November 30, 2020

I curl my legs underneath me and stare outside at the bleak morning. I wait for a glimpse of sunlight to ease me into my day. The drab colors of the gray sky match my mood.

Every car that rumbles by outside the house feels like a jackhammer inside my brain. Everything hurts. My entire body and every inch of my skin. This headache won't quit for three days now. I'm so damn tired.

I guess this is all part of early recovery, yet I can't help but feel it's some sort of punishment.

The gas fireplace roars beside me, giving off a small amount of heat. I shiver, craving more warmth. Glancing at the lights on the Christmas tree, I notice a single strand is broken near the top. I stare at the empty black hole, a strange feeling of closeness to the small absence of light inside the tree.

It's only six o'clock in the morning. I've been sitting here for an hour, and now my coffee is cold. I take a sip anyway.

The days between Thanksgiving and Christmas always feel dark and gloomy. That's why everyone knows these are the best days to drink. This cozy chair is my favorite spot to sit in the evenings with my wine. I never sit here in the mornings at this time of day. With coffee. Everything feels so off. So backward.

I've made it to my third day of sobriety. During last night's meeting of The Luckiest Club, the moderator, Louise, said the physical withdrawal I'm experiencing is normal. I didn't ask this question; I still had my camera off.

Whenever I've tried to cut back on my drinking in the past, I've felt this way. I'm no stranger to the discomfort. It's awful, almost enough to make me want to quit quitting, but not quite enough to necessitate a hospital or doctor's visit.

There's no alcohol in the house, and I voiced it out loud to my husband and friends, so this time feels significantly different from all the others. Louise also said sleep would get easier, which she better be right about because I'm functioning solely on cold coffee and shitty willpower. I probably slept a total of three hours last night.

I know there's no turning around. I've spoken the words out loud for the first time to myself, and I can't take them back now.

I just wish I knew what to do. There's no road map. Besides Louise and the people in the two Zoom recovery meetings I've attended, I have no guidance. I don't even know them, and they'll probably never know me. I wish there was a manual; a day-by-day guide I could download for my Kindle.

When I was pregnant with Brayden, I read *What to Expect When You're Expecting.* I loved the regular updates and would cradle my massive protruding belly as I burped up tacos and milkshakes. I enjoyed learning about how my baby was the size of an avocado one week and a mango the next.

I wish there were a daily sobriety guide that told me what to anticipate each morning. *Today, on day three, you will have debilitating headaches, despise your husband more than you have ever in your life, and will likely feel the world has turned on you completely. But keep going, you're doing great!*

I sigh and take another sip of my cold coffee. I need to do this. I need to keep going. I lay my head against the back of the chair. Chase abruptly appears, and he walks into the family room, rubbing his large brown eyes with the back of his fists. His dark hair sticks up in different directions, and he walks directly toward me in his favorite oversized Ohio State football t-shirt. Sluggish and still groggy with sleep, he drags his gray fleece blanket from his bed. He kisses me on the cheek.

"Good morning, buddy," I say.

"Hi, Mom." He settles into my warmth, and we sit looking at the lights on the Christmas tree. "You're up so early. Usually you're always in bed and only Dad is up at this time. Why are you awake?"

"Yeah, I couldn't sleep."

We sit in silence, his head on my shoulder. He yawns.

"Well, I like having you awake early with me for once," he tells me, kissing me on the cheek again.

"Thanks. I like being awake with you, bud."

Chase has no idea the real reason I'm sitting here and what's going on with me right now. It occurs to me that I haven't been up in the early morning with my children since they were babies. Not since I sat alone nursing them in my arms. These days, Evan gets up with the kids. In the last few years, I've always been too hungover to deal with the early risers of the house. I squeeze Chase tightly, and the familiar cloud of shame descends.

I cringe, wishing away the feelings in my gut. I can't believe I've been missing out on this. All those mornings wasted, being wasted in bed. I wipe a tear from my eye.

"Are you okay?" Chase asks.

"Yep, I'm okay, buddy."

I try not to think about it. That is what I usually do—ignore such thoughts. But it's hard now. Not drinking all the time brings feelings I can't ignore. Why do I want to cry all the time?

Chase wraps his arms around my waist and I feel better. A child comforting his mother. Everything is in reverse right now. But it's peaceful. Quiet. I am okay. I relax into his hug, smelling his shampoo from the bath the night before. I smile and squeeze him hard. This little person beside me, providing so much warmth and strength, propels me forward into another sober day.

The Basement (1989): Seven Years Old

As a little girl, I used to wake up early most mornings and go straight to my basement playroom. Aside from my backyard, it was in this playroom where my imagination evolved the most. The basement was a space just for my sisters and me, which our parents never bothered to go into. It was long and narrow, with a small window and a back door with steps leading up to the back patio. On one end sat an antique record player and a box TV that had belonged to my grandmother, complete with two large knobs to change the channel. The burnt smell of the furnace, the dark-blue hue of the carpet, and the dampness the dehumidifier never achieved to expel pervades my mind to this day.

My sisters and I usually played "family" in the basement, sectioning it off into three perfectly divided areas with a yardstick and silver duct tape. We built small rooms out of old furniture, unused chairs, and other handy items we found around the house. We created kitchens and bedrooms for all of our "babies," often arguing when someone crossed over their perfectly measured, cordoned-off line.

I had names for all of my children, and I tucked them into their beds at night. I woke them up to feed them breakfast in the morning, and I tended to their every need. I had my own little "house" that I took care of every day. It was a world I could escape into that was safe and unknown to anyone else.

Sometimes, my sisters and I turned the basement into a restaurant or grocery store, but this was always our private space, away from the grownups. This was where we could be who we wanted to be. We went down there on the summer afternoons when it was too hot to play outside, or if it was raining at the pool.

One particularly humid afternoon, the clouds rolled in, the wind picked up, and the sky took on an eerie glow.

"This feels like tornado weather," Mom said. "Everyone go down to the basement!" Anxiously, she ushered us all downstairs while she kept watch in the kitchen.

"Kimmy, turn on the music!" my sisters yelled in unison.

Pulling the black round record from its paper sleeve, I set the Andrew Lloyd Webber soundtrack into the large antique record player. Above us, the dark, gruesome sky took on that orangey glow of an impending storm, and the leaves on the trees curled under. The thunderstorms closed in, and as the storms raged above us, we laughed down below in the safety of our playroom.

We sang along to all of our favorite show tunes. I kept my eye on the solitary window, searching for funnel clouds like Mom told me to do. My sisters and I did a good job of distracting one another from the storms up above, but part of me was always a little scared. What if Mom was right? What if there was that unlikely chance that a tornado touched down? It was always better to just turn the music up, not think about it, and wait for the storms to pass.

Similarly, Jen sometimes shut the door at the top of the stairs when my parents' arguments could be heard down the narrow stairwell. We distracted ourselves from the tornado of anger coming from the adults in the kitchen and escaped to the safety of our childlike games. When there was darkness up above, our world of make-believe kept us safe down below.

Day 4: December 1, 2020

At six years of age, with long blond curly ringlets that fall down past her shoulders, my daughter looks nothing like me, either now or when I was her age. She stands beside me on her tippy toes, her body barely rising past my waist. She stares at her reflection in the mirror and purses her lips. These are the kinds of behaviors she learns from the YouTube makeup tutorials she devours whenever she thinks I'm not looking.

She puts her hands on her hips and peers over one shoulder. Blowing a kiss, she blinks her long, pale eyelashes several times. Then she leans over to grab my mascara and a single curl falls across her forehead. She tosses it back over her shoulder in her precocious way, gazes up at me again in the mirror, and smiles.

"Mommy, can I try some of this? Just this once?"

Sometimes, she's so beyond her years. Please, stay small. Please, don't get any bigger. I can't help but wonder, will she ever understand my mistakes? Will she be forever damaged by the things I've done?

"No mascara today, Parker."

She frowns at me, furrowing her brow. She is fiery. Determined. "Why not?" She stomps her foot and turns back to the mirror, puckering her lips, sighing dramatically.

I notice for the first time that the light blue-gray of her eyes matches the cobalt slate stones on the new chain around my neck. The chain I gave myself yesterday. A gift of progress. A reminder. These stones signify growth, resilience. A new chapter.

I study my reflection beside my beautiful daughter. My skin is pale and blotchy, and I look tired. My hair hangs limp around my bony cheeks. Parker's face is full of light, so delicate, joyful, and soft.

I squeeze her shoulders and stare back at her. Even though she doesn't resemble me on the outside, on the inside I know she's mine. She's feisty and strong-willed. She is powerful. Brave.

"You know the answer. You're too young for makeup," I tell her, willing her to stop growing up, to freeze time. Slow down, please. Be vulnerable and learn to live confidently without hiding behind a mask, my sweet girl. I wonder why she never plays with dolls like I used to. Why doesn't she play make-believe and create a world to crawl into as I once did? Why does she want to grow up so fast?

I've seen her strength and passion. The force in all of my children is one of the things that urges me to continue moving forward. I want to see the woman she will one day become; the men my boys will turn into. It is only alone, in the darkest hours of night, that I hope and pray my children haven't taken on the lesser parts of me.

But it is out of the darkness that I've begun to emerge. Hopeful. Removing the cloak, revealing what I know I can no longer hide from.

When I was Parker's age, I used to stick the notes between the couch cushions or into antique vases when I didn't get what I wanted. When I felt forced to do things I didn't like. When I didn't get my way. I was stubborn. Spunky. Just like her. But I was also scared, and I felt a need to hide. To escape to the basement to play in a world that was not like my own. To create a life around me that was safer than what I felt. When I was my daughter's age, I didn't know the secrets that were kept from me at the time, and all the lies I was told. I didn't know it would all be so hard for me someday. I wish my parents had been honest with me.

My eyes fall on the chain around my neck again. I hope Parker knows she's safe. I hope I can be an example of strength, someone she can turn to and look to for the truth as she navigates this difficult world.

I know that the path I've taken to bring me to this point has taught me something. I need to be here for her. For all of my children. I can no longer hide and escape to the imaginary world at the bottom of a bottle. I can no longer wear a mask of my own. I can no longer keep these secrets.

What is Sex? (1989): Seven Years Old

I never really heard the word sex until I was seven. My parents didn't talk about it, and even if I heard it on TV or in the movies, I didn't wonder too much about it. One day, my friend Megan was over for a playdate in my basement when she told me all about where babies came from. She described it in great detail. I was totally confused. I didn't understand any of it, but it sounded exciting.

We decided we just had to try it. Megan instructed me to lay down on top of the sleeping bags in the corner. We giggled as we practiced humping My Little Pony pillows side by side in the basement next to all of my baby dolls.

"I don't get what the point of this is Megan, how is this sex?" I asked her.

"Well, I don't know," she said, "but this is one of the ways."

Later that day, I proudly shared all of my newfound knowledge with my sisters. I stood on top of the plastic Fisher-Price picnic table in our playroom and described in vivid detail what Megan had told me as Laura and Jen stared at me wide-eyed.

"And then Megan said the man puts his wee-wee in the bum-bum," I said, dramatically waving my arms in the air and jumping off the table for emphasis.

Immediately afterward, Jen went upstairs and told my very conservative mother every single word I had said. Mom was horrified by what her youngest daughter had been doing, and she sat me down.

"Kimmy, that is very wrong. You and Megan were naughty. You will never do that again," she told me.

I felt ashamed. Embarrassed. And I was angry at my sister for tattling.

"Okay, but what is sex, then? Where do babies come from?" I asked, knowing I was crossing the line.

"God plants a seed in the mommy's belly, and that is all you need to know about that topic," Mom said. "Now, we will not speak of this again."

And we didn't. That was the end of it. We never again discussed the topic of sex or my shameful humping behavior.

I searched my children's Bible desperately for clues about babies and the word sex, much to no avail. I gave up eventually.

I felt guilty. I was embarrassed. And I was frustrated. Had I done something wrong? What did I do with the My Little Pony pillows? It had sort of felt good, but I wasn't sure why. I didn't understand it all, and no one explained to me why sex was so bad.

This was the first of many times that I was shamed into hiding when forced to confront something difficult—that I was taught it was better to run away from the hard truth than to face it head-on. That was how we always handled complicated, uncomfortable topics in my family. Instead of acknowledging that my curiosity was normal or that innocent experimentation was nothing to be ashamed of, Mom avoided the conversation. She wanted to move on quickly, as it clearly made her uncomfortable. *Put on your mask and hide.*

Green Jugs (1991): Nine Years Old

Mom was good at so many things. She was always there to pick me up early from school whether I felt a sore throat or stomachache coming on. I spent my afternoon on the couch watching Nickelodeon for hours with a cold pack across my feverish forehead while she tended to me. She enjoyed being home with us, and I appreciated having her around, especially on those days.

"How are you feeling, Kimmy?" she asked, leaning down to place her soft, smooth hand across my burning cheek.

I snuggled under the handmade wool blanket and moaned. Sitting beside me on the couch, her presence alone felt comforting and safe, and often she would spend the day knitting or cross-stitching by my side.

Mom always kept me company when I was sick, whether I was down with a sore throat or hanging my head over the garbage can. Not only was Mom there for every runny nose, but she also volunteered in our classrooms at school. She helped out with the PTA, whipped up cookies for charity bake sales, and stood waiting at the bus stop for us every afternoon. And at four o'clock, she stationed herself in the kitchen to begin the daily routine of dinner preparation and nightly news viewing.

At about this time, she regularly reached into the cabinet beneath the square box TV at the end of the counter, lifting a large green jug of wine and filling a tumbler with ice. She always needed three ice cubes. Slowly, throughout the evening, she refilled that glass, light-pink lipstick marks lining the dewy rim.

Mom made frequent stops at the liquor store on our way out of the Stop & Shop after an afternoon of grocery shopping, where she stocked up on her large jugs of wine.

"Why do we always need to stop here at this place?" I asked her. "Why can't we just go home?"

"I'll be super quick!" she said. "Just guard the groceries! Don't let anyone take anything."

"Who will steal the tomatoes and lettuce?" I asked, staring at the bags of food.

"You never know what kind of hooligans are out there!"

I waited patiently outside the liquor store, guarding the cartful of groceries, watching Mom through the window in the afternoon sun. The cold vegetables and fresh fruit began to sweat as I shifted my weight from one foot to another in the summer heat. Waiting. Pulling at my shorts, adjusting my tank top, desperate for air conditioning. Peering into the store and spotting her, furrowing my brow and urging her to hurry. She always came out with her wine, smiling. She seemed happy and relieved, ready to go.

"Okay, all set!" she said, delicately setting the bottles in the grocery cart's baby seat like precious little infants.

The jugs were always the same. Dark-green bottles with big handles and gold wrapping around the oversized corks. The liquor store clerks always stuck them in brown bags. I wondered, what was the point of those brown bags? And why did Mom always need such huge bottles?

As soon as we arrived home, not even four o'clock in the afternoon, even before she put the groceries away, Mom popped open that jug, its sharp aroma filling the kitchen.

Glug, glug, glug.

I heard the sound of the wine hitting the glass tumbler on the counter, followed by the jingle of ice cubes. Always three. Never more.

Standing at the sink, Mom took one long, drawn-out sip, eyes closed. Only then could she begin to unpack the groceries. Only then could she face the rest of the day.

I never thought much about my mother's evening wine routine. I never stood around too long or analyzed her actions. My job was done once I helped carry the groceries into the kitchen. Then I was free to shoot baskets in the driveway, ride bikes around the neighborhood, or play house in the backwoods.

Most often, I lost myself in a world of make-believe. My imagination was my best tool. I never realized that perhaps Mom was also escaping into her own world as well.

Day 8: December 6, 2020

I am awakened by the sound of my bedroom door swinging open, the familiar creak of the hinges, and the swift patter of tiny feet scampering across the hardwood floor. Without even opening my eyes, I know who this miniature intruder is based on the delicateness of her steps. A triangle of light shines onto the carpet, and I see the silhouette of my daughter, Parker. Her curls wild from sleep, she peers up at me. I sit up immediately and check the time. It's close to two in the morning, and I know the reason for her visit.

"I had a bad dream," she whispers.

"Okay, sweetie, it's alright," I tell her.

As I pull on my robe, I consider how long I've been sleeping. I went to bed at around nine o'clock—fell right into bed, sleeping deeply. I marvel at how easy it's been for me to fall asleep these last few nights. For a half second, I'm irritated about being disrupted from this nearly perfect rest. It's such a rarity for me, one I haven't experienced in decades. It is perhaps one of my most miraculous discoveries about sobriety.

I find my slippers beside the bed and tiptoe quietly out of the room, holding Parker's hand. These middle of the night awakenings seem to be happening a lot more frequently, more so than it ever did with her older brothers.

It dawns on me that this is the first time she's come to me in the night and hasn't had to shake me awake, or wake up Evan instead because she couldn't rouse me. Probably the first time I didn't push her away and mumble, "Go back to bed"—the first time in years that I'm coherent in the middle of the night.

We snuggle back in her bed, and I rub her hair. I breathe in deeply as she curls her body into mine, and I find myself overcome by a whirlwind of emotions. I feel angry at myself. I feel grateful. But I'm sad, as well.

I look down at the outline of my sweet girl. I consider how many moments like this I've missed.

I'm stunned by the revelation, and a sob escapes my lips.

"What's wrong, Mommy?" she asks.

"Nothing, Parker, nothing. I just love you so much."

And I wrap my arms around my baby girl, holding her tightly.

Ballroom Dancing (1991): Nine Years Old

S tanding in line, waiting to file into the gymnasium, I searched nervously for a friendly face. My eyes scanned the line as it snaked through the dark, unfamiliar hallway of the Brunswick Elementary School, the only all-boys private school in town. The majority of the children here were from Brunswick and Greenwich Academy, the accompanying girls' school. I felt as if I didn't know a single person, since I went to the local public school. The other kids chatted loudly in groups around me, and I shifted my weight uncomfortably, staring at my white tights.

The thick smell of sweat and men's cheap cologne hung heavy in the air. I looked up and spotted my only friend, Megan, up ahead of me, but she didn't see me. I noticed she had a pink ribbon in her hair, and I laughed to myself knowing how much she hated ribbons in her hair.

I pulled awkwardly at the lacey hem of the flowered dress Mom made me wear. I cinched the grosgrain bow tighter around my waist, as if this kept my stomach from heaving. I glanced down at the white gloves I was forced to wear, the uniform that all the young ladies were asked to adhere to when ballroom dancing. My once-white gloves were brown at the fingertips and already damp from my hot, sweaty hands.

I glanced to my right at the boy beside me in the line. This was the boy I had to attach myself to and have my first dance with that night. I eyed him up and down and took a deep breath. I didn't know his name. I'd never met him before. He was short, freckled-faced, and I was much taller than him. He breathed heavily, shifting his weight nervously. A bead of sweat trickled down his face, and he dabbed at it with a ball of tissue. A small piece stuck to his forehead, but he didn't notice. I stared straight ahead, horrified at my luck.

A few minutes before, in the car ride over, I'd asked my parents why I had to go to ballroom dancing classes. "It's stupid," I said. "Why do kids need to know how to ballroom dance?"

"Everyone does it. All young ladies should know how to foxtrot," Mom said.

"Do you know how to foxtrot?" I asked her.

"No, actually, but I wish I did," she replied thoughtfully. "I bet it would have been fun. But I was the captain of the cheerleading squad . . ."

"Yeah, I know, I know," I said, cutting her off. I'd heard that story before.

"You just need to do this because all the other kids are doing it," Dad said. "Remember to smile when you curtsy, and keep your shoulders back."

All at once, my partner and I were at the front of the line, and it was our turn to present ourselves to the ballroom, which was just the boys' basketball court. This meant we had to walk in together as a couple. He stuck his left arm out but didn't speak a word to me. We hadn't acknowledged each another once, and to this day I still don't know his name. Awkwardly, I threaded my bony wrist through his pudgy arm and stepped closer to him.

I was surprised to feel his body so close to me. It felt intimate. Uncomfortable. I could immediately sense his warmth. I felt the dampness of his clammy, cologne-soaked skin. His body felt doughy against my slender hip. We walked forward and approached the door to the gymnasium and waited our turn. I felt sick. Yet for the briefest moment, I considered that it also felt nice to have this strange boy beside me holding my arm because at least I wasn't doing it alone.

It was a curious sensation. It took over my belly and I no longer felt my dinner rolling around. Instead, butterflies danced at the weight of his body against mine. His closeness. His heavy breathing. I was taken aback by this utterly new sensation. I felt dizzy, even.

Then he snorted and coughed and I looked again at his face, which was nearly as white as the tissue stuck to his forehead. We were ushered ahead by the two large spotlights that shone on us. Hundreds of eyes were upon me. I hated the feeling of being on display. Onstage.

The band played loudly with horns that hurt my ears, and I couldn't think of what to do next. Where should I go? The boy breathed fast and heavy as he dragged me forward. Before I knew what was happening, we were moving across the gymnasium. But I wasn't ready, and my feet didn't move as quickly as his. My black patent leather Mary Janes dragged on the ground as I stumbled along almost a full two steps behind him. As I tripped, I saw the other boys and girls laughing and pointing. Hands cupped to their faces, they whispered to one another. I wanted to run away. Cry. I never wanted to see these kids again. I hated my dress, my hair, the bow, this boy, the feeling in my stomach. I wanted to hide and disappear into the shadows of the corner of the gymnasium. I wanted the darkness to swallow me whole. My parents had forced me to come here and do this. They wanted me to learn to behave like a young lady because that's what all the Greenwich girls did. Maybe it made them feel like they were doing a good job of parenting me, but I hated them for making me do it.

My anxiety and discomfort that evening was a familiar sensation that I would become accustomed to experiencing in most social situations throughout my life. Years later, I would discover that alcohol helped alleviate the stress that accompanied doing the things that made me nervous and going places that made me uncomfortable. One day, I would learn that I wouldn't have to experience these feelings alone as long as I had my trusted friend, alcohol.

Spofford Lake, NH (1991): Nine Years Old

"Kimmy, your turn now!"

I skipped down the dock at our lake house, holding my "kid sister" doll, past Laura, taking the life jacket from her. I felt daring and confident. This was the only time I was allowed out by myself in the rowboat—when Mom was sitting on the deck with her glass of wine before dinner. It was my chance to be alone on the water. I was the commander of my own ship, and I could escape into the wild. It was my favorite time of day: "the golden hour," as I would call it years later.

"Stay where we can see you, Kimmy!" Mom called from the porch, swirling her glass.

Snapping on the neon yellow and pink life jacket, I ignored Mom's pleas. Instead, I set my doll gingerly into the seat and began to untie the lines of the small metal boat. I cleared the cobwebs with my oar and sat down, the rusty metal hot against my tan legs.

I pushed off into the water, taking my doll out for an evening ride. I stared down through the silky murkiness at the shapes below and saw the black, jagged contours of rocks. The formations of the earth dropped off and dipped dozens of feet straight down, and I imagined a magical world far below me. It sent a shiver down my spine.

"Here we go, baby!" I said to my doll.

I rowed the boat along the shore into the pickleweeds, away from the house.

"This here is the famous pickleweed garden!" I said.

I was a tour guide now, talking to the passengers on my ferry like they did on the rides into Hamilton Harbour on vacation in Bermuda.

"Not too far, Kimmy!" Jen called from the end of the dock as I pushed on down the shore, ignoring her.

"Kimmy! Come back! Too far!" Mom yelled.

I pretended not to hear. "And over here to our right is the famous Idle-wild House, built in 1900," I told my imaginary passengers.

Glancing over my shoulder, I saw my sisters watching me from the dock a few houses back, my mother standing up on the porch, her hand shielding her eyes from the afternoon sun. I smiled to myself and kept rowing, remaining close to the shore but pushing myself farther along to the next house.

They all worry so much, I thought. There was a comfort in the ease of finding solitude on the lake, a thrill in doing something a little reckless. I liked the freedom, the peacefulness, and the time spent lost in my imagination.

But without warning, a large motorboat sped past me, sending a cascade of waves in my direction. I dropped the oars and grabbed onto the sides of the rowboat as the wake rocked me violently back and forth. The oars nearly slipped into the water, but I managed to grab hold of them at the last second. I sat stunned, staring down into the lake. The waves slowly receded, and the water grew calm again.

I looked back to see Mom and my sisters shaking their heads at me. I sheepishly turned the boat back around. I could almost hear their collective sigh of relief across the surface of the water as I headed back. I knew exactly what they were going to say to me. I didn't like scaring Mom, and ultimately, the depths of the lake frightened me. I just wanted to have some fun on my own, I told them.

My bravery was often short-lived, and my excursions always ended sooner than I dared. I wanted to prove to everyone that I was tough. I could do things on my own.

I wanted to show them I wasn't scared of that lake. But it would take many years before I would learn that being courageous doesn't mean you have to be fearless or that you must take on the world by yourself.

Sometimes, bravery means simply showing a little vulnerability.

Day 9: December 7, 2020

"I want to go for a bike ride alone," Brayden says to me. He is nine years old, and his need for independence is obvious these days. He spreads his legs apart slightly and crosses his arms as if to stand his ground.

"Where do you want to go?" I ask, putting the shirt I'm folding back into the pile of laundry. I turn to face him and give him my undivided attention.

"I want to go to the Needham Town Forest and bike down the rail trail," he states matter-of-factly.

"What? That's absurd."

"Why?"

"You want to cross High Rock Street all by yourself?"

"Yes."

"And go for a ride in the forest?"

"Yes, Mom!"

"No way. Absolutely not."

"You're so unfair!" he shouts. "Why are you so mean?"

We've had this conversation over and over again. He wants more freedom. I am so mean. He wants to be able to do more on his own. I don't allow him to do anything he wants to do.

He's been begging to explore the neighborhood. Play somewhere else other than the postage-stamp-sized strip of grass that is our tiny backyard. But the streets of Needham are busy and congested, especially the corner we live on. There are so many distracted drivers now, unlike when I was a child. People whip past our house, texting on their cell phones, not paying attention. I live in fear that one of my children is going to get run over, as there have been so many accidents in the area in recent years.

"I'm not arguing about this, buddy. I'm sorry. It's non-negotiable at this point."

"You're the worst mom ever!" he screams and storms out of the kitchen, stomping his feet heavily up the stairs to his bedroom. He slams the door, and I hear him tossing things around out of frustration.

I feel his pain and I know his need for freedom. To explore. My heart aches for him, but I know the constant arguments he and I are having lately aren't getting us anywhere. Engaging with him and yelling back is not productive for either of us. I feel so far away from him right now. I don't know how to reach him or how to fix this. Plus, I'm late for The Luckiest Club meeting. I can't deal with his constant disappointment. No matter what I do lately, he seems to hate me.

I need to focus on me for the next hour. I grab my laptop, sigh heavily, and head to my bedroom. I have to lock myself in the closet for the next hour and block out this noise, but I can't help but think how much I want a glass of wine right now. After a fight like this is when I would sneak off to the dining room and grab that bottle of Tito's.

Dares (1994): Twelve Years Old

My best friend Megan and I always found ways to entertain ourselves, exploring the neighborhood between our homes. She lived a few streets away. In middle school, our parents gave us the freedom and responsibility to come and go on our bikes.

One day, Megan and I were playing near the maintenance shack by the golf course. It was the off-season, and we discovered how thrilling it was to climb the rocks and trees up behind the pool. We sat down on a rock and Megan whipped out a pack of Marlboro Reds she'd stolen from her older brother's room.

"Check it out," she said.

"Woah. How do you do it?" I asked.

"Look, I'll show you," Megan said.

"I don't think I want to," I hesitated, looking around. There wasn't a single person nearby. We were alone, but I could still hear my mother's voice in my head. I knew it wasn't a good idea.

"Cigarettes are dangerous," Mom would say. "It will lead to horrible things. You will die from this."

"You don't have to, but I'm going to have one," Megan said. "Just watch me. It's fun." She flicked the lighter and skillfully lit the cigarette in one swift motion, blowing the smoke in my face. I coughed, and she smirked at me.

I was curious what it felt like because Megan seemed to be enjoying it. She looked like the girls in the movies. I liked the idea of trying something thrilling and naughty. I considered my options and scanned my surroundings for a minute. We were probably safe enough. I knew if I thought about it a second longer, I might lose my nerve.

"Fine, give it," I demanded. "I'll try."

"I knew it." Megan smiled triumphantly and handed me the cigarette. I stared down at the roll of paper between my fingers. Convinced it might burn me, I quickly brought it to my lips and inhaled, coughing deeply. It was too fast, and I'd barely even sucked in any air, but the taste was bitter and left a strange flavor on my tongue. It reminded me of the stale smell in the back of the old diner my family used to stop at in Deerfield on our way to Vermont on Friday nights.

I took another puff, coughing harder, and Megan giggled at me. I glared at her, but pretty soon I joined in on the laughter as well.

There was a pivotal shift in the types of childhood games I played from that point on. I no longer went to the basement to feed my dolls their dinner after school. Instead, I began to disappear to the golf shed with Megan on a regular basis. I went there so I could get away from my parents and escape into a different kind of world. Middle school wasn't easy, and it was in our secret hideouts that I was able to find a new type of comfort and safety with Megan. Experimenting with new things, I began to test out who I was. I also started to challenge all the principals my parents had ever taught me.

It was there amid the paths and roofs of the country club that I began to grow up faster than I could handle, and my life changed more quickly than I anticipated. It was also there that my secrets began to steal me away from myself.

The Sleepover (1994): Twelve Years Old

One weekend when I was twelve, I was invited to a sleepover with a group of popular girls, some of which I knew well but most of which I didn't. Megan was there, and I was thrilled to be included in the cool group. I wasn't often invited to large group parties, so it was exciting.

I was nervous, anxious, and overly enthusiastic. Mom was too. She packed my favorite stuffed animals because she knew I got homesick, but I was embarrassed by my pink fluffy monkey, so I left that one on my bed.

That night, the girls and I spent the majority of our time playing games in my friend Karen's oversized basement.

Once the movie ended, and after several rounds of "light as a feather, stiff as a board," some of the girls got antsy and began to play truth or dare. A few of them took it to a whole new level.

The smell of dark cedar wood filled the air inside the wine cellar. The smooth burgundy liquid sloshed around inside the dusty bottle every time the other girls tipped it back, holding it steadily with both hands. The first time Megan took me inside on a dare, I watched in awe, unmoving and terrified. I refused to participate, but I wanted to act cool. I didn't say a word.

As the other girls brought the bottle to their lips, over and over again, I considered what to do. I wanted to go back to playing Ouija and telling ghost stories. Why did they want to drink this nasty stuff?

The party wasn't feeling as fun anymore. The whole thing was getting uncomfortable. I was concerned for Megan every time she disappeared behind that wine cellar door, emerging with her red lips, giggling and sillier than before. I wanted the girls to stop. I just wanted to go to sleep.

A little while later, I sat alone on the couch in the basement, watching the girls go in and out of the wine cellar in pairs. I fiddled with the tassel on the pillow beside me and discovered a matchbook buried between the couch cushions. I picked it up and stared down at the small cardboard packet.

I hadn't gone back to the wine cellar since the first time Megan brought me in with her because I was too scared. But I wanted to feel part of the excitement. I was desperate to experience the same energy the rest of the girls were feeling.

I stood up with the matches in one hand. The girls giggled in a pile on the floor in front of me. I'm not sure what came over me, but I suddenly had an idea. Just like Megan once showed me on the roof at the club, I lit the match with a quick flick of my wrist. Then I held it out for them to see.

"Hey, guys, look at me," I said, waving the fire over my head.

The glowing match illuminated their faces as they looked up at me. They were quiet and seemed impressed, and for once I felt like somebody. Now I was the cool one, and everyone was looking at me.

"I want to light one!" one girl said, giggling.

"My turn!" shouted Megan, reaching for the matchbook.

"Do we have any cigarettes?" asked another girl.

All at once, a piercing alarm sounded. The girls screamed, and someone grabbed the match from my hand and blew it out. The smoke detector above my head began flashing and beeping. I was stunned. I stood looking all around as the other girls acted quickly, crawling and jumping into their sleeping bags to hide. I was terrified and mortified at the same time.

"*She* did it!" they said when the hostess's mother stormed down the stairs and saw me as the only one still standing up and seemingly not asleep.

The sleepover ended shortly thereafter, and all of the parents came to pick us up. Ashamed that I'd ruined the fun, I went home with Mom and Dad. I never told my parents what the other girls did that night, or that my mistake was not the worst of it all. I felt so guilty about setting off the smoke alarm that I didn't want anyone else to be even angrier at me. I was also afraid of upsetting the popular girls. More lies to tell. More answers that went untold. More secrets for me to stow away.

Locker Room Lies (1995): Thirteen Years Old

"Kimmy, just make sure you're home before it gets dark tonight, please! For once!" Mom said as I ran out the door to meet Megan. "Dad is actually coming home for dinner tonight on time, so don't be late!"

"Yeah, right, I'll believe it when I see it!" I called as I took off down the driveway.

Dad was coming home later and later in the evenings. He was always busy at work, and Mom seemed to deal with that by starting on her wine earlier and earlier. I didn't care. I had the afternoon to do what I pleased.

After chasing each other around the empty roads of the country club on our bikes, Megan and I found ourselves at the back door to the bathroom of the pool locker room. We listened for the sounds of people nearby, but there was no one around. The quiet of the late-fall afternoon and the crispness of the wind were all that could be heard.

"Let's try to get inside the locker room!" Megan said.

"What do you mean inside?"

"Let's sneak in."

"What? How? There's no door handle on this side."

"Let's see if we can find a way to get in," she said and began to look around on the ground.

"Okay, but why?"

"I just wonder what it's like in there right now," she said, looking for some way to open the door using a rock or a stick.

"Yeah, I guess it would be cool to see." I eyed her nervously. "But we could get caught, and I don't want to get in trouble."

Megan stopped her searching and turned to look at me. "Who's going to catch us? There's nobody here! Let's live a little!" She spread her arms wide.

"Fine."

Just then, she spotted a rusty hanger in the dirt. "Oh, look, this might work!" she said, smiling and raising her eyebrows. She jammed the hook of the hanger in the crack of the door, pulling it wide open. The door creaked loudly, and we froze.

We peered into the dark, musty locker room, the sun piercing a triangle of dusty light over our shoulders. There were cobwebs strung across the entrance, but we were intrigued. We smiled at each other.

We crept inside and looked around, seeing the familiar changing stalls and rusty metal lockers. This was a place that was always filled with children, their mothers, and the sounds of summer. With colorful towels and sunshine; joy and laughter. Now it felt unfamiliar and covered in a layer of dirt and dust. The blue and green pool furniture was stacked in the far corner, stored away for the winter until Memorial Day and the start of the summer. It smelled musty despite the November temperatures, but the familiar scent of sunscreen and chlorine still hung in the air.

Hoping to find some old forgotten relics, we investigated the lockers. Maybe we could find a lost bag or a pair of fancy sunglasses. After coming up empty-handed, we stumbled upon the cleaning closet.

What happened next was a blur. We unleashed our aggressions, abruptly and violently. Bottles of soap were squirted onto mirrors. Rolls of toilet paper were thrown across the locker room. We laughed maniacally at the mess we made. We threaded toilet paper across the rows of lockers like a giant spiderweb. There was powder flying and bubbles in the air. We giggled and spun in circles, marveling at our work. When it was all over, we ran away on our bikes, howling like hyenas at the chaos we had caused.

Later that night, I sat on the couch beside Mom and the guilt began to settle in. Maybe it was the shame of desecrating one of my favorite childhood spots. Or perhaps it was the weight of all the lies that were beginning to add up, but I couldn't stop thinking about what we'd done—what I had done.

"Mom," I said, "I feel really awful, but I need to tell you something."

"Okay, Kimmy, what is it?"

"Megan and I did something stupid."

"What did you do?" Mom turned the television down and sat up, putting her wine glass down heavily on the coffee table.

"We toilet-papered the pool locker room," I mumbled, staring at my feet.

"*What?*" she shouted. "You did *what?* Why?"

Mom's eyes widened, but before she could lash out any further, she reached for her glass. She tipped it back, closed her eyes, and took a long gulp, finishing what was left of her wine.

The next morning, we sat in silence in the car for the three-minute drive to the country club. Mom's fingers gripped the steering wheel, and she stared straight ahead as we navigated the tall picket fences at the entrance to the pool parking lot. When we pulled in and Mom saw it was completely empty with not another soul in sight, she relaxed, but only slightly.

"I told you there would be no one here," I said quietly.

She shot me an irritated look and said nothing. It was six o'clock in the morning, and I wished I were still in my bed. She probably did too.

We parked behind the pool locker room building, and she turned off the ignition. "Okay, so now what?" I asked, genuinely unsure of what I was expected to do.

I imagined Mom was more nervous than angry, and I stared at my hands, feeling ashamed. I should have just kept quiet the night before. I should have swallowed my secret and learned to live with the guilt.

Mom looked around, searching the parking lot one more time. "Okay, go and clean up the mess you made!" Her words were a half whisper, half shriek as she leaned over my lap and threw the passenger side door open. "And hurry it up! Make it look like you never set foot in there. Do it quickly! The last thing we need is to get caught after all this."

I slid out of the car and made my way around the back of the locker room as Mom watched me. I ducked out of sight, my insides burning from humiliation. I searched for the rusty hanger that we'd used to get in and found it on the ground where we'd left it. I stuck it in the crack of the door again, and just like yesterday, it swung open. I peered in, wishing I would find the locker room immaculately cleaned by some fairy godmother. No such luck.

My stomach sank. The mess was just as we'd left it. Toilet paper was everywhere. Soap dripped in partially dried streaks down the walls. I walked inside. I hesitated, staring at my smeared reflection in the mirror.

How many more times would I look into the mirror and wonder why? *What the hell is wrong with you, Kim?*

The soap suds had soaked into the area rugs in the dressing rooms, forming dark, foamy puddles. The smell of bleach mixed with pine hung in the air, making me feel lightheaded. I didn't stop to think. Instead, I began grabbing at the toilet paper as fast as I could. I threw it on the soap and got on my hands and knees and wiped at the puddles of foam.

I began to cry.

I climbed up onto the counter by the row of sinks and went to work on the mirror, shoving used paper towels into the large trash bins. I sobbed, thinking about all the times I'd spent here over the years with my family. All the memories created at this special place. Sunday barbeques at the pool. Swim lessons on Monday mornings. Camp everyday with my sisters on hot summer afternoons. And now this horrible mess. This was what I'd done to the place I loved so much. A place that had treated me so well.

I was angry with myself and disappointed by my stupid decisions. I was angry at Mom, too, for making me clean up alone. Why wouldn't she help me?

This was only the beginning. I had yet to experience true and utter self-loathing. Years later, without realizing it, I would slowly lose control. If only I had known then the number of times I would create such an awful mess of my life down the road. How many more times would I continue to stare at my reflection with disgust only to wake up and do it all over again the next day?

Day 10: December 8, 2020

"I would bring my wine with me as I tucked the twins into bed every night," Pamela from California says. I watch her kind, expressive eyes through my computer screen. I am crouched on the floor of my bedroom closet. It's my second alcohol support meeting of the day. I pull my pink fuzzy socks up high over my black Lululemon stretch pants.

How is this my life? I ask myself this question several times a day.

Looking at the shelves of neatly folded yoga pants, jeans, and sweaters, I spread my legs out and lie on my back. I stare at the ceiling, listening to Pamela continue. Her story's starting to sound eerily similar to my own.

I glance at the laptop to double-check that my video is off. Thankfully, no one in the virtual meeting can see me splayed out on the floor next to the rows and rows of heels and designer flats that have been collecting dust for the last nine months.

"And then, one day, I fell out of the top bunk bed!" Pamela says. "The cover came off my mug, and wine spilled all over the carpet! My cover was blown." She begins to cry. I wince, recognizing her shame. That all too familiar feeling of guilt starts to creep into my own mind.

"Oh, Pamelia, shit, I get it," I whisper.

From downstairs, I can hear my kids arguing over which TV show to watch next. It appears the one they were watching has just ended, and punches will likely soon be thrown over the clicker. I turn the volume up on the Zoom call and pray the kids figure it out on their own without interrupting me.

Please be good for Mom just a little bit longer, guys.

I sit up and look at Pamela's bloodshot eyes. I lean my back against my collection of evening dresses that are hung according to length, season, and occasion on the rack behind me. A red sequin gown brushes my cheek. I grab it and hold it out in front of me for a better look. I wore it to last year's hospital charity gala. I recoil at the memory of that night . . . or lack thereof.

The memories exist in fragments. I hadn't eaten dinner. One glass of champagne turned into many, many bottles. I woke up the next morning on the couch with a throbbing headache, a broken heel, and a somewhat quiet husband. Evan and I went about our business as usual, sweeping my shenanigans under the rug.

We often pretended there was nothing wrong with the fact that I woke up disheveled and hungover. Because ignoring the truth on a regular basis was easier for us both than dealing with confrontation every single Sunday morning. If I really misbehaved, he would sit me down to discuss it, but neither of us enjoyed those chats.

My friends and I laughed about our escapades as always. But that particular morning after the gala, a deep, faraway feeling sat in the back of my mind nagging at me. It wasn't just the hangover. I felt so angry at myself for getting so drunk, but Evan hadn't said a word about it. I can't decide if I wished he had confronted me that morning or not.

I sit up and listen to the next person talk as I snuggle into the clothing hanging behind me. It feels safe in here behind the closet door. I even feel like maybe I'm going to be okay. Someday. Far away from the rest of the world, things seem manageable for now. If only I can stay hidden inside my closet forever. My secret seems safe behind these walls.

But then I remember something Francy told me this week. "This isn't anything to be ashamed of. You're doing something incredibly brave. This shouldn't be a secret."

I know deep down that quitting drinking is a thing to be proud of. I'm doing something good for myself and my family. I'm finally choosing to face all the self-loathing that used to wake me up at three in the morning. I'm making a conscious choice to better myself. But it still feels so damn hard.

All the mornings of not being able to look in the mirror—I'm finally doing something about it. I'm not hiding anymore, and I'm dealing with the problem. I'm not finding comfort in a bottle of booze. Instead, I'm admitting the booze is the problem. I'm not drowning my feelings in alcohol anymore. I'm finally dealing with it all. But why am I so sad?

"Remember your why, Pamela. This is a good reminder for everyone. Don't forget all the reasons why you're going down this difficult road. Remind yourself every day why you want to stop drinking." Louise speaks sweetly with her English accent. "Our time is unfortunately up for today, though."

The Zoom call ends, and I close my computer. It is quiet. Eerily still, all alone in my closet. I contemplate Louise's words. I know I want to be a better mom, and my kids deserve that. I cannot be a good mom and keep alcohol in my life. I cannot manage both.

"This is my only option," I whisper.

I am sick of feeling hungover and depressed.

I am sick of feeling anxious and scared every day, obsessing about my next drink.

I am sick of blacking out and wondering what I did the night before.

I am sick of the guilt of lying to my husband and myself, sneaking around and hiding.

I am sick of wanting to do more for my kids but always falling short.

So I know why I want to stop drinking. That is slowly becoming the easy part. But I wonder why I even drank in the first place. Why did I think alcohol was making any of this better?

I glance around at my elegant, brightly organized wardrobe, and a feeling of urgent strength begins to envelop me. It cloaks me in a strange sensation. An energy takes over, and I feel like I need to fix what is right in front of me.

I stand up and pull open a drawer of neatly folded t-shirts and summer shorts that are perfectly organized in rows by color. I haven't touched them since Labor Day weekend, after the last drunken barbeque. Looking at them, I'm brought back to happy summer afternoons with friends. Sunshine. Corks popping. Glasses clinking. Tequila. Lime. Sand on my feet. Salt water on my arms. Laughter. Crisp Whispering Angel in my wine glass.

Without thinking, I reach into the drawer and yank out the clothes, sending a sea of cotton stripes and polka dots across my closet floor. I empty the rest of the drawer, flinging them up over my head. Then I move to the next row. Then the next. Soon the floor is carpeted in random nautical patterns and floral colors.

I take a deep breath and turn around, soaking in the scene before me. My immaculately organized closet is no longer perfect.

For the first time in my life, I smile at the crazy mess I've made. I laugh at the chaos, and it feels good. I have been unleashed, and I finally feel clear about what I'm doing.

Closeted Secrets (1995): Thirteen Years Old

One evening before dinner, I sneaked into my parent's closet, tiptoeing down the long hallway to their upstairs bedroom and into the large walk-in. Rows of shelves loomed above me, and I wondered what was stored inside the old-fashioned suitcases and worn-out boxes.

Yanking open the antique dresser drawers, I pulled out Mom's silk scarves and put them back just as I found them. I didn't know what I was looking for, but I was determined to solve a mystery, to find some sort of hidden treasure. It was as if I was on the verge of figuring out the key to a puzzle, the answer to a question I wasn't even sure I had. It felt wrong. Inappropriate. Daring.

I stared at Mom's exquisite dresses and imagined myself going out to fancy dinners in them. My favorite dress was the black-and-gold sequined gown she'd worn to Dad's company party the year before. She'd had one too many glasses of wine that night, and Dad had to take her home early before the babysitter had even put the three of us to bed.

He carried her up the stairs as she swung in his arms, acting silly. My sisters and I lingered outside their bedroom door, giggling as Dad attempted to get Mom undressed and into bed. I thought it was a shame she hadn't gotten to wear the beautiful gown for very long; they'd only been gone a couple of hours.

I touched the shimmery sequins with my fingertips, playing with the thread of the silky fabric. Then I tried on Dad's black patent leather dress shoes and danced around the hardwood floor. Sitting on Dad's small stool, I picked up the expensive ivory shoehorn that he never wanted me to touch and practiced sliding the shoes on and off.

I'm not sure why my parents didn't want me to play with their things or why I wasn't allowed in their room without an adult. I knew I shouldn't have been going through their drawers without them knowing, but I liked the intimacy of it. I pretended to understand them and know them a bit better. I felt closer to learning their secrets.

Holding Mom's clothes to my small body, I stared at myself in the mirror. I ran to the hallway once or twice to check and make sure that no one was coming. When the coast was clear, and the only noises heard were the floorboards groaning beneath the weight of my feet, I tiptoed back inside the closet to continue my private mission.

I eyed Dad's watch. His college ring. I tried on Mom's flashy jewelry. Played with her necklaces, brooches, and clip-on earrings that had belonged to my great-grandmother. It all felt so exhilarating.

Sometimes, I would lurk around in my father's private bathroom that was connected to the closet. It was pink tiled, and he had his own vanity with tons of cabinets to explore filled with various products. My mother, sisters and I never used this bathroom. Instead, Mom walked down the hallway to the other end of the house to use the toilet and shower that was for my sisters and me.

I returned to their closet every few months to linger and inspect. Over and over again. My parents never did catch me snooping through this part of the house, going through their things. I also never learned much from my exploring. What was I looking for? What did I hope to find?

It was as if there were clues buried in the drawers of my mother's closet, and I needed to know what they were. I was desperate to learn more about what was inside Dad's bathroom drawers, and to know what the adults in my life weren't telling me.

What was happening behind the closed doors? What did all the hushed whispers mean? What were all the averted eyes, quiet conversations, and stern voices really saying?

Part of me was always afraid of what I would discover there. Yet I kept going back, searching for answers I'd never find.

The Elusive (1990s): Teenage Years

Sometime in the 90s, Dad decided to buy a boat. No one in my family knew much about boating, but Dad thought it would be something fun to bring the family together. He was seeing less of us, as we were getting older. We all figured he was feeling lonely and bored. He wanted to learn a new hobby, so he decided to go for it. His audaciousness was inspiring, but Mom did not always see it that way.

Dad received his boater's license and started to navigate the waters off the coast of Connecticut. I assumed he wanted to feel young again like his buddy, Steve, who lived on the water in a big, newer house in Old Greenwich. Steve, significantly younger and with a few different boats, liked all water sports including jet skiing and fishing. Dad admired Steve and his fun, youthful way of living. It also made me feel less guilty for not being around the house and for hanging out with Megan and my other friends.

Mom was hesitant to get on board with the boating idea, but she reluctantly allowed Dad his fun. Right away, we realized our Saturday afternoon family boating excursions were not so bad after all. Dad's new reckless hobby was actually quite enjoyable.

It was a thirty-foot powerboat Dad bought straight off an ad in the newspaper, and it sat docked in the harbor in Greenwich. That boat was the one place we could all be together without the distraction of friends or boyfriends. My parents loved having us all to themselves for the day. Being together as a family of five made them happy, and I genuinely loved being out there in the sunshine, speeding through the open water. We named it *The Elusive*, after our favorite boat in Bermuda.

On the weekends, my family took the boat out from its slip in the harbor and deep into the Long Island Sound. We spent long, lazy days together listening to Bob Marley in the hot sun. I have fond memories of spending the afternoon on the deck of the boat watching the ships go in and out of Great Captain's Island then heading back to shore, salty and satisfied. First, we started the day off by picking up sandwiches and sodas in the late morning from Pisano's off Greenwich Avenue. Then we headed to the dock, my bag packed with my discman, Cape Cod Chips, and sunscreen. I used to love diving off the bow of the boat and swimming with my sisters in the questionable, often filthy brown water. I can still smell the motor as it revved and churned in the murky harbor. We didn't care that the water wasn't as blue as the beautiful oceans of Bermuda. We enjoyed every minute of it together.

Dad slathered on the sunscreen, leaving streaks of white across his nose before taking off into open water. One time, he forgot to untie the lines from the dock and almost broke the bow of the boat and the pier while onlookers shouted at us in disbelief.

"Here comes Chevy Chase! Always an adventure," Dad said while Mom covered her face in embarrassment, trying to hide in the cabin down below.

Another time, we got our anchor attached to an underwater electrical cable that ran out to Great Captain's Island, and we couldn't get it unhooked. My sister's boyfriend, Brian, had to dive into the water and cut the anchor off with a knife.

When we first got *The Elusive*, this time with my family was a treasure. But back then, I didn't realize it. Then one day, Mom stopped coming altogether, and it was never the same. I always felt she never really enjoyed going out on the water like the rest of us, but at least in the beginning she tried to have fun. She liked seeing us all together and happy, but she despised what the boat represented to my dad. At first, she went along and didn't complain because she loved spending time as a family. Then, over the years, I could tell certain things about the boat bothered her. Like when Dad drove too fast.

"Slow down, John! You're going much too quickly for the harbor!"

"No I'm not," he replied simply.

"People are staring!"

"It's fine, Gay!"

Mom also hated it when Dad invited his friends along, like his buddy Steve or his colleagues from work. She got angry when he had people other than us on the boat. She thought Dad drove the boat too fast on purpose, impressing his friends and spraying everyone with salt water. By the end, I think everything about the boat made Mom anxious and uncomfortable. She worried the whole time about our safety when we were out on the open ocean.

Sadly, one Saturday morning, Mom stayed home. She told us that her back hurt, and that she didn't feel like coming on the water that day. Dad shrugged his shoulders and didn't answer us when we asked about Mom's real reason for skipping out. Then, after that, she stopped coming out on the boat for good.

I really did love *The Elusive*, as did Dad. It was not long after Mom stopped coming that he decided to sell it and move onto a new project to distract himself from life happening around him. He took up swimming at the YMCA and weightlifting after that. That was when we began to see even less of him at home.

Day 14: December 12, 2020

It is late in the afternoon, and I settle in by the fireplace in the family room next to the Christmas tree with my daily pile of mail to open. December is my favorite month for opening letters. I normally don't even bother checking the mailbox any other month of the year because there's never anything interesting to be found. In the summer, envelopes usually just pile up and overflow from the mailbox, frustrating both the sweet old delivery man and my overly organized husband. But when December rolls around, it's game on. So many deliveries, letters, and packages: UPS, FedEx, and more.

I settle down with my can of seltzer. There's an unfamiliar comfort in my new version of happy hour, but at the same time a feeling of sadness and longing for what used to be. I dismiss the sensation, determined to find satisfaction in the faces from my past on the cardstock inside each envelope. I need to focus on the little things I have these days, and at this moment, holiday cards are it. The people I haven't seen or talked to in so long. The ones who always make me feel connected every year around this time.

I slice open the cards one by one, taking my time to admire the care and effort they took to design, stuff, and address. The entire holiday card process is a painful one, I know that just as much as anyone.

We took our family holiday photos two weeks before Thanksgiving in a park near our house. I had picked out the perfect coordinating outfits for the kids. I chose various shades of complementary reds, browns, and beiges. The photographer said, "Nothing too matchy-matchy" and suggested a soft palette that would pick up on the autumn hues in the trees and woods behind us. I chose a light-colored top, jeans, and booties. Casual and effortless. After all, the children are the focal point in these things.

"Okay, kids, don't poke each other in the eyes," the photographer said. "Let's all be nice and love each other. Let's be kind. Santa is watching! Oh, and don't pull your sister's hair, please?"

"Please stop," I told the boys. "You can do whatever you want this afternoon. You can play Xbox for the rest of the day. Let's just get through this. Smile for the nice lady."

I was hungover and had drunk half a bottle of wine beforehand just to get by. Through it all, I kept focusing on the next drink I would have as soon as we got home.

"Come on, guys, the faster you smile, the faster it's over for all of us," Evan said.

"*Smile*, God damnit!" I yelled.

I cringe at the memory.

Thankfully, the photographer was able to capture some beautiful pictures despite the chaotic process it took to get there. I looked composed. I had my hair blown out, and my makeup was impeccable. Inside, though, I was screaming. And slowly crumbling. Things were completely falling apart for me at that point, whether I was willing to admit it or not. It was a few weeks after that when I broke down and asked Evan for help.

I breathe deeply, trying to shake the shameful thought from my mind. I sip on my lime seltzer and stare back at the faces on the various cards before me. So many people from so many parts of our lives. Betsy from college, who now lives in Manhattan. I wonder if she still works at that ad firm. The Brown family from two streets over. Ashley from high school, who just had a baby boy named Jax. My cousin Jane, who lives in Texas and who I haven't seen in twenty-five years. The thoughtfully coordinated matching outfits on her children make me smile, as does the perfectly coiffed hair of Nathan, my friend Martha's baby boy. Card after card, the sentiments are the same. It's been a rough year, but we'll make it through. Peace. Joy. Happiness. I sigh. Screw Covid.

As I finish my afternoon mail ritual, I set the holiday cards on the counter and line them up one by one for the kids to see when they come home. I realize it's almost four o'clock and time for them to get off the bus. I pull out some bags of popcorn, goldfish, and apple sauce pouches and lay them out on the counter, ready to go. I throw on my coat and boots by the front door and turn on the Christmas lights on the trees, fence, and bushes. They love getting home from school and seeing the house lit up.

I pull open the door, and the December wind whips me in the face. I shiver, pulling my coat up high around my neck, and begin to walk up the street. I like to see the bus coming down the lane. Today, it's empty and quiet outside. There isn't a single person around. The sun is already setting over the trees behind the house, casting an amber light on the horizon.

I look forward to this time in the afternoon when the kids get home. Even though the hours that the kids are in school are necessary for me, I miss them. Evan spoke to their principal yesterday and got special permission for them to start attending school every day, full time. The hybrid Covid schedule they've been following up to this point has been inconsistent and unfulfilling for us all. But starting in a few weeks, after the holiday break, they'll be in school every day. No more of this alternating one week at home and one week in school. The irregularity of it all has been hard on us.

After a particularly rough time last week with the kids on Zoom trying to learn remotely and my attempts at remote alcohol recovery, I lost it. I yelled at Brayden for accidentally skipping his eleven o'clock Spanish class, and I cried when I spilled tomato soup all over the countertop at lunch.

The kids stood staring at one another, unsure of what to do. That night, Evan suggested we call the principal and make the request. "That way, you can focus on your recovery," he told me gently.

Evan was honest with Mrs. Peterson and told her what it is I'm up against, and she granted us special permission.

When the kids are out of the house, the quiet mornings alone are indispensable to my own learning process. I am a child again. A student. Introspective and inquisitive. Questioning my brain and body.

This learning experience is therapeutic, and I'm beginning to repair the broken bits. I'm a baby bird, fragile and wanting to fly. I found a therapist that's actually accepting new patients, which is unheard of these days. I'm growing stronger and gaining confidence in myself. I believe that by doing all of this, my kids will be happier and safer. This is all for the betterment of my family.

I'm starting to "work on myself," as they say in recovery. That's what it's all about. Because I can't just stop drinking and pretend everything in this world will be perfect for me. There's a bit of self-reflection to be done.

I keep my hands busy baking for the kids. I journal. And when I feel myself start to wonder what the hell I'm doing, I walk some more or log a few more miles on the Peloton, all while attending my daily Zoom support meetings. I'm doing all the things I'm supposed to do in the first month of sobriety like an obedient student. All in the name of not drinking.

I am trying to heal.

For myself.

For my children.

For my husband.

While I wait for the bus to arrive, I think about the holiday cards. Rachel with the five kids from Vermont. What's really going on behind all of those radiant, perfect smiles? Isn't her brother in jail? Vanessa, my college field hockey teammate. What's she hiding? Last time I ran into her over a glass of wine in Boston, her husband was sleeping in the guestroom.

I stop myself. Maybe they all have their secrets too. They could be hurting just like me. Things aren't always what they seem. Perhaps we are all just a little bit broken, in need of some mending, every single one of us.

First Sip (1996): Fourteen Years Old

In the fall of 1996, I transferred to the all-girls private school in town, Greenwich Academy, the partnering sister school to Brunswick, the all-boys school across the street. My parents decided I needed a smaller classroom size, better teacher attention, and to be more focused on my schoolwork. I'd always had a tough time keeping up in school and had mediocre grades, and my parents thought a private school environment would help me excel. I knew that I was privileged and fortunate to be attending G.A. I was grateful to leave behind the large hallways of the public school filled with throngs of mean girls whispering and staring.

I found myself actually looking forward to wearing a uniform for a change and not being judged by the jeans I wore each day. As much as I was going to miss seeing Megan in the hallways at school, I was excited about the small class size and the possibility of making new friends. Regardless, Megan and I would remain close for the duration of high school, continuing to see each other most weekends.

"These girls are more like you," my parents told me, and although I didn't exactly understand what that meant, I needed to believe it. I was ready to finally and truly fit in. I wanted what my parents were promising me.

What I knew about the kids from G.A. and 'Wick was only from my past days of ballroom dancing as a little girl. I didn't know many kids from there, and all I knew from dance classes was how awful and tight knit everyone seemed.

My friend Phil, who I'd known since I was in kindergarten, was going to private school along with me, attending Brunswick. I had a crush on him at one point in first grade in Mrs. Farrell's class when he sat across from me in art. Phil lived down the street from me, also near the country club. We spent our summers together golfing and playing Sharks and Minnows in the deep end of the pool. At least I had a familiar face in him. I was thrust into a brand-new world, terrified and intimidated. It was as if I were five years old and back at my first day of ski school all over again. I wasn't sure if I had anything to offer this place.

Right from the start, everyone acted like a sorority, hugging and lounging in one another's laps. I felt left out of it all. Both of my sisters had figured out their places there, so I wanted to be part of the sisterhood. But I didn't feel as though I fit in right away. All the girls wore collared shirts and matching bows in their hair.

The first day I came home from school, I told Mom I needed to have the brown loafers with the green laces from J.Crew. She looked at me with disbelief. I knew what she was thinking.

"We don't shop at J.Crew," she informed me. "Only the J.C. Penney catalog. Find something in there."

"I don't want to look at J.C. Penney," I told her, "I want the ones from J.Crew!" This was the first of many arguments about my uniform.

Like any private school, a hardworking competitive edge was ingrained in every one of those girls. They had been taught to work hard from day one in kindergarten, the very first day they'd put on the standard plaid kilt. I was worried I couldn't hack it, but as soon as I stepped foot on campus, I grew determined. I wanted to be a G.A. girl—I would figure out how to blend in and how to play the game. I would create my path.

Eventually, after much convincing, I persuaded Mom to buy me the loafers I wanted. I began dressing the part and acting like the girls I befriended. I learned how to roll my kilt at the top to make my skirt shorter, and I wore my hair in a loose pony with a ribbon just like the rest of the girls.

Pretty quickly, I made the field hockey team, which allowed me to eventually earn my spot as someone worth knowing. Someone that others wouldn't immediately forget. Athleticism earned you status. And by being on the field hockey team, I soon got looped into the party scene that not all were privy to.

It was at this school that I discovered a new side of myself. At the same time, I set course on a path of self-destruction, blind to the damage I was inflicting upon myself.

High school is challenging for most kids, and my experience was no different. I wanted to belong. I found myself turning away from the comfort and approval of my family and instead began searching for acceptance from the girls at school.

I didn't seek support from my older sisters; their allegiance was always to my parents anyway. I felt as if no one in my family understood me. I pulled away from them. I didn't confide in my mother like most girls did. I felt a burning desire to belong to something larger, yet I needed to be part of the crowd. I was constantly concerned how others saw me.

But soon enough, I learned that alcohol was the true gateway to acceptance. I also discovered that it was the best way to alleviate the social anxiety that had penetrated my existence since the days of ballroom dancing classes as a little girl. Alcohol made me worry less and not think as much.

The first high school party I attended was during my sophomore year. The party was at Phil's house, and his parents were gone. Megan and I showed up together. There were a handful of familiar faces there, and they were all drinking beer. This made me nervous because I'd never drunk alcohol before. I was only fourteen years old. My sisters would have never shown up at a party like this because they knew Mom and Dad wouldn't allow it.

The moment I walked into that house, I wondered if I should stay. I knew what my parents would have wanted me to do, but I didn't want to follow their rules. I wanted to fit in. It felt lawless and carefree hanging out in a house with no parents. The party was small and intimate, and I felt safe. This was going to be my little secret.

Suddenly, I saw myself back at the golf shack, my first cigarette in hand. I felt there was a bravery I needed to exhibit, and this was a path I had to explore. Dad always said, "You can't be brave if you don't feel scared."

An older boy I didn't know asked me what I wanted to drink.

"Kimmy, you don't have to have a beer if you don't want to," Megan said.

"Yes, she does!" Phil yelled.

"No, she doesn't! She can have a soda," Megan said.

I looked at the faces around me. I didn't know a lot of the people, but everyone was waiting for my answer.

"Sure, why not? I'll have a beer," I said, and everyone cheered. I felt powerful and cool.

Turquoise pool lights bounced off the trees in the yard, music blasted from the speakers on the side of the house, and steam rose off the surface of the water. I dangled my bare legs into the pool as the boys splashed water and threw a basketball back and forth.

Everyone was yelling and jumping around me, but for a moment, time stood still. I sat next to Megan on the edge, smiling and waiting. A beer can was placed in my hand. A warm Bud Light.

I hesitantly snapped it open, foam dripping over my fingers. Held back by a bit of apprehension, I waited. I felt like there was a spotlight on me. Was everyone staring at me? Would they make fun of me? But the music played louder, and the boys continued their game of pool basketball.

I contemplated what would happen if my parents found out. What would happen to me if my teachers knew what I was about to do? My coaches?

The wavering lasted a moment longer, but the music, the mood, and the laughter made me relax. Everything felt easy and calm. And for a fourteen-year-old girl, it was the perfect night for her first beer.

I was determined to be bold and strong. Maybe I wanted to blend in like the cool kids by promising myself that this was a secret. Slowly, I brought the can to my lips. I put my mouth on the rim and took a sip.

The warm, sour beer filled my mouth. It tasted rancid. I cringed, wondering if all alcohol was this gross.

Was that what Mom's wine tasted like? I thought about the green jugs under the counter. The pop of the cork and the smell wafting through the kitchen in the late afternoons.

I took another taste, this time pulling a longer, deeper sip. It felt strange, but it felt right.

Megan was staring at me, waiting for a response. I shrugged, burped, and we laughed. I took another big gulp. Almost immediately, my head began to spin.

I finished the beer quickly. Nausea kicked in fast, and I contemplated getting up and going for a walk.

Is this what drunk is? I wondered. *Drunk off one beer?*

I was scared for a minute. I sat still, and the feeling passed quickly.

"It's an acquired taste," Megan said, cracking open another can and handing it to me.

I took it from her and smiled. "Cheers!"

I didn't finish that second beer, but I took small sips, feeling my head spin ever so slightly. I was anxious and didn't want to feel any sicker than I already did. I also didn't want my parents to know what I was up to.

I didn't realize it at the time, but by lying I was creating my own treasure chest of dark secrets, just as my parents had subtly been doing for years.

I felt guilty for lying to my parents, but I buried those feelings and found a way to move forward after that night. I was a teenager, and that was what everyone was doing.

It was easier to pretend my behavior was normal, even though I knew it was wrong. It was easier to lie to myself to fit in than it was to stand up to the crowd.

I made a choice to be part of something. At that point in my life, I unknowingly set course on a dangerous path of self-sabotage, and there was no turning back. Because of that night, I would someday find myself on the edge of shattering.

Bermuda (1997): Fifteen Years Old

Seashells crunched beneath the tires of the taxicab as it pulled up the driveway of "Old House." I watched the decrepit brown van create a cloud of dust as I sat on the front steps, a feeling of disappointment enveloping me. No matter how many days we spent on the island of Bermuda, it was never enough. I never wanted to leave. It was our family's special spot. Our escape. A release from the confining expectations that our life in Greenwich asked of us. There was no place in the world like it. Time stood still, and all of my concerns from days back home seemed to temporarily disappear.

"I don't want to go yet," I said to Dad, who stood beside me, waving at the driver. The usual post-vacation blues were beginning to creep in, and we hadn't even left the island yet.

"I know you don't," he replied plainly. "Me neither. It's never easy leaving here." But he grabbed a suitcase and began to walk toward the cab.

I used my hand to shield the bright morning sun from my eyes. Watching my father, I saw him greet the Bermudian cab driver with a strong shake of the hand and a simultaneous clap on the back. The two of them chatted happily to one another as they began to load up the trunk with our belongings. I scowled at Dad's cheeriness.

"Does anyone want me to make a peanut butter sandwich before we go to the airport?" Mom called from inside the house. She was always dead set on using every last bit of food at the end of a vacation. She didn't like to waste anything.

I looked back over my shoulder at the white stucco building, a tiny green lizard climbing up the side momentarily distracting me. I sighed, stood up, and decided that a sandwich was probably better than the rubbery eggs they fed us on the airplane anyway.

Walking into "Old House" one last time, I took a deep breath. The scent of Dad's distinct Ban du Soleil sunscreen mixed with the musty dampness of the antique furniture gave me a familiar sadness. A longing to stay and remain in this place of comfort and continue this quiet existence. Bermuda living was easy. Simple. Life back home seemed busier and more complicated.

I looked around at the card table where my sisters and I played Hearts every night after long days of bodysurfing down at the beach. I glanced out the doors at the sprawling view of the Atlantic Ocean and listened for the crashing of the waves. I watched the Bermuda Longtails soaring high over the white caps out on the horizon, their pointy tails dancing playfully in the sun.

"We'll be back soon," I told the Longtails.

I was momentarily distracted by a door slamming shut and some shouting behind me. I could hear Dad's voice rising and Mom yelling back inside the small kitchen. Their words were muffled, but I didn't care to know what they were fighting about anyway. I didn't want it to ruin the end of the vacation. I didn't want it to discolor my final memory of "Old House."

Mom appeared at my side and pushed past me out onto the patio. She carried a large wine glass full of chardonnay in her right hand and a bottle of wine in the other. She slammed the bottle down on the table and tipped the glass back, draining the entire goblet in one long, exhausting gulp.

"We need to use up all the food. Go grab a snack or a soda, Kimmy," she said.

I stood there quietly. It wasn't even eleven o'clock in the morning, and she was drinking wine. The entire scene felt strange because we were getting ready to go to the airport. I was accustomed to her having wine in the evenings and at dinner, but it wasn't even lunchtime. All the arguing made sense now. It occurred to me why Dad was angry with her.

Mom's gaze was now on the same horizon I'd just been watching. The puffy white clouds floated above the turquoise waters, and she seemed as distant and distracted as the small sailboats way out at sea. She poured herself another large glass, avoiding eye contact with me.

"You know how much I hate flying," she said and walked back inside with the glass and the bottle.

I didn't follow her. I closed my eyes and listened to the familiar sounds of the ocean. I believed that if I stayed there and let the warm Bermuda sun wash over me a moment longer, perhaps everything would be alright when it was time to say our final goodbyes to my favorite island.

This was a pivotal moment for me. There comes a time in everyone's lives when they realize their parents are human. That day, I saw my mother as someone who was not steadfast and perfect or without fault, but instead she felt like a distant stranger. She was unexpectedly a person capable of making real mistakes; she was no longer just Mom.

A Bottle of Jack (1997): Fifteen Years Old

The first time I got really, truly drunk was also the first time I blacked out from alcohol. I was fifteen. I lied to my parents about where I would be for the night. Instead, I slept at my friend Jill's house, where there was a group of six boys and girls all spending the night. I knew what my parents would think if they found out who would be there and that Jill's parents weren't home. But I didn't care. I was excited to do something new and daring, and I didn't want to miss out on the fun.

Up until this point, I hadn't been to many big drinking parties. Alcohol still made me nervous, and I was working on the art of twisting the tops off beer bottles. I also hadn't yet perfected the craft of sipping without having foam spill out the sides of my mouth. I was nervous and reserved in social settings, always yearning to fit in. But I knew when I drank beer that a looseness came over me.

I was always careful not to let myself get too out of control, but I felt relaxed whenever I sipped on a Bud Light. I also knew enough to recognize that getting really out of control was frowned upon by other kids. In order to be cool, you had to know how not to make a scene when you were drinking. You didn't want the whole school talking about you on Monday. I also never wanted my parents to catch onto what I was doing. It was a delicate balance of pleasing my parents and my friends.

That night at Jill's, I told myself I'd just have one or two shots. I'd never drunk hard alcohol before, but I wanted to try it. I wanted to have some fun. I had the entire night ahead of me, and I was going to let loose. I felt safe with my friends, knowing that I didn't have to face my parents until the next day.

When I brought the shot glass to my mouth, the painful sensation of the Jack Daniel's stung my lips and burned my throat. It filled my stomach with warmth and my head was overtaken by a woozy sensation. My limbs felt like butter melting into the darkness of the pool deck. My friends laughed around me, morphing into an eruption of cheers and a thumping that startled me.

"You want another?" they asked me.

"Hell yeah!" I shouted.

I wanted to chase the warmth. The tingly happiness inside my brain. That buzz. I didn't want to let this euphoria slip away. I felt open. Detached. There was an untethered comfort, and I wanted to stay in this space forever.

I took another shot of Jack and let it smolder in my gut. I felt brave, for once. Excited. I reeled with delight.

This was going to be my night. I poured another, slamming the glass bottle back down onto the teak deck with conviction, spilling some of it on my jeans and shirt.

"It's fine, it's fine!" I said to nobody in particular. I laughed some more, alone in my thoughts.

I followed a boy I liked into the shadows beyond the grass, into the trees, our fingers touching and nothing else. His name was Jake. There was a pulse of electricity between us. A connection I'd never felt before. The laughter of our friends in the distance was muffled through the trees, and I could barely see the outline of his straight brown hair in the darkness.

Part of me wanted to go back to the group, afraid of what lay ahead.

But more of me wanted to stay. I wanted to be there with him. As nervous as I was, I felt wild and confident—a feeling as unfamiliar as the touch of his warm skin against my own.

Before I knew what was happening, we were awkwardly wrapped around each other, our teenage bodies fumbling in the moonlight. Unsure of what to do, I let him put his arms around my waist. With a confidence unknown to me, I stared into his eyes and felt myself melt away. And then he kissed me. He rubbed his body against mine, and I briefly thought back to the My Little Pony pillow in my basement. This felt so much more exciting than that pillow ever did.

I laughed and pulled away from him as he chased after me, out of the trees across the lawn toward the light. I needed more alcohol.

The music played from the speakers attached to the guest house. The Backstreet Boys echoed across the vastly manicured lawn, and we turned the bass up even louder.

Everyone continued to drink. We laughed harder. The sounds and colors around me created a simultaneous mix of slow-motion and fast-forward fragments of time.

I stayed beside Jake, and the noises grew louder. The music bounced off the tall oak trees. The cheering ensued. All the while, there were no parents around. No one to tell us to stop. No one to tell us that was enough.

I spun in circles, staring up at the stars around me.

Jake smiled at me.

Another shot lit up my insides.

I was indestructible.

I needed to keep feeling this comfort. Just knowing that I could do anything.

This pleasure was everything.

A sense of flying.

Of being unbound. I needed to feel it all coursing through my body. I didn't want it to stop.

But steadily, the sounds started to become a bit too heavy, the warmth began to blanket me in thickness, and the world started to slow down.

The spinning became constant, and I felt as if it wouldn't ever stop. I thought I was upright, but I was unexpectedly swaying sideways.

I hit the ground hard, smashing my face into the pool deck.

Pain shot through my limbs. No more butter or softness. Only sharp fire. And more darkness. The images became starless and indistinct.

And I was slowly being submerged into uncertainty. I was teetering on the edge. Unsteady and shaky, the spots in front of my eyes alluding to a darkness on the horizon. Until there were no more memories. The curtain had come down.

Things went dark. And the rest of the night was engulfed in a thick, velvety blackness. I was told I spent the whole night with my head over the toilet. The party came to a crashing halt for me. And my memory was blanketed in black, fuzzy confusion.

What struck me as alarming was that I wasn't concerned the next day about the fact I had forgotten several hours. I wasn't worried that, for the first time ever, an entire night of my life had been almost completely erased from my mind. I had blacked out, and I wasn't the least bit phased. Instead, I focused on the fun moments with a boy I liked, and reminisced and laughed with my friends about the silly parts I did remember.

I'd been nervous to take that first shot. But quickly, I found it to be the social lubricant I'd always needed. It was the magical elixir of fun, a potion that gave me comfort, confidence, and relief from my insecurities. It let me get outside of myself. It made me feel bigger than what I believed myself to be. It gave me more confidence in mind and body. And in reality, I was completely out of control.

But I wanted to do it again.

Soon after the party, Jake made me his girlfriend. He was the first boy I ever loved, and I loved him hard. Jake became the center of my entire teenage world. I gave him everything, including my virginity that fall of my junior year. He greedily accepted my love, devotion, and undivided attention. It began as a safe, mutual friendship in which we developed a loving bond. By the time we broke up, we were off to college, and I'd developed an unhealthy dependence on him. But those early years of our relationship, when we were first in love, things felt unimaginably perfect.

Over the rest of high school, I began to experiment with alcohol more and more. Soon, I was binge drinking every weekend with Jake by my side, because Jake always liked to drink a lot. I was a good girl at home for my parents and did what I was supposed to do. I kept my head down and focused as much as I could in school, kept my coaches impressed during the week, and worked hard in field hockey. That way, I was able to weave my way through the social scenes on the weekends.

I snuck around from each friend's house to the next, running from one sprawling pool house to another, drinking on docks down by the beach or in empty fields and playgrounds after dark. We were always drinking to get drunk, never sipping on alcohol because we enjoyed it. I mastered the art of sneaking around and stealing booze from my parents. I created a treasure chest of my very own secrets, ones I would keep with me for years to come.

I continued to bend the truth with my parents because the very same thing was unfolding before me at home. The relationship between my parents was deteriorating, and they were not being truthful. There was a lot of hiding, lying, and creeping around within the walls of my home. I decided it was easier to live with the shame of my poor decisions than to face my indiscretions, just as my parents were doing themselves within their marriage. Unfortunately, this would become a pattern of behavior for me for many more years.

Day 20: December 18, 2020

My feet pound the pavement, the icy surface cracking beneath every step. One foot in front of the other. My boots are heavy, my breathing deep in my facemask. This is my daily release. My escape. I walk the streets of Needham, and it helps to alleviate the overanalyzing I do in my brain. I enjoy the meditation and the clarity it gives me. I review my mission, my plan, and my reasons for quitting in the first place, but I keep coming back to the same question. How did I get here?

I look up at the bare, snow-covered trees and the cold sky above, pausing my sobriety podcast for a moment. I wait and listen to the silence and stillness around me, breathing in through my nose and out through my mouth like I've been taught to do these last several weeks.

There isn't a car or soul in sight. I keep walking, concentrating on the placement of each rubber boot. I search for patches of snow and mud in the hopes of not slipping and falling. But my left foot catches a patch of ice, and I start to slide.

"Shit!"

Instinctively, I hold my arms out to my sides to catch my balance, wobbling and tripping into a snowbank. You'd think that years of New England winters would have trained me better for these conditions. But this is actually the first year I've really walked these streets. Honestly, I've never walked so much in my damn life. In this new sober Covid world, there is a hell of a lot of time to do nothing but roam the streets of my small suburban town.

I find my footing again and continue on, more cautious and a bit slower. Today, my solo walk has a mission. I'm meeting a friend. I come to the end of the quiet road and find myself at a busy intersection, cars whizzing by.

I see Catherine standing across the road, waiting for the light to change. I wave to her, making sure she sees me, and I pull my facemask down and smile. She's early, or I'm late.

I haven't seen a lot of friends in a few weeks. I've been quiet, which is easy to do during these times. Everyone's hunkering down. No one really questions it or knows what's going on with me except for a handful of people. It feels nice to see a familiar face. As we approach one another, I realize just how lonely I've been.

"Hi!" I say.

"Hey!" she says, and we air kiss.

I feel awkward. I haven't seen Catherine in over ten months. Since before the pandemic began. This seems to be the pattern with a lot of friends lately. But a few days ago, I felt compelled to text and check in on her.

My last hazy memory of hanging out together was of a ladies' night that went painfully sideways. One glass of wine led to two. This led to us sucking back scorpion bowls at the Chinese restaurant in town, singing Journey's "Don't Stop Believin'" at late-night karaoke.

I point to the side street ahead, and we begin to slowly walk, pulling our masks up high around our faces. I'm happy to be out of the house. Excited to see someone I know in real life. Anyone. Any human other than my kids.

This is the only physical social interaction I get these days, icy walks in the twenty-degree December weather since I haven't been up for gatherings in people's driveways on Saturday nights around a firepit. I don't feel like answering the question, "Why aren't you drinking?"

I've been stuck in my strange sober bubble. Evan has still been going into the office, leaving me every day. He's one of the few people still not working from home.

Catherine and I have always found comfort in the fact that we can say whatever we want to one another without judgment. It feels like a breath of fresh air talking to her. I can speak openly and candidly about things, unlike with some of my other friends. She seems to always understand what I'm going through, and we've often found ourselves in similar situations over the years, with our kids being the same ages. I forgot what a good, thoughtful listener she is.

She knows by our text exchange that I've stopped drinking and wants me to tell her everything. As I begin my story, she listens quietly. I start to feel a comfort I didn't even know I'd been craving. The more I share, the more I feel a release and an openness.

"I don't know why, but I just woke up that morning and knew that I needed to finally ask Evan for help."

"Wow, how did you know?"

"I'm not sure. Some feeling just came over me. And it was as if a massive weight was lifted that I didn't even know was holding me down."

I feel a relaxation come over my body. By the end of my story, I'm exhausted—but in a good way. I feel like I do after a good workout or massage. We talk and walk for more than an hour, not even realizing the freezing temperature or icy sidewalks around us. Catherine shares her own struggles, and we come to realize that we're on the same page more than ever.

"I love how easy it is to talk to you. I miss this," Catherine says.

"Me too."

"I think I'm going to try to drink less. I know that I need to cut back."

"Really? That's great."

"Actually, ever since my dad died, things have been really hard. I've been drinking a lot more than I should. I guess I've been trying to moderate my drinking for the last several years, and I fail more times than not. I always drink way more than I want to. I can't just stop at one. I always want more. And dealing with my dad being gone. My mom has been having a tough time all alone. It's a lot."

"I can't imagine what you're experiencing," I tell her.

"I think maybe I can try to just take a break from drinking. Maybe take a month off. You seem so good. I want what you are feeling."

I can't help but smile. And for the first time in days, I don't feel so utterly alone.

Early Decision (1999): Seventeen Years Old

My parents' struggles only intensified during my later years in high school. Being wrapped up in my own teenage angst, I chose not to acknowledge that they were hurting. By the time I was a senior at Greenwich Academy, my life revolved almost entirely around Jake and my friends. My focus was on where I would get drunk that weekend. I didn't see what was going on at home between my parents, even if there were hints of distress happening at every angle.

Jen and Laura had gone away to college, and I was on my own. The green jug lived on the counter permanently, and Mom fell asleep on the couch snoring at seven o'clock most nights and often couldn't be roused.

Dad usually went to the gym in the morning after making his protein shake and came home late after swimming, post-work, in the evenings. He rarely made it home for dinner. I ignored the signs that they were spending less time together and that things were completely unraveling.

I didn't care. I had to deal with applying to college. Jake was going to Middlebury, and I wanted to be close to him. I believed that wherever I went, I'd just end up married to him in four years anyway, so it didn't really matter. Jake told me to apply to Colby College early, so I did. But Mom tried to convince me to aim lower and stay closer to home.

"Let's look at some different schools," she said. "I don't think your scores are good enough to apply to Colby, anyway."

Mom doubted my ability to thrive in a top school, and she wanted me somewhere I wouldn't be overly challenged. She said she wanted me to feel safe. In truth, I struggled tremendously with attention and anxiety, but I had no idea at the time. I wouldn't learn that until years later.

"Well, Jake thinks I can get into Colby. So I'm going to try," I replied simply.

"I don't know, I worry about you getting in over your head."

"I can look at Connecticut College where Laura is," I suggested. The idea of being near my sister was comforting to me, even if we didn't talk as much anymore.

"Yes, but that's still a reach academically for you. It might be hard to keep up your grades. I just don't want you to be disappointed," Mom said. "I'm just trying to protect you. Let's just go look at some more safety schools on your list. Let's aim a little lower."

She made me tour all kinds of schools in Massachusetts that I didn't care about because she thought all the New England small colleges like Colby and Middlebury were out of my league. She asked me to tour some larger state schools that weren't even on my radar. I spent weekend after weekend appeasing Mom, dragging myself from one college to another. Dad was busy at work, so he couldn't go with us on my college tours. He didn't know what schools I was even applying to. I almost didn't consider Colby out of fear of failure.

In the end, I did apply to Colby College, and I was accepted, early decision. I was led to believe that field hockey had played a huge role in that, so part of me worried I wasn't smart enough to go there. Mom had planted the seed of doubt, and that seed took root, completely consuming my mind and crushing my confidence by the time I arrived in Maine the following year.

A Shoebox Full of Secrets (1999): Seventeen Years Old

Dishonesty begins casually. And it often starts small. During my senior year, after I got accepted into college, I went through a phase where I kept a pack of Parliament Lights tucked away in a shoebox in my closet, along with love notes from Jake, condoms, and a small dime bag of weed that I bought off the streets of Port Chester, New York. These were some of my secret possessions that I never wanted my parents to find.

There was a craving I felt in the late afternoons after school when I thought about the cigarettes. Was it the nicotine I craved, or the need to escape the stress of school? Did I want to do something scandalous and rebel against the privileged lifestyle I'd grown accustomed to? Was I acting out because I had a feeling something was off between my parents? Or did I really just want to feel the dopamine rush as I breathed in the puff of smoke? I didn't know then and I still don't know now, but I craved those cigarettes often.

I opened the shoebox and pulled the pack out, turning it over and over again in my hand. I loved smelling it and practicing with the lighter on my bedroom floor. I feared that craving and obsessed over it. Cigarettes made me nervous; I knew they were bad for me. Images of the angry black lung my gym teacher showed us in sixth grade health class sat in the back of my mind, and I never wanted to be known as a "smoker." My friends and I made fun of girls like that. It was a nasty habit, and we laughed at the groups of teens that hung around on the avenue outside the movie theater surrounded by a cloud of smoke. I was better than that. I also knew what it meant to crave it. I didn't want to become addicted, so I only allowed myself to indulge every so often. I didn't want to die young from cancer, I thought. But it was also really fun to do something I knew I wasn't supposed to.

I waited for Mom to leave me home alone in the afternoons after school so I could sneak out onto the back patio and smoke. My black lab, Maggie, sat at the door wagging her tail, begging to come outside with me and play. I waited until I could see Mom's car heading away from the house, and I followed it down the road with my eyes and around the corner. As soon as she was out of sight, I lit the Parliament Light, expertly blowing the smoke up toward the sky, sighing deeply with relief.

I'm fine, I told myself. *This is no big deal,* I always said. *I deserve this.*

Eventually, I learned how to blow perfect smoke rings. Megan taught me how on one of our bike rides at the club. I watched them float slowly upward, and a feeling of elation momentarily took me away. I spun around in circles, laughing to myself, Maggie watching me intently through the window of the door.

Soon I grew nervous, searching the road for signs of Mom's car on her way back home too soon. I lived in fear of getting caught, picturing her returning unexpectedly for a forgotten checkbook or wallet.

I was terrified of getting into trouble. I loved the danger, but I hated it at the same time. I craved the dizziness the cigarettes gave me, but they also made me sick to my stomach. Exhilaration overwhelmed me as soon as I stepped foot outside. I wanted to feel that I was doing something naughty, but the guilt afterward was sometimes too much to handle. After a puff or two and feeling like I might pass out, I stubbed the cigarette out and crushed it with my shoe, hiding it under a rock. Then I went back inside, washed my hands, gave Maggie a kiss on the head, changed my clothes, and started my homework.

My parents never found the pile of crushed, half-smoked cigarettes out back under the pile of rocks. Years later, my husband would not find my stash of empty vodka bottles at the bottom of our recycling bin either.

As an adult, I'd sneak sips of vodka just like I sneaked cigarettes as a child, hiding from my husband before he got home from work. The same fear and exhilaration would cause my heart to pound in my chest as I wondered if I'd get caught.

Maybe all this time I wanted to be exposed. Perhaps deep down I knew I needed someone to find out about all the lying and save me from myself because I recognized that eventually, my secrets would suffocate me.

Goodbye, Yellow House (1999): Seventeen Years Old

In 1999, my parents decided to sell our house on Winterset Road. My childhood home. The place that contained all of the memories from the last seventeen years of my life—where I built forts in the woods and climbed trees in the front yard; where we went sledding down the stairs in sleeping bags and danced on the kitchen counter singing into spatulas with our favorite babysitter.

I should have taken it as a sign that things weren't going well between my parents.

"What? We're moving? Where? Why?" I shouted, exasperated, my teenage drama and angst brought to a whole new level of pain. Since my sisters were both away at college, the change felt especially directed at me.

"You'll be leaving for college soon," Mom told me, "so your father and I decided it's time to downsize. We bought a condo."

"A condo?" I cried, exasperated. "Are you eighty-five years old and retired? Who buys a condo around here?"

"The backcountry area of Stamford is more beautiful than Greenwich," Dad said, trying to sell me on the new neighborhood. "And not everyone living there is retired."

"I don't care," I said. "Why can't you wait a few years? This is my home. This is so sudden. This is so stupid!"

Being forced to leave my home broke me. As the movers packed up our things, so many happy memories seemed to evaporate into thin air. I watched them float away like the rings of smoke from the secret cigarettes on the back porch. Reminders of a simple past, gone forever. Perfect circles that expanded and disappeared into the sky.

Looking back, I don't know why I didn't see the writing on the wall. Dad was making his escape plan. Something dark and irreversible was brewing between my parents. Still, I refused to let it disrupt my senior year and my perfect plans for my future, so I kept telling people we still lived in Greenwich. I never talked about our move, and I would not be from "Stamford."

There was a pattern of avoidance that I was taught by my parents from an early age. We all pretended everything was normal, a song and dance we'd grown accustomed to for many years. It was a routine I followed into adulthood.

One night, in the new house in Stamford, I had a terrible nightmare about a pack of wolves that lived in the woods behind my old house on Winterset Road. They wore the faces of my friends. I was running from room to room, desperately searching for the switches to turn the lights off, locking every door and window. Outside, the wolves in people's skins stood at the periphery, watching me, waiting.

After I awoke from my dream, I ran to my parents' room in a panic. I was seventeen but I felt like I was five years old again, desperately pleading for their comfort. I felt ashamed for needing them in the middle of the night. I felt stupid for still having the same bad dreams about wolves in people's skins. But I wanted them to tell me it was going to be okay. I needed comfort in some way.

Rationally, I knew there were no actual wolves outside my bedroom window trying to get me, but things appeared off in my mind. Something was wrong. I was afraid. I felt like I was spiraling, out of control and caged all at the same time. I sensed I was on the precipice of something awful, and I couldn't control any of these emotions. I was terrified of what was going to happen to me. I was scared of what people thought of me and worried about how I was perceived, even in my dreams.

In retrospect, there was so much that was changing around me. My childhood was fading. I was growing up and heading to college soon. These things could not be denied. Yet, at the same time, there was more than what the typical teenager might have been facing. I was missing the comfort of a stable home. We were all hiding from one another in the shadows of our own secrets, crouched into our own corners. Scared, ashamed, lying, concealing.

Everything was slipping through my fingers, and I was desperate to hold onto it all with everything I could. Fighting the urge to crawl into my parents' bed that night, I cried at their door.

"Mom? I had an awful dream. Mom? Are you awake? Mom?" I asked, standing awkwardly in the doorway to my parents' bedroom.

She sat up and mumbled something, unable to form a coherent sentence.

"Mom?" I whispered to her again from the doorway, but she went back to sleep.

Maybe she'd had one too many glasses of wine. I wasn't brave enough to find out, and I let her be. I wanted her to sit with me like she used to when I got sick in the night, back when I was a little girl. I wanted her to lay beside me on the couch and scratch my back with the light of the TV glowing against our faces. I wanted her to rub my feet with witch hazel and whisper that it would all end up alright in the end.

Dad opened his eyes and glanced up at me, but he was never the one to care for me when I woke in the night. We stared at each other for a moment while Mom snored.

"Are you okay?" he asked groggily.

"Yes, I'm okay. I had a bad dream," I said and shut the door.

I wasn't a little girl anymore. I crawled back into bed, reassuring myself that everything would be fine. I needed to take care of myself because I was growing up. I tossed and turned the rest of the night. I was on my own now.

My behavior that night was strange even to me, and Dad never knew what to do with it. So he never mentioned it. That was what we did. Don't talk about your feelings or your problems. Keep your head down. Move on.

I think subconsciously I felt Dad might be leaving us soon. Maybe that night was my attempt to draw him out of the shadows—begging him for the truth, for some vulnerability and compassion. *Remove your mask, Dad.*

I didn't trust my parents to keep me safe anymore. Everyone was keeping secrets from me like the wolves in my dreams.

For years, it felt like I was playing a game of jack-in-the-box. Someone was slowly turning the crank on my life. I knew something was coming, but I just didn't know when or what was going to happen.

I was hanging on by a thread. There were cracks forming in my world, and the spackle that would hold it all together was alcohol.

Day 20 (Part Two): December 18, 2020

While preparing dinner in the kitchen, my phone pings and I get a text from Catherine: *Feeling inspired. Not drinking tonight. Let's see where this leads.* She follows up with a picture of two empty wine bottles next to her trash bin.

Good work! I write back with a bunch of bicep emojis and hearts. *Proud of you!*

I feel suddenly giddy. It's good to know that I perhaps inspired this change in my friend. Her dad passed away only a few months ago, and she is lost. Now we both don't have to feel so alone.

I find myself whistling along to the incredibly annoying theme song from *Alvin and the Chipmunks* that my kids are watching on TV, and I smile. I feel light and possibly even happy.

Then I think about how fun it would be to celebrate this moment with a glass of wine. Out of nowhere, I feel as though I've been slapped. I stare down at the cutting board full of vegetables.

"God damnit," I say under my breath.

Ursula, my wine witch, has reared her ugly head. The obnoxious voice that urges me to drink pops up out of nowhere. She reminds me about my old habits when I least expect it. She always starts quietly and innocently.

I've been listening to sobriety podcasts lately, and in one of them they talked about naming your wine witch. Give her a personality. I call her

Ursula because I picture her looking just like that awful, beastly sea hag from *The Little Mermaid*, one of my favorite childhood movies.

Hey, Kim, it's true. You're in a great mood, so a nice glass of wine would really top off this moment. Besides, what time is it? See, it's almost 5:00. You know most of your friends are already drinking by now, Ursula whispers.

She likes guilt trips. That was always her go-to move.

I push the thought out of my mind and focus on my children, dinner, and the tasks in front of me.

Hellooo . . . why don't you have a glass out yet?! There's no better way to cook than with a large glass of wine. Let's get this party started!

There she goes again, setting the scene. She always understood me. She was a good friend like that. She wanted to just keep me company.

I'm here, even when no one else is around to hang out.

But I can ignore this voice now. Because I'm sober. And stronger than I was twenty days ago. Plus, there's no wine in the house.

I just sigh and put my earbuds in and turn on my podcast of choice. Today's topic: How to beat cravings.

In the past, if Ursula got her way and I gave in, she wouldn't just stop at one glass. She was relentless.

Ah, now, doesn't that feel so good and relaxing? This is what it's all about! The initial buzz. Soooo soothing. Now pour another!

She wouldn't stay a friend for long. I know her game all too well. I can't go there anymore. She never really had my back, and she's a bit of a liar, actually.

I'm not going to give in to that bitch—not today. Not tomorrow. I know how to stand my ground now. Screw her.

I focus on prepping this dinner and portioning out the exact amount of carrots to each child so that they don't get grossed out and refuse to eat any of it.

I hear shouting through my earbuds, and I turn to see the boys wrestling on the carpet. Blood is pouring out of Chase's nose. Brayden sits back, smiling. These days, stuff like this happens almost nightly.

These kids are awful. Such spoiled brats. The only way to survive motherhood is with mommy wine juice. You deserve it. You need it, Ursula whispers.

It's okay.

I got this.

I toss the boys a box of tissues and turn the podcast back on.

Ursula will never win. Because I know her ways. She's self-centered.

Her tone shifts to a maniacal, pleading one. She won't give up, but she also won't succeed.

Oh, you should have had some wine, you would be in such better spirits by now. You're just going to blow a gasket soon instead.

In the past, the only way I knew how to deal with my wine witch was to keep feeding her. Drown her in wine.

If I tried to moderate and slow down, she became more insistent, more malicious and crazed. So I just kept drinking. And I couldn't see that what I was doing was remotely wrong.

I just wanted to chase that experience of what it felt like in the beginning: the relaxed, pleasant buzz.

Oh, just go take a few shots or drink a whole bottle, she would say. *It's never getting better until these kids go to bed. You're on your own, girl!*

Nothing I did ever stopped the voice in my head. So I just drank to shut her up and to drown her out.

Just then, Parker startles me from my thoughts. I watch as she accidentally dumps her cup of milk on the floor, and I feel my last and final nerve of the day sever.

I'm spent. My head is throbbing and I'm just about ready to throw in the mommy towel for the evening.

I get the dishrag without yelling at her, breathe deeply, and begin to wipe the mess up off the gleaming hardwood floors. I open the fridge to grab the milk jug and glance at the empty spot on the top right corner where my wine bottle used to sit. I sigh and close the door slowly.

I am okay. I am not drinking.

Ursula is never going to win.

The wicked wine witch is fucking dead.

High School Finale (2000): Eighteen Years Old

Mom sat alone most nights at the new house with a glass of wine in hand at the kitchen counter, the lights dim. Dad often stayed at a hotel in Greenwich. He said it was easier to get to work the next morning and to be closer to the gym than to drive the thirty minutes from Stamford.

I hid in my room talking on the phone with Jake, pretending my life was fine. But I had a feeling something drastic was on the horizon. I was waiting for that jack-in-the-box to pop out, scare me, or change things forever.

"The Stamford condo was a lot farther away than we realized, huh?" Dad laughed one evening when he made it home early for dinner.

"Why the hell did we move so damn far?" I asked him.

"Don't swear, Kimmy," Mom said.

I let it go. I didn't question the situation more than that, but in hindsight I know I was choosing to ignore the obvious.

Where was Dad? Mom was drinking more than she should have. I pushed all of this to the back of my mind and focused on myself because that's what teenagers do.

I spent a lot of time at friends' houses, away from my own home.

It was easy to be consumed by my own high school worries since my entire world revolved around my boyfriend and friends. I wasn't going to let my parents' adult problems ruin all the fun I was determined to have in my last year of high school.

I was going to take advantage of the fact that they were less present in my life, wrapped up in their own personal matters. I seized the opportunities to stay out later, sleep at Jake's house, and sneak out to parties.

Toward the end of the fall season of my senior year, Mom took me to a field hockey team dinner. We were at one of my teammates' house with all my friends and the other moms and dads, but my own dad wasn't there.

We ate pasta and salad in preparation for the big game the next day, all of the players crowding around on the floor in the family room in front of the oversized flat-screen TV. We watched a movie while the parents chatted in the kitchen over cocktails.

I had driven us in my new Land Rover Discovery that I'd received for my birthday, and when it was time to go, I struggled to pull Mom away from the adult conversations.

"Mom, let's go! Coach says I need to get some sleep!"

"One minute, Kimmy!"

"Mom, time to go! All the parents are leaving!"

She tipped her glass back and finished her drink, giggling. She was drunk. She slurred her words on the ride home and kept telling the same story over and over.

I was frustrated and embarrassed by her. As soon as we walked in the house, she flopped down on the couch in the family room.

I left her alone in the dark, calling out my cat's name and singing to herself. I went upstairs to my room. I wondered what exactly she had said or done at the dinner and what all the parents thought of me for being the only player there without her dad present.

As my senior year started to come to an end, I began to panic and grow fearful of leaving Jake. I was happy I'd gotten into Colby, but I didn't want to go. I felt like it was all happening too fast, and I wanted more time.

Megan was attending Colby with me, which was exciting. I also had my friend Phil, who had been with me for years. But I wanted Jake to come with me. A huge part of me also worried I wasn't smart enough to hack it there.

I escaped from the reality that high school was over and drank a lot that summer. I obsessed over my love for Jake and avoided accepting the truth that there was no way we would stay together forever.

There was also a deeper truth I wasn't yet ready to face. Mom was drinking too much, and Dad wasn't around to care.

I was the last of their children to leave home for good. There were huge changes happening, and I was unable to recognize what was going on right in front of me.

Colby College (2000) Eighteen Years Old

The day I arrived at Colby College, I resented my parents for bringing me there. I behaved like a toddler forced to eat her vegetables and had a fit when it was time to pack up my bags and head out. In all honesty, I was petrified to leave my parents and live on my own.

"I don't want to do this!" I cried at the continental breakfast at the Best Western off I-95 on my first morning as a freshman.

The campus was set atop charming, picturesque Mayflower Hill, prominently towering in the background of the old mill town of Waterville, Maine. There were pristine grounds with beautifully maintained brick buildings and attractive students gathering in every quad. Visually, the campus had seemed ideal to me during the visitors' weekend the year before. The people were euphoric and exuded total happiness and joy. But when I arrived that morning in late August, it seemed dark, expansive, and completely overwhelming.

"College sucks," I mumbled as we drove up to the athletic center.

"You'll love it!" Dad said cheerfully.

Everywhere I looked, everyone else seemed excited to be there. I, on the other hand, wanted to be back home in the safety of my small bubble at G.A. I wanted to be back in the comfort of Jill's pool house, sneaking vodka and driving with the top down in Stephanie's Jeep, winding along the road around Tod's Point with the sunshine on my face overlooking the Manhattan skyline. I ached to feel Jake's body pressed against mine as we snuggled on the couch in his basement watching baseball with his friends, sipping Bud Lights. I wanted familiarity. I wanted safety. I wanted to go home.

Instead, Colby felt strange. Unknown. Swarming with too many students. So many eager, animated kids happy to get away from their homes. Was I in over my head?

"Why is everyone so excited?" I asked Mom as we pulled up to the field for preseason field hockey. "This place feels so weird. People are all smiling and laughing."

I waited by the car, assessing the groups of girls warming up by the track. My parents stood beside me, ready to walk me over and deliver me to the coach for the timed run—the first test of my college career.

"We'll be waiting at the car when you're done!" Mom said. "We'll watch you from here!"

"Please don't. I think I'm going to puke," I told Mom. "I'm not going. I don't want to run. I don't care about playing field hockey. I just want to go home."

Maybe I could get her to sneak me out of there.

"Yes, you do," Dad said. "You love this sport. Let's go. You have to go meet the coach. Come on, we will walk you."

"I can't. I just can't do it." I felt weak and dizzy.

Mom looked just as panicked. I could see she was thinking this whole thing was a bad idea. Maybe she wanted to interject and tell Dad that I should have stayed in Connecticut and gone somewhere closer to home, like UCONN. Maybe she wanted to remind us once and for all that Colby was too much of a reach for me in every way.

"Let's just all walk over there first," Dad said. "Let's go check it out."

Mom and I exchanged looks.

I followed Dad to the track, staring straight down at the ground, my shoulders hunched. After a few minutes of small talk, I begrudgingly said hello to the coach and captains and agreed to do the test. The nerves I felt were enough to make me pass out.

"It's just butterflies, Kimmy, you can do this!" Dad said encouragingly. I looked up at him, wanting to throw up on his shoes.

I ran, but I stumbled my way around the track. I jogged when I should have sprinted. I walked when I should have run. I got a bad cramp on the last lap and stopped for ten seconds to dry heave right before crossing the finish line. I barely completed the stupid thing.

My parents awkwardly sat in the stands together, watching me. But I did it, and it was over.

Afterward, Mom and Dad lugged the endless Tupperware bins from Bed Bath & Beyond all the way from my Land Rover down the long hallway to my small dorm room.

I had been so focused on myself and my own needs that I never considered the fact that Mom was going to be alone at home with no one else to take care of anymore. Dad would be there with her, but my parents were empty nesters now.

I didn't consider how my leaving might impact them both. I was so angry with them for making me go to college, which in retrospect was very selfish. I knew I wasn't actually going to stay home since all of my friends were leaving too, but I couldn't help feeling upset. I think I knew deep down that things were about to shift drastically for us all.

"Let's put your clothes away," Mom said. "This is the fun part!"

She began unpacking, hanging up my shirts and pinning my Jimmy Buffett posters to the walls for me, all in an attempt to make my cement block of a room feel cozier. I would later find out the kids on campus called my hallway "the virgin vault" because it was the only all-girls floor on campus.

I felt numb. I was tired. I looked around my new room and watched Dad set up the brand-new TV, VCR, and stereo that he'd bought me from Circuit City.

Mom put my underwear, socks, and shoes away in my closet. My new home was organized and unpacked in less than an hour.

Mom attempted to distract me by reading about the orientation dinners and meetings from the pamphlets. "Oh, how neat, they have a DJ in the student center tonight!"

"Cool," I shrugged, staring at the cement wall in front of me.

A little while later, I watched from the window of the common room as my parents drove off.

I couldn't hold it back any longer. I sobbed uncontrollably, my face pressed against the glass. I didn't want them to leave, and I immediately felt homesick for them both.

Mom smiled and gave me two thumbs up from the passenger seat. She was trying to stay positive for me, but I could see tears in her eyes as well. I knew that things would never be the same after that.

Day 22: December 20, 2021

As of two days ago, I now know at least two women who don't drink. I have real-life sober friends that I can text, call, and talk to, other than my husband. Two people that just seem to understand and know how I am feeling, without any judgment. It's nice.

Things seem different between me and some of my other friends. The ones that know I stopped drinking, a few of them have stopped returning my texts. I thought certain friends would have been more supportive with my decision, but they've gone silent over the last several days. With Francy and Catherine, there's a compassionate understanding. These ladies just seem to know what I'm going through.

"It gets easier," Francy says, walking along beside me on the path near my house.

"Physically, I feel better," I tell her. "The booze is out of my system, so I no longer think about it nonstop. But I feel a little lost. Disconnected from life. I'm scared I won't be able to even enjoy Christmas because it won't feel fun. It won't be the same. What is Christmas without a nice bottle of red wine?"

"There's so many better things you can do with your life than numb yourself with wine," she says. "You can actually be there for your kids. Not being drunk is the best gift you can give them."

We keep walking until we find ourselves in front of my house with nowhere else to go. Francy turns and faces me, placing her hands on my shoulders. She looks me in the eyes and pushes her sunglasses onto her head. I smile at her suddenly serious demeanor.

"It's like a best friend that's absent for the first time for the holidays. A family member that's usually always there every Christmas but is dead. He's passed away, and you're mourning his loss. Your buddy, booze. Done. Alcohol has died. See ya, fucker! And it's sad that he won't be there to celebrate with and be part of the festivities, but it's time to create new memories without him. You need to leave him in the past. He taught you a lot about yourself, but it is time to move on."

I chuckle and contemplate this for a moment, biting my lower lip, watching the trucks whizz down our busy street. There's a large part of me that knows Francy is right. I am better off. I need to just get used to things this way.

"You're right. I need to fast-forward whenever I get a craving," I say. "Play the tape forward. Remind myself of what it's like when I drink. I need to remember last Christmas when I had too much wine the night before and spent all morning hungover in the bathroom puking. I missed the kids opening gifts."

"You were not present for the presents," Francy says and smiles.

"I was anything *but* present," I concede.

"Yup. You'll see how much better the holidays are this year. Just you wait."

I know Francy is right. I believe this deep in my core, but there's that little voice that questions it all. Something deeper than Ursula the wine witch. I can feel the little girl inside of me. That adolescent child who still throws a tantrum because she isn't getting her way. The little girl who hides angry notes in her mother's vases because things aren't going how she wants them to. This wasn't how she planned her life. Things feel murky, strange, and unfamiliar. I think she's pissed. She's confused. She's scared. She's lonely. But she doesn't know how to manage any of this, so she wants what she's always used as a crutch to get her through the difficult stuff. She wants her booze back.

The Start of the Next Four Years (2000): Eighteen Years Old

Once my parents left me at school and the initial shock wore off, I began to adjust. I got my feet on the ground and was forced to settle into college life. I got along well with my roommate, Marisa, and within a matter of days, I realized college wasn't going to be too bad. I discovered a new type of independence along the beautiful sidewalks of Colby College, and it was here where I forged a different path, exploring a side of myself I hadn't yet met. Jake and I agreed to see other people, and I was intrigued by this newfound freedom. It was refreshing to uncover this inexperienced side of myself.

I learned that life at Colby revolved around the weekend. I started to see this place was going to be a lot more fun than I'd ever expected. The eagerness and energy the other students exuded began to rub off on me. How could it not? There was freedom unlike anything else I had ever known; that unique self-determination you only experience the first time you leave home.

Maine was my home now. And Colby was full of immense excitement and fun. It was an endless loop of amusement. I called and spoke to my parents now and again, checking in to let them know I was settling in, but I didn't feel the need or the want to talk all the time. The distance started to feel comfortable. I had to establish my autonomy, and I knew I needed to prove that I could do life on my own.

"Where is the party this weekend?" I asked my new friend, Mandy, in Psych class Thursday morning during the third week of school.

"We will start at the senior apartments. Then go off-campus to the Farmhouse," she said.

I got a prickle of excitement and a few nervous butterflies in my belly. I knew I needed to be drunk to show up to those kinds of parties. There were going to be a lot of people, and a lot of upperclassmen.

"What time?" I asked, biting my lip.

"Get off campus by eleven," said Derek.

"Hopefully, the cops don't show up this time," said Marisa.

My friends didn't seem as nervous when talking about preparing for these nights. I was up for anything, but I always felt anxious.

College was a constant party, and I felt pressure to fit in. I wanted to have fun but also find my way into the right crowd. Classes and field hockey were supposed to be my focus, but I had bigger distractions. Attending parties became the highlight of my week, and the events of the weekends sat at the forefront of my mind ahead of all other priorities. We discussed where we were going starting Monday morning, as well as the theme of the Saturday evening soiree. We communicated with one another on AOL Instant Messenger all week, planning our outfits.

"Can we really sneak into the senior apartments?" I asked as I put on my makeup that Saturday night.

"Freshmen can always get into any party, so yeah, why not?" Marisa replied.

At Colby, you either got on board or you missed the boat entirely. To keep up, I learned who to be seen with and what crowds not to associate with. The football parties were the rowdiest, and those boys loved freshmen girls. The soccer guys were quieter but friendly. It was fall, so the baseball boys were off-season and always down to drink. I was told to steer clear of the hockey boys, as they were only looking for sex and nothing more. And finally, everyone knew that the off-campus underground frat parties were the best and drew the biggest crowds.

Getting drunk was my end game every weekend. And because of the focus on partying, I began to see alcohol as the magical medicine necessary to get me where I needed to go. It soaked me in confidence and was my gateway to fun. With my trusted friend vodka there to guide me, I felt at ease. I became self-assured when I got my buzz on, especially since some of my new college friends had never really tried drinking before. I was able to show them the way because I'd already dabbled in it in high school.

Gathered around a small table on our knees in my dorm room, I looked around at my new friends. Mandy poured Malibu Rum into a cup of Coke. I cringed and grabbed a bottle of vodka off the floor next to Maura.

"Ladies, ladies. Let's try something different. This is how you take a shot, like this. Watch," I told them.

They all put their drinks down and watched in silence as I poured vodka into one of my shot glasses. I tipped it back quickly and let it slide into my mouth. It burned, but I swallowed it anyway. I slammed the glass back down onto the makeshift coffee table and smiled, my eyes stinging and watering. I forced myself not to gag, grabbing a swig of Sprite and shoving a handful of Cheerios into my mouth.

"See? Easy!"

We all laughed.

I had skills, and I found that I could teach some of them how to get drunk like a proper lady. I gained confidence when I drank. I became a new, more self-assured girl.

It seemed that a light turned on inside me every Friday and Saturday night. That was when I emerged from my shell and came alive.

When I wasn't drunk, I didn't know how to let loose. And unless I was drinking, I felt like I wasn't getting "the ultimate college experience" and didn't know how to get through my weekends.

I struggled through my introductory freshman courses, attempting to study hard in the library most evenings, trying to prove to everyone that I belonged there.

I searched for the confidence so many of my friends had, but I only ever felt true strength and comfort on the weekends when I was drinking. I never considered stepping foot into any of the parties we attended not completely wasted. I needed to have a generous buzz before setting out for the evening.

We liked to pregame in my room, and I needed to have plenty social lubricant before facing any upperclassmen boys. I was petrified by the idea of showing up clear-headed.

I was always questioning how people perceived me, terrified of who I might run into during the day when I wasn't drinking. I felt insecure about so much of myself until I got hold of my trusty friend, Smirnoff, on Friday and Saturday nights. Only then did I relax into my body and stop questioning myself. Only when there was alcohol did I stop wondering what people thought of me and began to feel confident in who I was.

I had been taught since I was a little girl not to allow myself to show any cracks. But there was so much that scared me that first year and threatened to hold me back. I began to figure out how to try and keep myself from breaking. Freshman year at Colby, I knew I had discovered the absolute glue to hold it all together for the next four years. College was going to be fucking awesome.

The Semi-Naked Dance (2000): Eighteen Years Old

Blacking out was a regular occurrence for me. It happened almost every single weekend at Colby and continued well into adulthood. Memories sometimes came back to me in chunks the next morning, but I often lost entire portions of my night—blocks of hours gone, that I'll never get back no matter how hard I fight my brain to locate them. Moments in time evaporated into the cold Maine air.

We started by pregaming in my dorm room. I loved to host the party, and people always came to my room. It was the ultimate gathering spot.

"Shots!" I yelled as Mandy lined up the glasses.

Marisa poured the handle of Smirnoff Vodka across the row.

With the music of Nelly playing through the speakers on top of the closet shelf, we scooped up the shots, swallowed them fast, and cheered loudly. Immediately afterward, I grabbed a handful of crackers as my solid chaser.

"Who wants another one?" I called, arranging the next round, the confidence and excitement building in my chest.

"We need more solid chasers! More cereal!" I emptied a box of Chex onto my desk in front of my laptop while simultaneously fiddling with Napster. We often blasted the same three songs on repeat until we were all sufficiently drunk.

We were dressed in a theme that night. Wherever the party was, we were game. The less clothing it required, the better the costume and the more attention from the senior boys. That night, we were going to the semi-naked dance with the football team, where you had to pay one dollar for each item of clothing you were wearing before you were allowed through the door. I wore a short dress and underwear. No bra. Two dollars.

I felt self-assured with my trusty cloak of liquor. We were going to see Kevin, the boy with the blue eyes that always said hello to me at the gym. He knew my name, and he was a senior on the football team.

By the time my friends and I finished our pregaming ritual, we were well intoxicated. Stumbling down the narrow path in heels, I found my way to the senior apartments with my friends. We always made a point to look out for one another and stick together. There was an unspoken rule about this.

I was adequately lubricated as we walked into the party at Kevin's apartment. It was hot and stuffy, and the only light was from a strand of Christmas lights around the perimeter of the ceiling. Bodies were crammed into the common room, laughing and moving to the loud music. I felt confident and comfortable. I began talking to everyone I bumped into. I walked up to boys I didn't know and grabbed their hands, pulling them close to me.

"Hi! Come dance with me!" I said to Kevin, wrapping my arms around the back of his waist.

He was tall and handsome, and he laughed at my flirtation. Our bodies moved against one another on the dance floor, the sound of the music drowning out the noise of the people around us. I didn't care who was watching me. I liked how assertive I was feeling.

Mandy grabbed my hand and spun me around, but Kevin pulled me back close to him. I laughed and sat down on his lap in the corner, basking in his attention. He was kind and smiled down at me. He told me I was beautiful, so I kissed him. My fingers moved through his long blond hair, but before I knew it, I was thrown off by the intimacy of it. At first I liked it, but then it occurred to me that the only other person to tell me I was beautiful had been Jake. The last person I had kissed was Jake. Kevin's lips felt fuller, and he tasted different. Suddenly, I had enough of the kissing. I said goodbye to Kevin. He gave me a kind smile and told me he'd had fun. I scampered home back to my dorm, laughing with my friends, feeling strange yet excited.

The next day in the dining hall, we rehashed the events of the night. Someone had pictures from a disposable camera developed that afternoon at Walgreens, and we whipped out the evidence of our debauchery. I was embarrassed to look at the photos, but I did anyway.

We began to piece together the rest of the night, laughing about the silly things we each did. I had forgotten that we ordered pizza once we got back to the dorm. Many of my friends had forgotten segments of the evening like I did, which made me feel better. I wasn't the only one blacking out. For us, the photos were invaluable. They gave us clues as to where we'd been, who we'd seen, and what we'd done.

As we huddled around the photographs, Kevin walked past. "Hi Kim," he said, smiling. We broke into a fit of giggles, and I waved to him. I turned bright red and looked away. There was no alcohol in my system to fuel my confidence right then.

The excitement I got from rehashing our nights the next day was worth the anxiety I sometimes woke up with when I couldn't remember my whole night. Seeing Kevin made me want to go out and do it all over again, though. My friends' excited reactions validated the decision to keep getting drunk weekend after weekend. And we continued to do it consistently for the next four years.

New Home (2000): Eighteen Years Old

On that idyllic campus atop Mayflower Hill, we told ourselves many lies. Looming far above an old run-down mill town in the middle of rural Maine, it was here that I began to lose my footing. In those early days of my freshman year, my friends and I all found comfort and confidence inside a bottle of alcohol. We were freshmen girls just looking for fun. I was six hours away from the secure bubble of my hometown of Greenwich, the only other home I'd ever known. At the immature age of eighteen, I was just trying to find my way.

I continued to work hard and partied harder, using alcohol to reassure me on the weekends. I was certain never to be overly promiscuous with the opposite sex, careful to keep my reputation in check. I never had sex, but I liked to flirt and I enjoyed the attention it gave me. I kissed lots of boys, but I wanted to be looked at with respect. I didn't want other people that didn't know me to look down on me. I judged other girls that slept around, so I was careful not to do the same. Reputation was everything at

Colby. I spent so much energy focused on impressing others, only secretly terrified of disappointing myself.

Careful not to go home with just anyone on a Saturday night, I felt in control of my decisions. As drunk as I got, I believed I was safe. I liked to think that I commanded respect from others, but I was allowing others to dictate my self-worth. I let them decide how I should look at myself. I was not in charge of my own feelings. Everyone else was. And when I was drunk, my inhibitions were lowered whether I wanted to admit it or not.

Regardless, I trusted the boys at Colby every weekend to respect me. It was a small community, and safety was never a concern for me. Sexual assault never seemed like a possibility. Those things didn't happen inside our Colby bubble.

I'd been taught self-defense at Greenwich Academy and learned about how to protect myself against a sexual predator. It was a mandatory class for the graduating seniors. I remember kicking our instructor, who was covered in padding, in the groin and neck, pretending to break his nose with my hand.

We had all giggled throughout the tutorial as each of us demonstrated in front of our classmates on stage how to take down our perpetrator. We learned about the fight-or-flight mode, and I always remember thinking I would just run away if ever in that situation.

"I'm such a flight girl," I joked. It felt awkward practicing against the handsome instructor in front of all my friends. "Besides, that will never happen to me. I don't need to know how to do that," I told Mom when I got home later that night at dinner.

"I hope not. You never know. You always need to have your guard up and be prepared. I think you should carry pepper spray with you at all times," Mom said.

"Colby will be in the middle of the woods in Maine, Mom. I'm not going to New York City," I said.

As a freshman, I never imagined I would need to utilize the things I learned in that self-defense class. I never believed I would be targeted. I never thought it would be me.

Day 30: December 28, 2020

I settled down in front of the fire pit beside my friend Trish. The heat of the logs feels hot on my face. I back my chair up and wrap the fleece blanket over my shoulders. *It's colder when you aren't inebriated,* I think.

"Hi! How are you?" Trish whispers.

"Good! We just got here."

"How does it feel?"

"What do you mean?"

"This is your first sober party," she says. "Are you surviving?"

"Yes. I'm fine."

"Is it weird being here and not drinking?"

I hesitate and look up. All around us, groups of people huddle together to keep warm by the fire pits and heat lamps as other couples gather on the outdoor paddle tennis courts—a popular sport at New England country clubs in the wintertime, especially during Covid. It seems like it's the only thing people do lately. That and drink. Our friend John hands out beers like I'm back at Colby.

"I'm fine," I tell Trish. "But I just got here, so maybe ask me in an hour."

We sit in silence. I feel strange, wondering why it feels so different to be here simply because I'm not drinking. I want to stand up and walk around, but I don't know where to go or who to stand beside. I feel like I don't fit in. There's something missing. It's almost as if someone is absent. I feel so lost. I think back to last winter when we came to the paddle courts and I was organizing everyone into flip-cup teams and managing the Spotify playlist. I actually ended the night doing keg stands with some of the men.

Tonight, I'm very aware of my hands. What do I do with them? Why are hands such an awkward appendage all of a sudden? It feels as if there are a thousand sets of eyes on me. Looking across the paddle courts at the groups of people gathered in circles, I wonder if all their voices are whispering about me. Are they wondering why I don't have a drink in my hands? No one else will come and talk to me. The others know I'm not drinking, I am sure of it. They're judging me.

So I sit on my hands and hide under the blanket, unsure of how to formulate even a simple sentence to one of my closest friends.

Beth and Megan are standing with their heads together, quietly talking. I don't know them very well, and we haven't hung out since before Covid. I bet they're talking about me. I can just imagine the gossipy words they're whispering.

Evan comes and sits down beside us. "How's it going?" he asks with concern, snapping me out of my trancelike state. Checking in on me like I'm a child.

I stare at my husband and smile. He leans in close and kisses me on the cheek. "I'm fine," I say, "but maybe we can play some paddle when a court opens up."

"Absolutely," he says rubbing my leg.

"So tell me about Christmas, you guys!" Trish says.

"It was great," Evan tells her. "Really low-key. Lots of quiet time with the kids. Kim cooked a wonderful breakfast, and we went for a long walk as a family. We saw the Christmas lights down in Foxboro at Patriot Place. We started some new traditions. Right, Kim?"

"It was wonderful." I try to add something to the conversation. And my husband is right. It was truly incredible to be present for my children this year. To not be hungover or hiding behind a bottle of wine. "It was a nice, quiet day! How about you guys?"

I try to listen as Trish tells me a story about her family's Christmas and travel excursions over the past week. I can't help but think about my own children.

Christmas morning was the first time I was able to watch them open their gifts without feeling like I needed to run to the bathroom to throw up. I watched each child tear through the wrapping paper, one present after another, surprise on their faces. And I didn't feel like hiding.

"Mommy, look what Santa gave me!" shrieked Parker, holding up an

American Girl doll.

I sat on the floor beside them, watching the red and green paper build up on the carpet, feeling their curiosity. Their joy. Their excitement. I wasn't thinking about if we might start mixing mimosas or when I could begin to tend to my own hungover needs. I didn't think about myself at all.

I giggled with the boys as we took turns riding a rollercoaster on their brand-new virtual reality goggles. I cooked an elaborate spread of bacon and eggs for breakfast, something I never was able to do in years past.

After the morning rush, I did a Peloton ride while the kids watched Christmas movies on the couch. I found myself sobbing uncontrollably to Sia's "Unstoppable" while simultaneously wiping sweat from my forehead. There were so many varying extremes of emotions that day.

I shiver in the cold December air and look around the party. I scan the faces of the people surrounding me. Everyone is engrossed in their conversation, and no one seems to notice how uncomfortable I am. Not a single person is looking in my direction. No one knows the worry I feel. The thoughts swirling around in my head.

I hear Kate tell the same story for the third time in a row to the same group of people. I think she is pretty drunk. Does anyone really listen to anyone else? Is everyone else just as obsessed with their own thoughts like I am right now? I look back at Trish, who's laughing at her own story. She and Evan are talking and not even paying attention to me at all.

"Do you guys want to play paddle?" I ask them both, feeling rude for interrupting her.

"Yes!" they both say. Trish hands me a paddle, and Evan grabs my hand and pulls me to my feet, wrapping his arm around my shoulder.

That Night in January (2001): Eighteen Years Old

I met Jonathon at a football party in the Heights dorm at the end of January. The temperature was well below freezing, as it often was in the winter in Maine. The parties were more of the same, with nothing to do but gather in the common room of a dorm around a keg. The girls and I decided to get dressed up to make the night interesting and break up the monotony. I wore my pleather pants, a backless silk shirt, and my tall leather boots. We'd been hitting the tanning booths regularly, so I had a nice sun-kissed glow.

After our regular pregaming ritual in my dorm, we were perfectly drunk like usual. Things were going as they normally did for us, and I found myself kissing Jonathon on the darkened dance floor in front of everyone. He didn't say much to me that night, and we had never spoken before then. There was a determination to him, though. He was a quiet but handsome boy. It seemed fun. Harmless.

The disco lights flashed in my eyes, and I stumbled around in my tall boots. There is very little that I recall of that night, but there are vivid scenes that stand out. The red, green, and blue strobe lights in my eyes. A smoke machine. His warm hands on my bare back. The distinct smell of cheap keg beer sloshing down the front of my shirt.

I'd had a crush on Jonathon since the day I laid eyes on him that fall at a football party in Taylor. He was a guy's guy, laughing with the boys often and rarely making an effort to speak to me or my friends. I thought he'd looked at me once with interest in the dining hall, but I may have been just telling myself that. He was quiet and not the friendliest whatsoever, but he was incredibly attractive. His eyes were dark, piercing, and sexy. And he was choosing me that night.

I leaned into Jonathon against the wall in the lounge, the lights dizzying me and forcing me to hold onto him for support. I was alone. I couldn't find my friends. I held his hand when we left the party. Where was my jacket? Did I even bring a jacket? I didn't remember. I wasn't sure I wanted to leave with him, but the party was over. I was so intoxicated, and I didn't know what else to do.

I wrapped my arms around my shoulders when we stepped outside. It was cold. Jonathon laughed when I slipped on the ice and slammed my back against the snowy ground. The black sky looked ominous behind him. The stars were bright against a vast inky canvas as I lay in the snow, waiting for him to help me to my feet. His face was illuminated by only a single streetlight on the sidewalk.

I wondered if he would help me stand up. Instead, he just stared at me while I crawled onto my knees, watching me struggle. There was a coldness to his laughter, an iciness in his lack of concern for my well-being.

Then after that memory of being on the ground, there was deep, dark emptiness. A huge shadowy hole of nothing. I blacked out.

I awoke in a strange bed with someone lying on top of me. I wondered how I'd gotten there. Who was this person? And then it came rushing back. The Heights. Kissing Jonathon. Falling down in the snow. I started to remember.

But he was now on top of me. Moving against me. And I was naked. How did I get here? He breathed heavily into my ear. His body was pressed against mine, and I felt weak. Tired. I was suffocating because of his weight. Did he realize this? Where had I gone? Was I here the entire time?

He was trying to force himself inside me, and I abruptly became conscious of what was happening. It was like awakening from a bad dream.

"What? What's happening?" I mumbled. It felt like my body was slowly being pulled from underneath dark, murky water. Like a wave had crashed into me and I was coming up for air. I had been drowning, but now I was finally able to breathe.

"What are you doing?" I whispered, but the weight of his body was stifling. Making it hard to move or breathe or get the words out clearly.

I willed my brain to begin to make sense of the scene, like an engine revving in the cold Maine air, trying to warm up. I wanted my mind to start working faster. But it wouldn't. I couldn't focus. I tried to figure out how I got there, but things wouldn't make sense. Why was Jonathon naked on top of me?

This is not right! Alarms were sounding inside of me. Piercing, screaming and forceful alarms, deep within my belly. This is not right.

To this day, it's a memory that is incredibly sharp and vivid. I wonder why my body has been able to hold onto that particular recollection and feeling for so long. How am I able to evoke such graphic details of this moment but I can't recall the feeling of my son's newborn hair or his gentle baby cry in the hospital years later? Why can't I elicit the feeling of my daughter's tiny infant body as the doctor first laid her against my naked breast, or the joyous sensation that enveloped my heart when Evan proposed to me on the Connecticut shoreline at the age of twenty-four? Why instead do I clearly remember these awful sensations from that night?

I searched to find my words and tried to get control of the situation. I didn't want to make Jonathon mad, but I also knew I didn't want to have this boy's hard, naked flesh pressed between my legs. All I knew was that the situation I was in felt very bad, and I was scared. I thought perhaps I was choking, and the weight of him on top of me made it so I was unable to speak.

"What's going on?" I asked him again, thrashing my legs a bit, as the hair on his chest rubbed against my bare breasts. I finally managed to get his attention, because he stopped moving for a moment. The weight of his body suddenly felt even heavier. He froze and didn't move for what felt like ages. Then he spoke quietly in my ear.

"Oh, hey, umm . . . do you have a jimmy cap?"

I felt paralyzed. I didn't know what to say back. It took a second to understand that he was referring to a condom. I tried to move out from underneath him, but I couldn't. I didn't want it to happen and I wanted it all to stop, yet I didn't want to make him angry. I lay there petrified.

"What?" was all I could manage.

"A condom? Do you have one?"

"Umm. Uhh. I don't, no, I don't want to do that," I told him.

And then I closed my eyes. All I remember is blackness. Indistinct darkness. And everything faded away.

The Morning After (2001): Eighteen Years Old

The next memory I had was of waking up in Jonathon's bed, still naked, the morning sun shining in through a window. My clothes were strewn around the room. I looked beside me to find him fully dressed and asleep with his back to me.

I didn't know if we'd had sex, but my body was sore in places that told me we had. Had he even used a condom?

I pulled my pants on and wrapped my shirt around me. I grabbed my boots and crawled around quietly, looking for my underwear. I didn't look up, hoping he'd remain asleep. I wanted to get as far away from that room and from that boy as quickly as possible.

I tiptoed out the door without my underwear. I ran down the hallway and out of the building, refusing to lift my head or look behind me. Once I was outside, I realized where I was on campus and began to make my way back to my dorm.

Shame washed over me. Had I asked for this? Did I drink too much? Maybe it was my fault. This was never anything I would have allowed myself to do sober. But I'd been too drunk to stop him and was way too blacked out. Maybe I shouldn't have worn that shirt. I had so many conflicting emotions. At the same time, I was mad at myself for screwing it up with this handsome boy, but even more angry that he'd turned out to be such an asshole. Looking back now, I was clearly confused. Why wasn't I more concerned for my own safety and the fact that I had been raped? Why didn't I go straight to the health center and report what had happened to me?

I was always taught to avoid and hide from the truth. Remaining in the shadows was the safest form of self-preservation. And this was no different.

Burying Trauma (2001): Eighteen Years Old

When I got back to my dorm, I put on fresh pajamas, crawled into bed, pulled the covers over my head, and tried to pretend none of it had happened. I slept for most of the day, willing my hangover and mistakes from the night before to disappear. Later that evening in the dining hall, I learned that I couldn't hide from it forever.

I was sitting with my friends, and we were chatting as usual about the events of the night before, picking at plates of pumpkin chocolate chip cookies. I was still trying to put everything with Jonathon out of my mind and simultaneously nurse my hangover when Phil, my friend from Brunswick, sat down tentatively across from me. I had known this boy since kindergarten and the days of my 1980s bowl cut, back when I used to only wear neon pink stirrup pants and tie-dyed scrunchies.

"We need to chat, Kim," he said.

"Okay," I said plainly, unnerved by the expression on his face.

"Jonathon from my baseball team has been talking about you."

"Okay." My hands began to sweat.

"It's not good."

"Well, what's he been saying?" I asked, my stomach dropping.

All of my friends' ears perked up, and everyone was staring at Phil. He leaned in close and whispered that Jonathon had been telling everyone that we'd had sex the night before.

"This doesn't sound like you," Phil said, "and it definitely doesn't sound like anything you want being talked about, regardless."

"I'm going to throw up," I said.

"Also, Jonathon hung your thong from his doorknob, you know. He's been asking the guys to come by and check it out. It's like a trophy or some shit." Phil was barely able to look me in the eye.

I was livid. I was mortified. And I felt lightheaded. But more than anything, I felt deep down in my gut that something was seriously wrong. Yet at the same time, I hoped Phil was lying. Or maybe that Jonathon was just exaggerating and trying to impress his teammates. Absurdly, a screwed-up part of me hoped Jonathon really liked me and that all of this was just a big misunderstanding.

I wanted to run and hide from it all. But I had too much self-respect to stand by while this guy ruined my reputation. With the support of my friends, I was urged to face him.

I left the dining hall with three of my friends and went straight to Jonathon's dorm to confront him. He was stunned to see me, and he was unprepared to deal with the conversation that took place.

With my voice shaking, I demanded he give me my underwear back. Then I asked, "Did we have sex last night?"

I don't know what I was hoping he would say or what kind of response I would get out of him. He hesitated, uncomfortable and awkward. He didn't like being confronted in such a way.

"No, we didn't." He stared back at me, his hands across his chest threateningly. He didn't know what to make of me, but he steadfastly denied any wrongdoing.

"Good," I said awkwardly, "because I remember last night telling you I didn't want to, so if we did, then we have a real problem."

"We don't have a problem at all," Jonathon said confidently, challenging me with his stance, glaring from one face to the next as my friends stood behind me.

I knew at that point I had shown my cards, and I felt disappointed. I was sad that a relationship with a handsome boy I'd lusted after for so long wasn't going to work out. I was embarrassed it had escalated to this, and I wanted to cry. I ran back to my dorm, ignoring the most salient aspect of it all. I had been sexually assaulted. Jonathon had raped me. But this was a fact I would never consider.

Later that night, alone in my dorm room bed, I finally broke. I allowed myself to cry into my pillow. I cried because my reputation had been tarnished. I cried because I would never be Jonathon's girlfriend. I cried because people were talking about me, had seen my underwear, and were calling me a slut. I cried because I was angry for getting too drunk. All of that shame scared me. As soon as I began to feel those terrifying emotions and the crying became unmanageable, I forced myself to stop. It was over.

I wasn't going to think about it anymore. It was time to move on, I decided. He wasn't going to bring me down. I forced myself to put on a mask and wrap this secret up tightly in the back of my mind. I was done feeling sorry for myself.

I focused on the one thing I could gain control of again: my reputation. That was the more manageable option. My reputation was something I had worked hard to maintain. My self-worth was truly wrapped up in how others perceived me. Perhaps, in the back of my mind, I knew if I went to the administration, I would be cast aside by so many, including my friends and classmates. Everyone would be angry at me for shining a light on the drinking culture at Colby. That was why I chose to ignore the most important aspect of all. That was one of the many reasons why it was never a possibility for me to acknowledge the hardest part of that night.

The administration had turned a blind eye to so many of the antics happening on campus, and if I became a whistleblower, people would never forgive me. My classmates would never allow me into any more senior apartments or off-campus parties. I would become "that girl." No more attention from the football players or baseball boys. I would be ostracized by a place where I had finally fit in.

I didn't want that role. I couldn't allow that to be me. I wouldn't be the person to take everything down. There was too much responsibility in blowing it all up. So I buried the pain deep inside. I lied to myself and pretended it was all going to be okay. I convinced myself that Jonathon hadn't hurt me. I was fine. Everything was fine. *This isn't a big deal.*

I didn't talk much about the trauma of that night. But it was a trauma. So instead of dealing with it, I pushed it down deep, and I drank to forget about it. I continued to get drunk, weekend after weekend, until the images of that night with Jonathon began to blur and fade. I buried the painful truth beneath bottles of booze. But the truth can't stay hidden forever.

A Family Shattered (2001): Eighteen Years Old

As I immersed myself in college life, I seldom spoke to my parents or sisters. So one afternoon in March when Jen called me, I found it odd to hear from her. I listened to her voicemail on my dorm room phone telling me to call her at the house in Connecticut. A feeling of dread came over me. I knew something was wrong. She was home for the weekend visiting her boyfriend, Brian, from college, and she wanted me to call her back.

I tentatively picked up the phone and dialed home. Jen answered.

Concern and sadness came through in her voice. "Kimmy, Dad moved out." There was no sugarcoating it.

"What do you mean?" I said.

"He packed his bags, and he left."

"How do you know?"

"He took artwork off the walls. He packed up his side of the closet."

"I don't understand," I said. "Why? Where?" I was dumbfounded.

"I don't know where he went, but, Kimmy, don't you get it? He's finally gone. He finally left Mom. For good." I was silent. "He did leave her a note on her dresser for her to find for when she got home from visiting Grampy in New Hampshire for the weekend. So at least he did that."

"Well, what did the note say?" I asked.

"I can't bring myself to read it. He's gone, though, Kim."

I couldn't make sense of the words I was hearing. Why did he go? How could he just leave? There were so many unanswered questions. So many thoughts. So many feelings. I knew my parents were unhappy, but for Dad to just give up on Mom like this was so confusing to me.

My heart was racing. All at once, it felt as if this was happening to someone else. This wasn't my life. This was all a movie, and I was watching it from afar.

Jen continued to talk, but I was floating. Detached. I was staring down at the scene, witnessing it as it all unfolded. I pictured his side of the closet, empty and bare except for a few wire hangers. The image ripped me in half, and I felt so sad and lonely for Mom.

I wanted to know why Dad just walked away from it all without having a conversation with her. I knew there had to be more that I didn't know about. It seemed to me, even at only eighteen, that it was a completely pitiful and unfair way of handling the situation.

It was selfish. He'd had plenty of opportunities to confront Mom and do this face-to-face with her, but he chose to slither off into the shadows instead. I felt he owed her a little more respect after over twenty years of marriage. To ransack the house in the night, stealing the paintings off the walls, packing up all his clothes, and taking our dog, Maggie, felt more like the move of a man on the run from some heinous crime.

It was a pathetic, hateful violation of our family. I wanted him to pick up the phone and explain it to me. I felt lost. My family was no longer—rising like smoke rings into the sky, slowly separating from one another.

I ended the call with Jen and went right to my Colby girls. I threw on my best jeans, put on some makeup, and headed to the biggest party I could find. I surrounded myself with kegs, vodka shots, and "normalcy." Alcohol was my only source of comfort that night.

I was angry at Dad, and I felt frustrated with Mom. I believed this was something they could have worked through if they'd tried harder. If they both cared more. If they loved me more. There seemed to be little to no concern for my well-being, either. I was off at college, and neither of them felt the need to call me. I was an adult in their eyes, and I was living my life. In actuality, I was still a child, and I had no idea what kind of road I was headed down.

The one constant in my life was drinking. The booze kept me from feeling vulnerable; kept me from feeling anything, in fact. Most of all, it kept me from my sadness and anger toward my parents. I didn't talk about their separation, but instead I focused on having fun. I wouldn't let the demise of my parents' relationship ruin the rest of the best four years of my life.

Day 35: January 2, 2021

"What are you feeling after getting all of that off your chest?" Ronni asks.

I don't answer. My eyes begin to tear up, so I stare down at my lap, fidgeting with my wedding rings, something I do when I'm anxious.

How does she always do this? It's like a magic power that my therapist has. She seems to know exactly what to ask every time I'm really beginning to get somewhere. How did she get me to say all of that? I don't even know where it came from or how she got it all to come pouring out of me. It's like the floodgates just opened up!

After talking for over thirty minutes just now about my parents' relationship, she gets me going on a completely different topic—one that I never seem willing to discuss with anyone, not even Evan. How did she get me to even think about that jerk Jonathan from college?

I had never met Ronni before last month. I stare back at the computer screen and focus on the face of the woman that a few weeks ago was a complete stranger. This is only the fourth time we've talked and she already knows some of the biggest secrets of my life. The things that I don't even talk to Evan about. I've divulged some of the darkest parts of myself to her—things I didn't even know I needed to talk about. Things I've been hiding from and avoiding for years.

She waits patiently for an answer. I sigh loudly. "I don't know! I have a lot of fucked-up memories from college that I don't remember, so it's not a big deal! I never thought it was a big deal what happened. I just forgot about it."

I try to laugh. She waits. I realize it isn't funny. This makes the tears come. "I blacked out a lot. It's fine. So what?"

"It's not fine, Kim. You were raped. That boy Jonathon, he raped you. You blocked it out due to the trauma. As a response to the fear, your body chose whether to go into fight, flight, or freeze. Your sympathetic nervous system initiated the freeze response. You were scared, and that was your body's response. You cannot blame yourself. Your brain was responding appropriately. Your body holds onto trauma though to protect yourself from letting it happen again, which is why you can remember it so vividly."

I wipe my cheek and can't bring myself to look at the computer screen. "I know. I know." I twist my rings.

"And I'm very sorry that happened to you. But just because you were drunk, it's not your fault."

"I know."

"Do you know that, though?"

"I don't know."

"You didn't want to have sex, Kim. You didn't want to be naked in his bed. You need to show yourself some grace, some compassion for managing things the way you did in the coming days. You were a child. And you didn't have the tools to deal with it all at the time. It was a major trauma. You can't blame yourself. And your parents weren't present for you because they were distracted by their own secrets."

I start crying harder. And I allow my body to feel. For the first time since that awful night with Jonathon twenty years ago, I begin to mourn for that young eighteen-year-old girl. The girl who was raped. I'm able to realize that I was in fact just a child. It was not my fault, and I cannot blame myself for what happened to me. I cannot blame myself for getting too drunk. I cannot blame myself for hiding.

These awful pieces of my past haunt me at night when I'm alone with my thoughts. Those fleeting memories that would pop into my mind, causing me to drink for so many years in an attempt to forget it all.

"If you could talk to her now, what would you say to that girl back at Colby? What would you say to eighteen-year-old Kim right now?"

"I would say . . . Don't be such a fucking coward."

I begin to cry harder than I have in days.

Evan (2001): Eighteen Years Old

I spun in circles as my best friend Mandy wrapped the Saran Wrap around my body. I looked down at the see-through makeshift tube top.

"Can you see my bra?" I asked.

"No, not really. You can't see much." She stood back, admiring her work.

We were headed to the Anything But Clothes party in the senior apartments, and we were determined to make a statement. We liked being *those* freshmen. We enjoyed the attention from the older boys, and we didn't mind the irritated stares from the senior girls.

"Shots!" I shouted as my roommate lined the glasses up, all part of our pregaming ritual.

As the music of Britney Spears blasted from the speakers on the closet shelf, we grabbed the drinks and swallowed them fast, cheering loudly.

"Who wants another one?" I called, arranging the next round, the confidence and excitement building in all of us.

I checked my Instant Messenger and put up my away message for the night: *See you later, but I probably won't remember!* It was true. The evening went dark, parts remaining fuzzy still to this day.

The night I met my husband will forever exist as an empty hole in my memory. A secret unknown to me for the next twenty years of my life. Even Evan has little recollection of meeting me. He remembers a whole other party and a totally different night altogether.

Ours is a forgotten history, lost in time—a love story that exists as a jumbled distortion of echoes of the past.

Today, when my kids ask for the tale of how we met, I often create an elaborate, detailed description of the night pieced together from various parties we'd been to—one that didn't really exist in anyone's experience. It's a fairytale; a romantic fable I've made up to entertain them. I once told them that I'd been wearing a beautiful dress, conveniently leaving out the Saran Wrap tube top, and that Daddy and I had met at a fancy ball in the student center one rainy night.

Another time, I told them that Mommy and Daddy met at a college party across campus. There was a horrible snowstorm. Daddy offered to walk Mommy back to her dorm room. He was such a perfect gentleman.

Each time they ask, I fabricate a new and slightly different version, the guilt of not remembering any of it eating away at me. The fact that I can't tell my daughter what her father said to me the night we met because I was too drunk is enough to make me want to scream. There's a dark velvet curtain hung in place of the memory. It's as if there are tiny snapshots in my brain from a polaroid camera. Only fragments remain, left for me to piece together like a puzzle.

Yet one image exists, sharp and distinct: Evan standing outside the senior apartments, snowflakes drifting in the lamplight around him. The black of the night sky surrounded us. In my memory, it's only he and I, completely alone even though I know we weren't. He stood, probably shivering, hands in the pockets of his jeans. He wore his favorite Cleveland Indians hat, the edges of the rim frayed and faded. I would grow to know this hat. I would seek it out in the dining hall, the library, and across the quad.

Evan held my gaze and smiled confidently at me, indicating an interest, a wonder, and a need to know more. I had been warned of those hockey boys, but he seemed sweet.

So much was unknown between us at the time. So much that we were to face and pull out of one another. So much to conquer together. A snapshot. A moment in time, perhaps inconsequential to us then.

He had an attentive smile and a kind demeanor. He was a boy from Ohio who had gone to military boarding school but was recruited to Colby to play hockey. He was passionate. He was independent. And he was smart and thoughtful.

Evan and I exchanged Instant Messenger names and I found myself constantly on the lookout for him, wanting to be where he was, showing up at parties where I knew he would be. He often left clues on his away message as to where he'd be later in the night. I was immediately drawn to him, and we just worked. He liked me, and I liked him.

He was kind and easy to be around. I felt understood by him, more so than any other person I had met at Colby. Our relationship was born in a world of binge drinking, and in the beginning a lot of our time together involved alcohol. Because that was what everyone did at Colby, it seemed. He drank just as much as anyone else I knew.

I was desperate to be loved and to be cared for. I craved protection, and needed someone to rescue me. Evan seemed worthy of the task. Eventually, we began to spend time together without the mask of booze. He was the first person I confided in about my parents' situation. He was willing to listen to me and seemed interested in what I had to say.

"My dad moved out," I told him. "I guess you could say my parents are separated."

"I'm so sorry," Evan said.

I didn't like talking about my home life, and I didn't want his sympathy. I didn't want to be reminded of the darkness that I'd worked so hard to put out of my mind. I didn't like thinking about the pieces of my life that were falling apart back home.

"Yeah, it sucks. But I'm fine, really," I insisted. "Tell me about your family."

"Well, I've lived away from home since I was fourteen, so I don't see my parents much anymore," Evan said. "I know what it's like to feel alone."

I didn't feel judged by Evan. He made me feel safe—understood for the first time in a very long time.

He was different from Jake and every other boy I'd known. He wasn't arrogant, and he wasn't threatening like I'd come to feel about many of the boys around me. He was compassionate, which seemed so rare.

I had grown weary of the opposite sex without knowing it, and that night, I realized just how intimidating I found all boys to be.

Eventually, I found myself in Evan's arms and experienced a comfort and safety I'd needed for a long time. I was broken, but Evan slowly began to fix me.

In my memory, our love was born amid a world of heavy alcohol consumption, incessant partying, and endless hangovers over the next few months.

My memories from the rest of that school year are filled with snapshots of nonstop parties, tailgates, and other spring events with Evan by my side: beer die tournaments, off-campus day drinking, and hanging out late into the night in his dorm room with his teammates.

When it was time to pack up and head home for the summer, I didn't want to leave the safety of my Colby bubble. I didn't want to go back to Connecticut. Things felt lighter and easier in Maine, but back home, everything felt covered in a layer of gloom.

Dad's Roommate (2001): Eighteen Years Old

"Evan, this is my mom," I said as Evan walked through the door of Mom's house a few days into summer vacation.

"It's so nice to meet you, Mrs. Betz," Evan said, shaking Mom's hand.

"Hello, welcome!" Mom ushered him inside. She was excited to play hostess, happy for the distraction from the empty place her life had become.

After I was home for about a week in Connecticut, Evan came and visited me. I was excited to introduce my new boyfriend to my family. At this point, it was a bizarre time of transition for my family. My world had been flipped upside down. I'd come back to a life that was very unlike what it used to be.

Mom was now living alone. She seemed sad a lot of the time, but she worked hard to pretend she wasn't. I felt trapped between two separate worlds.

When I was at Colby, it was easy to pretend that what my parents were going through wasn't real. I could essentially put it out of my mind because it didn't directly impact me when I was away from home. But I was forced to confront the realities of their withering marriage head-on that summer, and there was no more ignoring it.

Dad had moved out and set himself up in a beautiful penthouse apartment in downtown Greenwich that sat atop the avenue overlooking the Long Island Sound. He even had a roof-deck. And he had found himself a roommate.

After spending a few days at Mom's house, I brought Evan to Dad's place for dinner so he could get to know him and meet his friend and roommate, Richie. Yes, it felt like a midlife crisis. Yes, it was all very weird. But we went with it. I had to go because I was a good daughter. I felt like I was doing that a lot lately—going along with what was expected of me.

"Why does your dad have a roommate at his age?" Evan asked me when I told him, unable to hide the skepticism in his voice.

I had wondered the same thing, but I didn't know the full story. I also didn't have the audacity to ask this very pertinent question. "I think he's lonely, and he hasn't lived by himself since before he married my mom," I surmised. "He doesn't know how to do laundry or cook very well, and Richie does. He likes someone to help with that kind of stuff."

It was a hot evening in June. We parked in the private lot among the Porsches, Lamborghinis, and the other fancy cars outside the apartment building. Dad gave us the grand tour as soon as we arrived. He made a point to show us their separate bedrooms.

I knew Richie. He'd been a good friend of Dad's for a few years. He had also been my boss at the café where I'd worked the summer before. Back then, Dad stopped in for a sandwich or a bowl of soup, leaving me fifty-dollar tips after the lunch crowd had thinned out. He sometimes sat around after, quietly talking to Richie at the counter.

Richie loved cooking, baking, and all things food related. A few years before, he'd brought us cookies at Christmas. Another year, he stopped by for a drink at Thanksgiving. I could always tell Mom didn't like him coming over, but much to her dismay, Richie continued hanging around.

That night for dinner, Dad brought Evan and me up to the new roof-deck, and we sprawled out on the couches, admiring the hot summer weather and devouring the cheese spread laid out before us.

"Who wants an appletini?" Richie asked, serving us in a formal white apron. He proceeded to cook up a massive, extravagant dinner. It felt nice to be wined and dined, and the food was delicious. He even served a large homemade pie for dessert.

I felt confused by Dad because he was so engaged and present, something that I hadn't seen in him for years. He seemed to be playing house with Richie. I stared at the two of them, watching their interactions. Something felt different about Dad, and it occurred to me that he seemed truly happy, which was also new. I wondered why Dad was so content living this bachelor lifestyle with his friend. He was so excited to show off his strange, new life, and he seemed to have completely forgotten about Mom sitting at home alone.

I was skeptical of Richie and what he was up to, living with Dad. He wasn't working at the time, so I wondered if he was just looking for a free place to stay. Something felt off to me, and I couldn't put my finger on it.

On the way back to Mom's house in Stamford after dinner, I sighed with relief. I was happy to be done, and I was tired. *Maybe all this will feel normal someday,* I thought.

"That meal was damn good!" I said.

Evan turned and looked at me for a long moment. He hesitated. "That was a little weird," he finally said.

"I know. You're telling me."

"What has your dad told you about Richie?"

"Nothing, really. Richie stopped working, but I guess he's looking for a job." I said.

"No, what has your dad said about their relationship?"

"What do you mean?"

"I'm pretty sure there's something going on between them," Evan said gently.

"Huh? I'm not sure what you're trying to imply, but—"

"I think your dad might be gay, Kim."

"What? Gay? My dad is not gay!" The word felt foreign on my lips.

Evan's comment hit me hard. I sat quiet for a moment, fuming. I was shocked to hear him say this about my father. "Kim, it would all make a lot of sense if he was, don't you think?"

"No! I mean, he and Richie have separate rooms, for God's sake. There's no way they're gay!"

"Yeah, I don't think they use both rooms."

I began to think about what Evan was saying, and we sat in silence for the rest of the car ride.

I believe my dad had secrets. Deep, painful secrets he'd been hiding from me his entire life. Maybe this was it—the answer to the question I never even knew I had. It felt as if everything I knew in my world was slowly unraveling. I was confused and completely terrified.

My father. The man who used to take me fishing on Spofford Lake in the rowboat when I was twelve. The man who threw the baseball with me in the yard on Winterset Road when I was five. The guy who captained our boat every summer on Long Island Sound. The one who rode the waves with me on Horseshoe Bay Beach in Bermuda. The man who sat beside me on the chair lift at Stratton Mountain.

There was no way this person, who I'd known for the last eighteen years, was lying to me. It was unfathomable.

But the fact was, John Betz was not telling the whole truth. This was evident to me from an early age.

I knew ever since I was a little girl that there was something he didn't want us to know. Maybe it was even something Mom knew. I wondered if my sisters had any idea.

I recalled the pain behind Dad's eyes as he captained *The Elusive*, staring out at the horizon. The sun was setting. He seemed sad. Contemplative. Distant. Lost. There was a hurt buried deep within. He always seemed to be running. Hiding. Keeping something to himself. And he managed to do it for my entire childhood.

At that moment, I knew in the depths of my soul that Evan was right. Finally, here he was: my father, a seemingly completely different person. Was this the missing puzzle piece?

I was angry at Evan. It was the easier option: take my aggression out on the boy I barely knew instead. I told myself that Evan didn't even know my family or my parents and was making assumptions. It seemed unfair that I'd been forced to confront this without any preparation. It was all just entirely confusing.

Things were awkward between Evan and me the next day after dinner with Dad. I refused to speak to him about it.

He flew home to Ohio a few days later, and we didn't talk much more that summer. I avoided his phone calls and this frightening truth, just as I'd been taught to do my entire life with difficult situations.

I pretended everything would be just fine.

Day 37: January 4, 2021

I've been sleeping so well these days, waking up rested and full of energy, that I've decided to start some new projects. One of my sober tasks of the new year is to clean out some closets. I feel the need to purge, sort through old junk, and donate clothing to the less fortunate. My sobriety support groups suggested keeping busy with projects, so I thought this might be a good one. Ronni approved it as well, and I feel good about the job if she does.

I start by cleaning out the clothes in my closet. I pack piles of shirts, dresses, bags, and shoes into shopping bags to donate, and then I move on to the kids' closets. Eventually, I tackle the playroom. It becomes an obsession, and pretty soon I'm cleaning out the entire house, one closet and storage bin after another. It feels cleansing. Therapeutic.

In the upstairs hallway, I sift through a bin of books from when I was a young girl. I stumble upon a diary. The pink, yellow, and orange plaid cover looks vaguely familiar. I open it up and the spine cracks, having been closed for years. It's from 1990. Written on the front page is a familiar scrawl: *This belongs to Kimmy Betz.* Upon seeing the large, curvy handwriting of my youth, I'm immediately drawn back to my childhood. It's a diary I kept on one of the many vacations to Bermuda. I was eight years old.

One of the houses in which we vacationed on the hills off South Street, which faced the south side of the island of Bermuda, was called "Tree Tops." We stayed at this house for several weeks one summer before I went into fourth grade. The mornings were spent at the beaches, and during the afternoons we lazed around in the house's private pool. I spent hours searching for lizards and frogs in the thick grass and running from my sisters during long games of hide-and-go-seek on rainy mornings. There were endless places to hide in that home, as it was full of nooks and crannies to get lost in.

One morning during that trip, we went to our favorite beach on the other side of the island called Horseshoe Bay Beach. We packed a picnic lunch and set up an umbrella and chairs in the morning. Dad took us on a hike over to the other beaches along the shore, searching for small tide pools and crabs. Jobson's Cove was one of my favorites, as there was a large lagoon that collected behind a wall of rocks that kept it sheltered from the ocean. It felt like a private sanctuary on a deserted island, and it was a hike to get to, so it felt like our own personal beach.

Mom didn't like to go for beach walks. Instead, she stayed with the chairs and towels, reading her book and observing the other people nearby. It felt like an adventure to me, climbing over the sharp coral rocks.

After Dad brought us back from the hike, he took off on one of his long solo strolls, leaving us alone with Mom. I never liked it when he left us. It made me frustrated that he wanted to be by himself.

Dad haphazardly rubbed another layer of sunscreen on his face and tossed on his Ray-Bans. Then he marched off down the shore in minuscule speedo bikini bottoms that barely covered his behind. He was gone for over an hour, walking for miles and miles it seemed, lost in his thoughts. I sat waiting for him, staring down the beach, bored.

It was hot there that summer. Mom and Dad complained of the heat often. We hung out back at "Tree Tops" a lot, and my sisters and I played inside with our dolls and Barbies to stay cool when Dad needed to do work in the office.

At the end of the three-week trip, Dad abruptly changed our flights and forced us all to go home a day early. He became very agitated late one morning, and he claimed he had heatstroke from a long round of golf at the Mid Ocean Club. He needed to get back to work, he said. He was stressed, he told us. Over the years, I recall that the story changed a bit. I am not sure when he started talking about the large English-style portraits on the walls in the foyer of "Tree Tops." But eventually, over time, he started to blame those pictures for why we left early.

"The eyes on the paintings! They were following me around at night!"

As we got older, my sisters and I always liked to reenact this, dramatically pretending to have heatstroke just like Dad said he did. He claimed the eyes of the four little girls were looking at him and had come to life. He had become delirious from too much relaxation, Mom said.

"I could feel them. They used to watch me," he would reminisce. It was a family joke . . . or so I thought.

As time went on, I surmised that perhaps Dad had simply had enough vacation and decided it was time to go, like Mom said. But according to my diary, there's more to the story that I simply forgot about over the years, I guess.

Now, standing in the upstairs hallway of my home as an adult, I feel lied to all over again. My dad always did a good job of letting us believe it was the creepy paintings that caused our trip to end early, but he'd decided to leave the island for an entirely different reason—one I forgot all about.

I flip the pages. I thumb through them over and over again, scanning every word for more clues. I look for the story about the little girls in the paintings. I look for talk about his heatstroke. The eyes following my dad at night. I want to laugh and feel the familiar nostalgia from my childhood. But the story of the paintings is not in my diary. And as I search the words, looking for clues or any kind of mention of it, a feeling of confusion comes over me. The eyes. The portraits of the four little girls. Where is it?

Am I thinking of the wrong trip? No, this is the one. I had written in my diary every night, chronicling exactly what we'd done each day right down to what we ate for breakfast, lunch, and dinner. The paintings and the heatstroke—that was all at "Tree Tops." I'm sure of it.

But that was not the reason we left Bermuda early. What I'd written about instead was that Dad was angry at his best friend, Steve, who was supposed to be visiting us on the island for the last few days of our trip, but Steve had called the house and canceled at the last minute. There was no talk of paintings or heatstroke. Dad was mad and sad, I wrote. Mom and Dad had a fight. Dad changed our flights, and we had to end the vacation early. Through the words in my journal, I can tell how upset I was with my parents.

It dawns on me now that perhaps Dad created the elaborate story about the paintings after the fact to mask his secret. Steve maybe meant more to Dad at the time than any of us knew. Thirty years later, reading my eight-year-old scrawl, I see that there were signs even then that pointed to the pain Dad was experiencing. I had no idea.

I can imagine that Dad probably struggled with his sexuality for most of my childhood, and there were clues right under my nose all along. He was even struggling when we were in our happy place in Bermuda, the most beautiful place on this earth.

My heart breaks for both my parents. I sit down on the floor, allowing the diary to spill open on my lap. I sigh heavily as tears spill down my cheeks. Pounding my fists against the wall before me, I scream.

"Fuck! Fuck! Fuck!"

So many lies told to me for so many years. So many secrets kept from me even to this day. Everything feels like a lie.

I start laughing at the absurdity of the situation; a hysterical, maniacal laugh. And then I wonder if I've truly lost it. I roll on the floor, allowing the strangeness of the emotions to settle, until my body falls silent and still.

I stare into the distance, allowing my eyes to focus on the pattern of Brayden's carpet across the hall. I scan his photos on the wall. His framed hockey jersey. The picture of Evan playing hockey at Colby. His striped bedspread, the mess of laundry that spills out of the hamper.

So many emotions have poured out of me these past few weeks—feelings that I'm unaccustomed to experiencing. There has been too much lying and hiding from myself for so many years. I consider my own husband. My own children. All the lying and hurt I have done to them with my drinking.

"No more fucking lies," I say out loud to the empty rooms around me. "No more secrets in this family."

PART II

A Broken Home (2001): Eighteen Years Old

Dishonesty starts casually. It often begins as a small omission of fact, or a lack of specificity in the details that allows one to get away with not telling the truth. But it grows, swelling and spreading like an infection. The roots originate from the lie you first tell yourself. In the end, though, it's almost impossible to deceive your subconscious mind. The truth always prevails. Most secrets never stay buried.

Shortly after Evan left Connecticut and went back to his home to Ohio, I confronted Dad about Richie and asked him if there was anything special about his relationship with the man he called his roommate. I couldn't stop wondering what Dad was hiding.

I'd been home from Colby for only a few weeks, and nothing felt right. I couldn't stop thinking about who my father was. Everything I knew about him up to this point in my life felt like a lie. I felt lost, left alone in the dark.

Laura and Jen didn't have any answers either. Whenever I asked them what they thought of the situation, they shrugged their shoulders and avoided the conversation. They were even more uncomfortable discussing the topic than me. I, on the other hand, was determined to try to understand it all. I didn't dare ask Mom anything in her fragile state, so I felt it was my job to approach Dad.

One evening in June, my sisters and I sat on the plush, velvety couch across from Dad and Richie in the library at the yacht club before dinner. We sipped martinis, waiting for our reservation. The room was empty except for the five of us and the rows of antique books on the walls. Richie sat perched in a tall wingback chair next to Dad, and my sisters and I were crammed together on a loveseat. We all looked out at the setting sun, the sky a swirl of pink and orange beyond Greenwich Harbor.

"Is there anything you want to tell us, Dad?" I asked casually.

"What do you mean, dear?" Dad replied.

"What exactly is going on between you and Richie?" I continued. Everyone fell silent, my sisters staring into their drinks. Richie stood abruptly and left the room.

"Excuse me?" Dad asked.

"We want to know," I said, determined to get some answers. The alcohol in my hand fueled my words and gave me courage. Jen and Laura sat still beside me.

"That is absolutely none of your business!" Dad roared. He had only raised his voice at me a handful of times in my life. He stormed out of the library after Richie, and I was left feeling completely ashamed and abandoned. Jen and Laura were mad at me for confronting him.

"Why would you bring that up before dinner?" Laura said. "That was so awkward."

"Things were okay the way they were. Just let it go," Jen added.

My entire family wanted to pretend life was fine and that everything was normal, when in reality there was nothing normal about the situation. My sisters wanted to play along with Dad's game. They were prepared to just accept this arrangement between Dad and Richie as it was, without further explanation. My sisters were afraid to point out the obvious, and they were equally frightened of confrontation. Maybe my sisters felt safer hiding in the shadows with Dad than stepping into the light and facing the truth, but this didn't sit well with me. I wanted to understand it better. What had happened to our family? I didn't like being lied to.

After about ten minutes, Dad cooled off and came back with Richie to fetch us from the library, and we pretended the argument had never happened. We settled in for dinner together on the waterfront, my father and sisters chatting amicably about the weather and the upcoming summer. They pretended everything was normal, like we hadn't just had one of the most intense confrontations of our lives. I was flustered. I remained silent and drank several more martinis, stewing in my own discomfort.

Dad's brief display of anger toward me in the library showed me a great deal about our family dynamic and about the shame I imagine he was feeling at this time in his life. He couldn't acknowledge the truth or manage any type of discussion about it, and it only pushed me further away from every one of my family members.

Mom avoided any and all conversations about Dad and Richie. She was mortified that her husband was now living with another man. She was lonely, sad, and embarrassed. I tried not to talk to her about my theories. I felt awful for the pain she was going through. Much later, I found out that she'd had her own suspicions for years. She'd known what Dad was facing, but she kept the secret buried out of her own humiliation.

My family, in their own self-preserving way, was teaching me how to hide from the truth. Don't talk about the hard things. Don't ask questions. Hide in the shame. It's easier to live a lie and remain in the shadows than to confront it all head-on.

I believe Dad was on his own road of self-discovery. He was trying to figure out how to be his most authentic self, but it was a struggle in the beginning. It isolated him from all of us. I don't fault him for having to do this. It was part of his journey, but it hurt me. And I didn't have the tools to manage it on my own.

That was a strange summer for me. Nothing felt the same; everything felt raw and new. There was no way to deny what was happening with Dad and Richie, and I wonder if deep down, I knew before Evan even mentioned it. If I did, I denied it for a very long time, along with the rest of my family. After that evening in the library, I avoided talking about it with Dad or anyone again for months.

Another secret kept hidden. Don't talk about it. Don't discuss it. Dad still maintained for months that he and Richie were simply just roommates, and they went on living their lives. They were friends, and it was something we had to get comfortable with real fast. One thing I knew for certain: Richie was here to stay, and I needed to get used to that idea.

It was an abrupt and sharp change to everything I knew, but my parents seemed to think I should be fine with all the disruption. So I tried. Everyone was hurting in their own way, I guess. And I was just expected to behave like a grownup. After all, I was eighteen and pretty much living life on my own.

At one of the hardest times in our lives, my sisters and I should have been able to look to our parents for guidance, but we couldn't. Neither Mom nor Dad gave us any idea of how to move forward. I felt stuck. I felt abandoned. I felt alone. I was still a child, and I needed my parents. But they weren't there.

All of this made me miss my Colby home. My college life. My friends. My bubble. I desperately wanted to go back to school because my world at home in Connecticut was nothing like I remembered it to be. I longed for the routine of classes and weekend parties, the simplicity of dining hall chatter and planning out Saturday evening outfits. Drinking and partying with my friends, and the simple fun of lying around hungover on Sunday mornings offered a respite from the stress of living at home for the summer.

I didn't realize it at the time, but I was deeply hurt by my father. He had crushed our family dynamic and left us to pick up the broken pieces of my mother. Mom had hurt me for not being stronger, and for making me feel so alone. Neither could show me how to move forward in this new life.

When Dad moved in with Richie, he maintained that he'd left Mom because he fell out of love with her. He also alluded to her drinking as part of the reason he no longer loved her. This made me feel utterly sad for Mom, and my sisters and I encouraged her to get help. We begged her to go to Alcoholics Anonymous, which was the only support group we knew of at the time.

That first summer our family fell apart, we went to an Al-Anon support meeting for family members of alcoholics. Jen decided it would be good for the three of us to go, but I recall feeling strange sitting in the basement of the church. I wondered what the other people thought of me and my sisters, and I didn't like feeling so exposed. I felt ashamed, and I refused to go back after one meeting.

Back then, I never thought my own drinking habits were like my mom's. I never drew a parallel line, because in my mind, I drank to have fun. Mom drank alone to drown her sorrows. To my immature brain, there was a huge difference. Even sitting in the Al-Anon meeting, there was no guilt on my part. I was different from all the sad alcoholics that we talked about and pitied. I could never be one of them, even though I was drinking to get drunk every single weekend.

All the while throughout that summer, Evan kept calling me. At first, I answered his calls, but I was distant. Removed. I didn't want to talk to him. I didn't want to hear any more of his opinions. I could barely grasp what I was going through, let alone explain it to someone I'd just met a few months before.

Jake was there for me that summer. I believed at the time that he understood every part of me. He was my very first love, and he knew me better than most people. He took care of me when my parents wouldn't, and he didn't ask questions. He was the only constant in my life from when my parents were still married, before it all changed.

I drank a lot during those summer months instead of preparing for the upcoming fall field hockey season. Finding comfort in drinking beers on Jake's couch in his basement or at Tod's Point took priority over going to the gym and conditioning at the local track. Drowning my sorrows at the bottom of the bottle, I skipped workouts. I ignored the weight training schedule my coach had sent home because I was hungover. I wanted to be with Jake and lie in his arms and pretend all the realities of my situation didn't exist.

August rolled around, and it was time for me to head back to Colby. It was bittersweet this time. The departure from Jake was sad, but it was nothing like the separation the year before. I was excited to leave home and get back to school, my friends, and my college routine. I was okay with saying goodbye to him.

I didn't know what was in store for our relationship, but I was alright with that. I think deep down I may have hoped our paths would someday bring us back together again. But in the end, this is where our relationship was officially laid to rest. Maybe he came back into my life for those few months that summer to simply serve as a soft place to land for a while, a bridge from my past to ease me into the next phase of a new, unfamiliar life—a life where my parents no longer played a role; a world where I could no longer rely on them to guide me forward.

The Calamity Continues (2001): Nineteen Years Old

That fall, I moved onto the first floor in a dorm on Frat Row called Johnson. Evan just so happened to be living on the third floor. The first day I ran into him on campus, he turned around and walked in the other direction. I hadn't returned his phone calls all summer, and we hadn't spoken in months. Despite seeing Evan, being back on campus felt familiar, and after months of discomfort and sadness, it felt good to be home.

The smell of the eggs in the Dana dining hall and the sounds of the Patagonia-clad kids tossing frisbees in the quad were welcomed sensations. The thumping music coming from open windows of the brick dorm buildings amid a sea of dark-green trees with their leaves beginning to change felt like a reassurance that life goes on.

Field hockey held a fresh set of challenges that semester. There was a new coach on the scene, which meant I had to try out for the team again. At that point in my life, my passion for the sport had disappeared. I had other things to worry about, and I no longer experienced the thrill I used to whenever I stepped foot on the field hockey field. A huge part of this was because my parents had stopped regularly attending my games.

That fall, I was cut from the team, and it seemed as though my field hockey career had come to an end. But there were bigger things in the world for me to worry about.

A week after field hockey was stripped from my life, I watched the events of 9/11 unfold on the tiny television in my dorm room. After that, my trivial concerns over my personal matters didn't seem so severe anymore, and for a long time, my focus shifted. My friends and I stayed glued to our TVs for days, desperate to understand what was happening to our nation, which was under attack.

Eventually, the country began the slow process of healing, as did the Colby community. Our classes and learning were consumed by the affairs of the world for a while, but we all came together in the only way we could. We drank. When we were together, we felt safe and removed inside our college bubble in rural Maine, far from the pain and suffering of so many others. So, at the end of every day, we did what we did best: we got blackout drunk.

That fall, I stayed in my dorm a fair amount, and I skipped my morning classes. I drank and smoked a lot of weed with my friends down the hall. I started smoking cigarettes during the day and hung out on fire escapes between classes in the academic buildings with the other smokers. My parents were further away than they ever had been in my life. I never called them. They left me messages sometimes, but I rarely checked in. There was little effort made on anyone's part. I hardly spoke to my sisters, either. They were probably maintaining their independence as a form of self-preservation, focusing on their own lives as well.

Dad and Richie visited me for parents' weekend that fall. They brought a brand-new rug from Pottery Barn as a gift for my dorm room.

"Who is your dad's friend?" my pot-smoking buddies down the hall asked me, leaning against the doorframe as Dad and Richie dragged the oversized rug in together.

"It's his roommate," I shrugged, averting my eyes.

"Interesting," they said, smiling.

I thought it was unfair to keep going along with Dad's game, and a part of me resented him for making me do it. But I never said anything. Riding in the back seat beside my friend Maura as Dad and Richie sang along to

ABBA on the way to dinner, I kept quiet.

Maura looked at them with wide-eyed disbelief. "How do they know every word to this song?" she whispered to me.

"They love the *Mamma Mia!* soundtrack," I said, rolling my eyes.

It was bizarre that they thought no one knew their truth. But Maura and I played along.

That fall, I was lonely. After the parents' weekend visit, it was as if Dad had completed his fatherly duty. He didn't call much. At the same time, I never called home to check on Mom, because I didn't need to be reminded of the sadness she was regularly facing. Evan still avoided me, holding a strong grudge for leaving him hanging over the summer. We ran into one another off and on but mostly kept to ourselves. He was one of the few people from Colby besides Maura and a few other friends who'd had a glimpse into my life at home and saw my situation for what it was: a secret I was trying to keep. Maybe that was why I avoided him. It was an open wound I was trying to keep concealed.

Eventually, Evan and I found our way back to one another that winter. There was a void that only he could fill; a compassionate understanding he had for me; a kindness and a tenderness no other boy was able to provide. We rarely spoke about my past, and he never judged me for what I had to do that summer before. He understood and accepted me. He loved me.

We couldn't resist spending every moment together, and soon I was attending all of his hockey games and hanging out in his room every day. I buried myself in my relationship with him. We identified with each other. We were both independent souls that had been forced to grow up fast. Forging ahead without much support from parents and family, we had only our self-reliance. Focusing on our future was the only option. Evan had been on his own since he was fourteen, emerging from boarding school with force and determination. Not many understood what I had gone through in the past year, but Evan somehow had the compassion to see me. In each other, we found reassurance and comfort.

With Evan, everything felt safe. It felt right. He was the ultimate escape, the truest form of avoidance. And I was fleeing the reality of what was

139

waiting for me back at home. The debris that my parents had left behind in the wake of their destruction were all pieces of my past. I was able to escape to a safer, more protected place with Evan.

I fell in love fast and hard. And through Evan's love, I learned how to move beyond my comfort zone. He pushed me to try harder. To be better. I had begun to forget how and had started to doubt myself. My self-worth had dwindled. The world had become a dark, dangerous place again. I couldn't trust anyone, most of all myself. Eventually, in the coming months, Evan encouraged me to do one of the hardest things I ever had to do.

Understanding the Truth (2002): Twenty Years Old

In 2002, things became difficult academically and emotionally. There was something off for me. It was like a puzzle piece was missing. There was a constant darkness clouding my mind. Alcohol was the only thing that provided any sort of relief. My only escape.

I was struggling more than ever with my courses, and I found it hard to focus on the work to the point that skipping class was a regular occurrence. I began to grow fearful and anxious whenever I had to attend large seminars, because I was terrified of speaking in front of groups of people. I doubted myself and my abilities more than ever. Things were coming to a head.

One morning in an English seminar, I was assigned a presentation on some reading material with two other classmates. When it came time to share our ideas with the group, I took my spot at the front of the room alongside the other girls. Even though I was prepared, my mind went blank. I couldn't read my notes, and I felt the room closing in on me. My heart raced, my body began to sweat, and it was hard to breathe. There was a loud thumping in my ears, and I thought I was going to faint.

There were dozens of eyes on me, waiting for me to speak. My body betrayed me, and I couldn't formulate any words. One of the other girls took over for me when she realized I was panicking. My face turned a deep shade of red. I excused myself to get a drink of water and skipped the seminar for the next three weeks. I barely passed the course at the end of the semester.

I called my doctor, afraid there was something wrong with me. She told me to start seeing a therapist. She thought it had to do with my parents getting divorced. Talking to a therapist didn't help, and I dreaded going to the sessions. I also developed debilitating migraines around this time. Medically, my body seemed to be trying to tell me something, but there was so much I refused to do about it.

My parents had no idea what was going on with me. My doctor put me on an antidepressant, but I avoided taking them, thinking it was more important to drink than to take the pills. It was on the weekends, when I was drinking, that I felt the truest escape from all the panic and anxiety.

During the weekdays, I became overwhelmed with schoolwork, and everything seemed out of my control. I was helpless and afraid. I'd just been home for the holidays, and I was frustrated by the charade Dad was still playing. I hated his lies. His secrets seemed to have gone on for so long.

"Why does my dad keep lying to us? Why can't he just be honest with me?" I sobbed to Evan one night. "It's so unfair that he's still living this lie to all of us—to my mom and to the world. It's obvious that he and Richie are in love. It's practically laughable that he hasn't admitted he's gay yet."

"So go talk to him," Evan told me. "What have you got to lose? Maybe that'll make you feel better. Maybe that's what's causing a lot of this stress. Maybe you need to face this shit. Hash it out. Talk it through."

Dad was still living with Richie, and it had been well over a year since our confrontation in the library at the yacht club.

"He owes you more of an explanation," Evan continued, nudging me. "Call him and tell him you want a weekend at the lake with him to talk."

I knew Evan was right. I needed some sort of closure. Everything about that part of my life still felt like a bloody open wound, raw and exposed to the elements. I was ready for the truth.

I took a weekend away from school and drove to our lake house in New Hampshire. Dad and I sat down by the fire, overlooking the lake where I'd spent every summer as a child swimming, boating, and fishing.

"I've been having a really tough time lately," I told him. "I need to know the truth. Are you gay?"

The moment was eerily similar to that time at the yacht club. But this time, there were no secrets. Dad didn't walk away, yell, or deny it. He wasn't ashamed or angry or upset. He did seem nervous and hesitant. But he sat calmly, looked me in the eyes, and took a deep breath.

"Yes," he said. "I am gay."

He seemed prepared for my question. He crossed one leg over the other and folded his hands in his lap. We were sitting far apart on separate couches. Pushing his glasses up on his nose, he cleared his throat and started explaining.

"I love Richie very much, and I have loved him for a long time." He went on to say that it had been the hardest thing he'd ever done, accepting this about himself. But he was finally living an authentic life, and he was happier than he'd ever known he could be.

There was a peacefulness in his eyes, a joy and relief behind his words. His eyes grew watery at one point, but I believe that he was feeling so much happiness as he spoke. It was as if there was a feeling of being free.

I told him I supported him. "I'm happy for you, Dad."

"My biggest fear in all of this," he said, "was that you three girls wouldn't accept me. That you wouldn't love me if you knew the truth. I've worried about that from the start. For years."

"I only ever wanted the truth," I said. "I don't care if you love Richie. I'm happy you're happy. I just wanted you to be honest."

I reassured him that I would always love him. We stood, and he put his arms out toward me in a gesture of forgiveness. I gave him a big hug, and a slight sob escaped his lips. Dad asked me to keep the secret to myself. When he was ready, he would tell Laura and Jen. It wasn't for several months that he found the courage to do that, though.

Looking back on this weekend, I felt a huge weight was lifted. We had taken a big step and made progress toward understanding each another. We were able to talk openly and honestly like never before. But at the same time, instead of getting the support I needed, I was there to lift him up. I reassured him that I still loved him, which was absolutely the truth. No matter what, he was still my dad.

When I left, I felt hollow. I was drained. I didn't know where to go from there. Now what? I still had questions, many that I couldn't even articulate at the time.

I was happy to be going back to my Colby family. On the drive, I self-ishly thought a lot about how this might be perceived by others once it all came out. I didn't know anyone who had a gay father. I didn't have a friend who had been through an experience like this.

What would people back home in Greenwich say about this? What would they think about my parents? Even though I was genuinely happy for Dad, I was also a bit embarrassed by how it all fell apart. What happened to our perfect family? Mom had never alluded to knowing any of this. What were my sisters going to do? Why was Dad still keeping secrets? It was a lot for me to carry at the time.

On the other hand, I was proud of the brave move Dad and I had taken. We had stepped out of the shadows and confronted the truth together. We'd faced his secret head-on and were talking about it. This relieved some of my anxiety, and there was comfort in finally seeing the big picture.

It would take decades of sleepless nights before I found peace, though. I buried my feelings at the bottom of a bottle before I realized that getting the answer I needed that weekend didn't fix everything. There was still so much pain for me to work through. I was drifting along in a swirl of sad-ness, anger, and resentment, floating away from everyone and everything I had ever known.

Something was still missing. I wanted to fill a void, but there was an emptiness that couldn't be filled. When Dad walked out on our family, something changed. He had relinquished his role as head of the family to begin his own quest. I knew it was a journey he had to take, but that didn't make it any less damaging to me.

When I got back to Colby, I got blackout drunk with Evan and my friends. I returned to alcohol, like always, thinking it would fix everything. That was what we always did.

It was around this time that Mom sold the house in Stamford and moved to Keene, New Hampshire, to be closer to her father and sister. This was God's plan for her, she claimed. It was out of her control, so she made peace with it. I believe it was easier to escape the memories and painful reminders of her past by moving away.

She claimed she wanted to start over. She joined a new church and said goodbye to her old life in Greenwich. It was just another excuse for me not to come home to Connecticut because I no longer had a home there. I felt like a drifter. It was during the next several years when I began to see the real effects of Dad's decision on my family. That was when I noticed the toll it had taken on Mom, when I truly saw how much she was drinking.

I was alone on an empty, quiet lake, rowing away from my past, into a world of confusion. So many questions. Very few answers.

Summer in Boston (2003): Twenty Years Old

I hated running. With every step I took, I only felt more tired. Evan told me early morning jogs invigorated him, and that I should feel the same way. They should help me wake up, he said, but I wanted nothing more than to stay snuggled in the queen-sized bed we shared together until I was forced to head to the T for my summer job. Evan was always a morning person. I, on the other hand, was not.

My muscles ached and cramped, proving just how out of shape I truly was. Every time my feet encountered the pavement, my body began to hate me even more. Yet every morning, we continued to do this, and I let him drag me out there.

After three months of these early morning runs, it never got any easier. If anything, my continuously slow pace had only proven to him that I was, in fact, not a runner.

But deep down, I knew my legs were growing stronger, and I was getting there. The muscles of my thighs and calves had grown long and lean, and my stamina had slowly progressed. Maybe I was ready for field hockey tryouts after all. Evan was determined to get me back out on the field, but I would never give him the satisfaction of knowing he was succeeding.

I glanced over at Evan. His easy stride, his effortless gate. I looked down at my gawky legs as they scuffed the path before us. My lungs screamed at me, and my chest burned. It took every ounce of energy to keep up with his pace, and I knew this was slow for him. We were practically walking.

I dodged the other runners coming at us along the crowded esplanade. I felt people creeping up behind me and getting ready to pass us, their sweat and hot breath closing in on me.

But I felt safe. Protected. I never felt judged by the pace I kept or the lack of running prowess I possessed. I never felt Evan was annoyed that I could barely breathe when we were hardly moving more than a swift walk. Because he loved me. He was proud of me. When I had that man by my side, I kept going, for him—as much as I wanted to stop and stand there in the middle of the crowded sidewalk and explain to him, hands on my hips, that he was wrong about me and my running capabilities.

"See? I'm not built for running! I'm just not a runner! Can we please stop this charade already?" I wanted to say, lecturing him the way I so often did. But no. Instead, I kept going. I didn't give up, because the faint burning in my belly was something *he* had taught me. He smiled at me. My biggest cheerleader. So I kept pushing myself. For him.

"You got this! Keep running!" Evan said, barely out of breath.

I gave him a thumbs up, unable to speak, half smiling. I looked at the Charles River alongside us and the sun that was coming up. I was grateful that this painful trek was nearly complete and we could head back to our apartment and sit down for coffee before we left for work at our respective summer jobs.

It had been a perfect few months, living together. Playing house. Pretending to be actual grownups. I wanted to stay in the safety of that summer dream forever. I didn't want to go back to Colby in the fall. I didn't want to go back for field hockey tryouts again or face any of the challenges the next year had in store. Because it was our last year at Colby. Our final year together in college. I wanted summer to stay, and I wanted to remain in the secrecy of our private bubble. I craved the simplicity of this life in the apartment by Fenway Park, listening to Red Sox games through the open window in the heat of the summer nights, forever safe in his love for me.

Day 45: January 11, 2021

Stepping off the platform of the T, we walk east toward the water, the Boston skyline to our left. I instinctively hold Chase and Parker's hands more tightly. It's been a while since we've been in the city. Evan walks along the other side of me, and Brayden marches independently beside us all, hands in his pockets. I feel content to be here, away from the suburbs. It feels like an adventure.

I smile proudly. We are a unit. A team. This is my family.

I'm cold, but the frigid air feels cleansing. Parker skips along, her curls bouncing across her shoulders, and Chase tries to run ahead, dragging us along behind him. The wind whips around the buildings, and I bury my face inside my jacket.

"How long of a walk?" Chase asks, and I can sense his excitement waning.

"It's not too far, let's just try to enjoy the sunshine!" I say as a bus honks loudly beside us.

"It's cold!" Brayden complains, his feet dragging across the pavement.

"So let's walk fast!" Evan suggests.

We make our way to the waterfront, and I marvel at the changes to the Seaport district since the last time we were here, a year ago. There are skyscrapers that have gone up while other buildings have come down. A bit more green space and fewer parking lots. So many changes.

"Look at all the restaurants now," I say to Evan.

"Is that an indoor beer garden?" he asks me.

"Yes, I actually heard this went in here." I'm unable to hide the disappointment in my voice.

"What's a beer garden?" Parker asks.

I ignore her question, and we stop to watch a crowd that's already gathered inside a warehouse with the garage doors open to the street. We gawk at the picnic tables full of people at eleven o'clock in the morning, listening to a live acoustic guitarist. The adults gather around the space heaters by the doors, and the brightly colored tables and decor invite us.

"Can we go in?" Chase asks. "That looks warm!"

Two young men are tossing a football back and forth from table to table. A few people are lounging in Adirondack chairs, playing cards. There's a corn hole game going on farther inside.

"Are they drinking beer in the morning?" Brayden asks.

"Why, yes. Yes, they are," I say, gazing at the pale ale in the hands of the man in front of us. We continue to stare, looking at them like animals in a zoo. I love a good brewery. This is my jam. Interactive drinking is the best kind of drinking, I used to say. Back during my heyday, this would have been our first stop, and we probably would have made ourselves comfortable here all day. I would have felt it was quality family time exploring the city then saddling up for a nice, warm lunch. *Look, games for the kids!* But I know it wouldn't have ended well for me. One beer always led to another. Then a third. I was never content with having that single drink, and my mind was never on my children's needs after the floodgates opened. Once I had that first sip, it was like I became brainwashed and selfishly focused on one thing and one thing only: to get drunk.

I take a few steps back, away from the smell of stale beer and fried food. I try to breathe in the fresh air but smell the exhaust of a nearby truck instead. Seeking relief from the memories of my past, my mind whirls. I feel as if at any moment I could be sucked in through the garage doors into the brewery, toward the strum of the music, lost forever. It's like a vortex. The force inside is strong, and like a hand it grips my insides tightly and squeezes. The frothy plastic cups call my name. The laughter of the people rings, seductively calling to me through the doors. There's a collective energy I can't let go of. And then *bam!* I'm thrust back into reality.

"Okay! Let's go, everyone!" I turn and start to walk into the cold, Boston wind, taking my children's hands. Watching these people, it's like I'm back in the senior apartments at Colby, or I'm back in quarantine, drinking with the neighbors, alcohol fueling my every decision.

I used to believe getting drunk was the pinnacle of fun, and I feel the familiar shame cycling around me. I consider for a moment what it is that I am experiencing as we keep walking.

I notice the anger. The sadness. I let it wash over me. For so long, I needed to immerse myself in this world of drinking. I needed to get drunk to just feel. To laugh. To cry. To experience anything.

I feel tingly, and I am very aware of everything now. My skin prickles, almost vibrating at the sudden realization that I can't be that person who finds happiness in a bar. That person who escapes her responsibilities with alcohol. That is *not* me anymore.

We are not drinking today.

We will not be ruining our day by getting wasted.

We are not those people. I really do not want to be that kind of mom anymore.

I am here. With my children. With my husband. It is a new chapter.

And then the sudden outrage seems to dissipate, and the sad feelings begin to settle. The irritation and shame that's forced me to slam my feet into the pavement are no longer.

The vibrating subsides. After a moment, I realize I'm speed-walking and dragging my kids behind me. I slow my pace and smile at them.

I should be enjoying the day and this very moment. There's nothing to be ashamed of right now. Not anymore. I can find joy without the bottle in hand.

I must start to forgive myself at some point.

I am not that girl anymore.

That isn't going to be my life anymore.

Casual Dishonesty (2003): Twenty Years Old

During the fall of my senior year, my friends and I lived about five minutes off campus on Sheldon Place. I lived in one house, and Evan lived with his teammates a few houses down the street from us. There were other residents of Waterville that lived on Sheldon Place that weren't students at Colby, making us feel very grown-up. We felt like we were on our way to becoming adults. We were responsible for paying the electric bills every month and taking out the trash each week. We grocery shopped, cooked dinner every night, and even cleaned sometimes. Evan and I took turns staying over at each other's house, never sleeping apart.

One night in October, I tossed and turned in Evan's bed, waiting for him to come back to his house. He had gone to dinner without me, and it was my turn to sleep at his place. It was late, well past midnight. He was having dinner with my field hockey coach, who happened to be a former classmate that graduated a few years before. She was my old captain and teammate, and a friend of Evan's.

She had been hired that fall as the new assistant coach. She was familiar with the Colby party scene, but she wasn't allowed to come to the on-campus parties as an employee. Plus, all of her friends had graduated, so she knew very few people anymore. She and Evan had a close friendship, and I was determined not to be the jealous girlfriend. Besides, she was my coach, so there was nothing to worry about. I trusted my boyfriend completely, unlike I had ever trusted another person. I thought it was sweet that she'd invited him over for dinner.

"You should go! At least for a little bit. She sits at home alone most nights," I told him.

"But I need to be up early tomorrow," Evan said.

"Well, just go for an hour to be polite."

Evan came home several hours later, well after midnight, smelling like booze. He didn't talk to me, but instead he went straight to take a shower. After he was done, he crawled into bed.

"How was dinner?"

"Fine, I'm tired," he replied and pushed me away.

He didn't seem interested in talking anymore with me that night.

There was a small part of me that wondered why he was giving me the cold shoulder after coming home much later than he said he would. If anything, I should be mad at him.

And why did he shower before getting into bed? He never took showers at night. That was a little strange, but I was too afraid to let my mind wander. Instead, I rolled over with my back to his back and forced myself to go to sleep.

When we awoke the next morning, everything seemed normal between us. We headed to campus together like usual. We went about our day and continued this charade for the rest of the week. But for months, I had a sick feeling in my stomach.

Sometimes, if the voice inside my head would bring up any feelings of concern I'd had that night, I would drink to forget about it.

When I began to feel like maybe that shower he'd taken when he came home from her house was a red flag, I would keep the thought from creeping in by turning up the music in our kitchen and lining up the shot glasses on the dining room table. I wouldn't let myself go there. Evan would never hurt me.

There was one big question that I was always too afraid ask myself. Had Evan cheated on me with my coach? I never confronted him.

Dishonesty starts casually.

It begins simply by running from the truth. It's impossible to lie to yourself, though. Secrets never stay hidden.

Up until that year, I had been dealt my fair share of punches in college, so maybe I knew I couldn't handle another painful blow. On the other hand, I was accustomed to a certain amount of fiction in my life, and a blind eye had served me well in the past.

So I chose to remain in the shadows, staying unaware of the truth. We finished college less than a year later.

Big Transitions (2004): Twenty-One Years Old

I graduated from Colby in June of 2004 alongside Evan and the rest of my friends. Moving away from college was one of the most difficult things I ever did. It was like the people I cared most about were abandoning me all over again. Every one of my friends was headed in different directions. The campus had become my favorite place in the world, and it broke my heart to leave somewhere that was full of so many memories. Colby had given me a new family and a sense of comfort when I was most alone. It was my refuge, and I grew in ways I never imagined I would. Even though there was great difficulty and struggle packed into those years, I also found them to be the best of my life.

Mayflower Hill was full of strange truths. Dark secrets. Desperate lies. Even far-fetched stories. Just like the cozy walls of my youth, the dozens of dorms on that college campus came to define who I was. Nestled above the town of Waterville, Maine, this was the place I called home. The place I trusted and relied on for some of the most life-challenging years of my existence.

But my home let me down almost as much as it raised me up.

Behind those walls, I was assaulted. Taught to believe it had been my fault. On that campus, I was cut from the field hockey team but learned to come back fighting harder. After watching the planes hit the World Trade Center on September 11, I along with the rest of my classmates learned the meaning of resilience. It was behind the walls of Colby that I felt more alone than ever, and I was forced to stand on my own—finding comfort and support through a brand-new family of friends and classmates; a family that laughed with me, cried with me, and protected me. A group that partied hard but loved even harder.

It was also at Colby that I fell in love. A love like I never knew I could feel. Evan encouraged me to confront and push myself in ways I never had the courage to do before.

I lost myself.

I found myself.

And through it all, I drank myself stupid every weekend, believing that was the key to experiencing it all. So often I used alcohol to numb the pain. To feel joy. To escape fear.

Even by the end of my senior year, I was still just as lost as when I began.

"I will never do this to my kids..." (2007): Twenty-Five Years Old

Evan and I managed to make our relationship work long distance. Evan attended law school in Ohio, and I headed to New York City, then Connecticut for graduate school. In the summer of 2007, Evan and I moved in together in Boston after getting engaged, and my life began to come together exactly how I had always wanted it to be since I was a little girl. At that time, I longed for connection, and I was anxious to begin the storybook life I had envisioned for so long with Evan.

One weekend, Evan and I arrived at Mom's house in New Hampshire for a weekend visit from Boston. We often escaped from the noise of the city up to the mountains or the lake. We'd decided to get ahead of the traffic one weekend, and it was four o'clock when we arrived at Mom's.

"Mom, are you okay?" I asked.

"Yes, I'm great," she replied.

I briskly walked out of the house, letting the screen door slam behind me and went to get our suitcases from the car, and Evan followed me outside.

"Why can't she just stop for a few days?" I said, exasperated. "Can she really not go a whole weekend without drinking?"

"I mean, I guess she can't help it," Evan said.

Every time we visited her, she drank. Often in secret.

"Does she really think we can't notice?"

Those days, Mom lied to us over and over again, pretending that she didn't even have wine in the house. I could tell by the way she spoke and the look on her face, though. I was growing more and more infuriated with each passing visit. She always excused herself to her room for a while, somehow thinking we were unaware of what she was doing up there. She would emerge later, hiccupping, eyes unfocused, smelling of Listerine and perfume.

Another weekend, my sisters and I were snooping around and found bottles of wine hidden in her closet. There were empty wine bottles under the trash in the recycling bin, and bottles stashed behind boxes in the garage. I snuck around in the evening hours after she'd gone to bed, searching for all of her hiding spots, feeling like I was the one doing something wrong, nervous that she'd catch me. On the way out, before heading back to Boston the next day, I pleaded with her to stop drinking so much.

"Please, Mom, just consider drinking less for the sake of your future grandchildren."

"I'm fine. You don't need to worry about me," she said, slurring her words. "It's your father who has his priorities all out of whack."

It was exhausting and frustrating, and I thought to myself, *I will never do this to my kids when I'm a mother.*

I didn't consider at that time that my own drinking was a concern. I believed the way I drank was acceptable because it was how all of my friends drank too. We went out on the weekends and enjoyed going to bars just like everyone else I knew. I battled weekend hangovers, but so did all of my friends and coworkers. I never drank during the week, and we rarely kept alcohol in our apartment. Also, I never drank alone. There were so many distinctions in my mind that separated me from my mother and her habits.

By the time I was twenty-five, I stopped seeing my parents as two flawless beings who could do no wrong. They were not the ultimate, faultless Mom and Dad I always believed them to be. They were humans capable of making their own mistakes. They'd both been hurting for a long time and had tried to keep it together for our sake. But the choices they made to repair the damages of the past only ended up hurting me more. I stopped waiting around for them to figure things out, and I finally accepted the fact that they were done parenting me. It was as if my parents' jobs were complete.

Being able to see this, I thought that meant I was strong, and that I was moving on with my life. I could stand tall and be a better adult and wife to my future husband because I had seen the flaws in my own parents. I believed I would begin my own family feeling wiser and more knowledgeable. I pushed ahead and thought I was leaving that pain in the past. My parents' secrets and past mistakes would not define me. I wanted to move beyond it all, and I had to create my own life. I needed to let it all go.

Little did I know that it was impossible to walk away from the past. You can't deny pain. You can't escape the hurt. What I was doing was burying it. I was simply storing the damage their secrets did to me and taking it with me wherever I went.

Day 63: January 30, 2021

"Hi, Mom, I have something to tell you."

I am alone in the woods, my feet crunching into the snow beneath me as I meander along the rail trail by our house. I press the phone awkwardly against my cheek with my bulky winter glove.

"What is it?" Mom asks. "You aren't sick, are you?"

"No," I say, hesitating.

"Are the kids okay? It isn't the Covid, is it?" Concern builds in her voice.

I need to continue down this path. I need to just come right out and tell Mom what I've been experiencing with sobriety. I can't be scared.

As I go through my days, I manage to feel all the feelings. In my recovery meetings, I'm told it's part of the healing process. I feel everything: happiness, anger, frustration, pride. It's a constant cycle of emotions. And throughout it all, I have not shared any of what I'm going through with my mom, and that is hard. I know why I haven't been able to talk to her about it, and I've been avoiding this. It's easier to journal or talk to random strangers on the internet than it is to speak to my own mom about my problems with alcohol.

I'm two months sober, and it's still a secret. Mom has no idea about any of my struggles. With the daily texts and phone calls, I remain silent with her about all of this. She doesn't know the kids are going to school full time. She has no idea the pain I've been feeling, or the rawness I've been experiencing. She doesn't know anything about my life right now, and I'm starting to realize that the secrets are what got me here in the first place. Yet I continue to keep them.

I want to be able to talk to Mom about my sobriety, but I don't think I can go there yet. I'm afraid of what she'll think. She may not be able to see past her own experiences. Will she take it personally? Is she still drinking every day? Will she think about her own life and have regrets? I don't want to hurt her by shining light on her problems if she's not ready to face them. Or maybe it could go the other direction, and she'll judge me and be disappointed. I don't know what to expect, but it terrifies me to tell *her* more than anyone else in this world.

I don't want to think about talking to her yet. It would be easier to just not deal with it. It's not worth going there. What's the point in telling her? It will only hurt her. Or upset her. Or makes things weird. And then I realize I'm in the same habit loop from before, repeating the same things I used to do.

I hear the voices of my past. *What's the point in attempting this conversation? You can't do this. Talking about this stuff with Mom is too hard. Don't even bother. It's not worth it.* And I realize these are the thoughts that got me here in the first place.

Up until now, I've put my mother into her own small corner. I've boxed her in to protect myself. I've put her there so I can mentally prepare myself for her judgment. I've distanced myself from the pain until I'm ready.

"I'm fine, everyone is good," I tell her, wiping my nose with a tissue. "I just need you to know, I've been going through something recently."

"Oh?"

"I've been getting support for alcohol addiction."

She's quiet for a moment. At times in the past, I was angry at her and blamed her for not being stronger and doing more when I begged her to get help with alcohol. These days, I often blame others for my problems. It's just easier that way. I've complained to Evan that Mom could have set a better example for me so I didn't end up like this.

Then I take a step back and remind myself that she has always been just like me. I can't fault her or anyone else for where I am right now. I can't blame her for my choices. I can't condemn her. It's not her fault. This isn't about blame, just as no one can blame Dad for his secrets.

I need to reserve judgment and recognize that Mom has tried to fight this and has lost the battle before. Maybe she looked at herself in the mirror and tried searching for the strength but couldn't do it. Maybe she attempted to face her subconscious demons and recognize the damage alcohol was doing to her life but succumbed to the voice inside her head instead. Maybe she tried but failed time and time again. Maybe she couldn't give up alcohol when she wanted, and here she is today. Still drinking. So I tell myself to give her grace, find a place for her outside that box that I've put her in, and be strong for the both of us instead.

"Okay," Mom says, "are you alright?"

"I'm okay, but I just want you to know that I needed to cut alcohol out of my life. I've been struggling, but I'm doing better."

There's an awkward silence, and I can tell she doesn't know what to say. This is also what I was scared of. Creating a larger divide in the ocean between us that's been growing for the last twenty years. I want Mom to understand what I'm going through, but I fear she won't. And I worry this will make it more difficult to ever understand each other.

"I'm sorry you've been having a tough time, but I'm glad you've decided to do something about it," she says, then falls quiet for a moment before speaking again. "What are you doing this weekend? Do the boys have hockey games?"

Just like that, the conversation moves on. We pick up and move ahead, pretending all is fine in the world. Like usual. But at least I was able to say my part.

Relief floods over me. No more secrets weighing me down. Freedom. We talk about the weekend plans. The weather. The regular stuff we normally discuss. And for the first time in days, I feel like I'm not drowning.

Goodbye, Spofford Lake (2008): Twenty-Six Years Old

A s a child, I thought my father's heart and soul belonged to New England. Most of our weekends were spent on the ski slopes of the White Mountains in New Hampshire, racing down the mountain, trailing after one another. In the summer, Dad would fire up the motorboat on Spofford Lake and pull us in circles on a big red innertube across the smooth, glass-like water. Dad poured his blood, sweat, and tears into that lake house. He took such pride in painting the dock a new shade of blue every spring and watching us grow up on the water each summer.

But once Richie settled into the picture, things changed. Dad started visiting Spofford Lake less and less, limiting his visits to once a month, then only a few times a year. Soon, the house sat empty. He began spending more time in New York City, then Florida, spending months at a time in Sarasota and Palm Beach.

One day, he sat me down. "I've decided to sell the Spofford house. It's gotten so old, and it's too much work for me. I don't want to spend the rest of my life painting the dock, dragging the floats in and out of the water, and pouring money into replacing shingles and broken bilge pumps on the boat."

"But . . . what? You love that house," I said.

"I used to love it, but not anymore."

"How can that be?" I asked, dumbfounded.

"It's time for me to try something new," Dad replied.

He sold that house a year later. It broke my heart to see him give it up so easily and never look back. I wasn't ready. I wanted to keep the lake house in our family. I wanted to hold onto a piece of it forever, somehow.

It shook my understanding. I thought I would have the Spofford house to one day bring my children to, and teach them how to row in a canoe, fish off the dock, and waterski just like Dad taught me. I wanted to always come back to stargaze off the deck and watch the Fourth of July parade in the summer. I had so many happy memories there. We had a history within those walls. The house held a piece of my heart. And it had been my one true home after our house in Greenwich was gone. It hurt knowing this house was no longer ours. I grieved for the loss of our lake house, and I was shattered as I said goodbye to this piece of my past.

But I didn't complain to Dad. I kept quiet. I had to be supportive. I always had to be silent, keep my head down, and act like it would all be okay. My little secret sadness.

"The cold weather isn't good for Richie's back, and the mold at the lake is always bad for my sinuses, you know," he reminded us.

"No, I didn't know," I said.

"That lake house is a money pit! And the town is such a dump. It's really gone to hell."

Where was the man I knew? Did he still think about the memories of our past as I did? Where was the man who stood on the end of the dock and taught me how to fish?

"Okay, Dad. I understand. It's a bummer you're selling it, but that's cool. Whatever." It was easier not to confront him and let it go. I had to pretend it was all okay.

After that, Dad stopped traveling up to the lake for good. He never went back. He also hadn't visited the mountains where he taught me how to ride the chairlift as a little girl in well over twenty years.

Our lake house was like a metaphor for our life; our family; my relationship with Dad.

Day 68: February 4, 2021

There was a sense of relief after talking to Mom a few days ago, a freedom from letting my secret breathe. A lightness and vulnerability. An authentic realness, knowing that this is me. I am doing it all and feeling it all, and there's no hiding anymore.

I put the phone on speaker and set it down on the kitchen counter.

Alone in the house, I listen to Dad's deep voice echo off the walls of the kitchen. I can hear the wind whistling into his phone as he walks along the shores of Palm Beach. I envision the warmth of the sun on his face, the sand between his toes. It's strange that he resides in a part of the country that we never even visited when I was a child. When I was a kid, Dad felt Florida was too crowded for a vacation destination. He refused to ever take us there.

He drones on about whatever news story recently caught his eye. I let him tell me his latest political opinions, and I nod along. He rambles on about the real estate market in Palm Beach county. I lean my face into my right hand and stare at the lines in the marble countertop. This is how my conversations with my father are these days. He speaks, I listen.

He goes on to talk about selling his condo. He and Richie are about to embark upon a new venture. I don't give him my opinion. I don't speak up. I let him do the talking. It's easier that way.

"So I think we'll sell this place and rent part time in Palm Beach and part time in New York City, six months here, and six months there," Dad says.

"Oh, really?" My ears perk up. This is interesting, but I don't really buy into it. "But why? I thought you guys loved Florida full time."

"We do! But we miss you kids so much, we want to be closer to you some of the time. To the grandkids," he tells me.

"Okay." I don't believe him. I can't help but think there's an ulterior motive.

Every time I talk to Dad, he has a new plan, and it has never once involved me or my kids. He can never stay in one place too long and is never satisfied living in the house he's in. He and Richie buy and sell their home constantly, and since the day he moved out twenty years ago, Dad has never made me or my sisters a priority in his plans. Not since he took all the paintings off the wall in Stamford and left that note for Mom.

He talks about renovating, redecorating, and what he envisions for the next project they plan to invest in. This is what keeps them busy. Happy, I guess. Yet this is the first time in many years that he claims he wants to come back north.

"Richie misses the city and wants more culture," Dad says. "And we want to be close to the University Club. And everyone down here—they're all such Trump supporters. I need a break."

There it is. Boredom. Conservative America is wearing him down. Other motives, indeed. But maybe he does want to see me more. See my kids. Maybe there's some change coming down the road.

"Dad," I try to interrupt.

"Richie wants to be closer to Kate and the kids, too."

I breathe heavily, relaxing my body into a counter stool. I continue tracing the gray, black, and white lines of the countertops with my fingertip, creating tiny looping patterns.

"Dad, that's great," I tell him after a few more minutes have passed.

I'm tired now, and it's become like talking to a stranger on the other line. I don't believe Dad will ever move back here. And if he does, how is this time going to be any different than the last twenty years? But I need to tell him my piece. There was a reason for this phone call, a point to this conversation. But my mission has been derailed, and I feel as though I'm losing steam.

I want to just say goodbye and be done with this call. But instead, I hear Ronni's voice in my head, and I know I cannot just walk away. I need to push forward. I can't stay stuck in the same habit loop from my past, avoiding the hard stuff. I need to tell Dad what's been going on with me these days. I need to just do it. Like a Band-Aid.

"Dad, I have something to tell you."

"Oh? Is everything okay with you? Evan?"

"Yeah, we're fine. I just wanted you to know I stopped drinking. It's a choice I made. I felt that I was developing an unhealthy relationship with alcohol. So I'm getting help. I'm doing some support online. Getting therapy. I'm good, and I just wanted you to know."

"Wow, really? Kimmy, I'm so proud of you. That's some really big news."

"Yeah, I know."

"Truly, I mean it. You know Richie and I don't drink much anymore. I try to work out twice a day, and alcohol is such a toxin."

"Right."

"I was really thinking you drank too much the last time you visited me and Richie in Palm Beach anyway, so this is probably really good. Much better for you."

"Okay, well that's not very productive for me to hear, Dad."

"Right. True."

"But I have to run now, Dad. Kids are coming home soon. I just wanted you to know this news. I'm doing well, though."

We finish our phone call and say our goodbyes. I press the end button on the call and lay slumped on the counter. I feel some relief, but like always, I'm left wanting more. I'm feeling overwhelmed for some reason. I said my truth, and I feel a bit lighter. This is no longer feeling like a secret I need to keep from him, which is freeing.

But still, words have gone unspoken. I feel defeated by the entire exchange. Exhausted. The hollowness between my father and me seems to echo throughout my empty house.

Shipping Up to Boston (2008): Twenty-Six Years Old

Evan and I found our own rhythm as we settled into our new life together as real adults. We purchased an adorable condo in the South End of Boston, a trendy section of the city filled with young professionals. We lived in the most desirable area, called the Golden Triangle, as this part of the South End bordered some of the best restaurants and backed up to the bustling Back Bay portion of Boston. The South End was filled with historical row houses and brownstones from the late 1700s, most of which had been renovated to fit the taste of the young professionals that had slowly gentrified the area. Our condo was a three-story row house that we entered at garden level through a small staircase down from the street. We ducked our heads and walked through a wrought iron gate and down several stairs to access the front door.

It had charm and personality, and we spent days making it our own. We painted the bedroom and bathrooms, picked out furniture, and even bought a patio set and grill for our outdoor space. We were doing it, and we were truly on our own. We loved our apartment and living in the city. Things seemed perfect.

The first year was centered around the planning and execution of our wedding, working hard and playing hard on the weekend. We maintained that Colby mentality through and through. We still enjoyed drinking with friends, but we were working, so we didn't drink during the week. Evan especially took his job seriously. He worked around the clock and barely had time to enjoy a beer on a weeknight.

When we visited friends on the weekends and attended other people's weddings, it was like we were back at Colby, and I always got drunk like the good old days. All bets were off anytime the Colby crew got together. Evan never got to the point that I did, though, and he was always my designated driver.

Often, Evan would tend to me on Sunday mornings, making me bacon and eggs to relieve my hangover. We sometimes went out to brunch, where he urged me to order a Mimosa or Bloody Mary to relieve my headache, but I didn't see the point. He figured one drink on a Sunday would get me back to normal, but I only ever wanted to get wasted. A single drink seemed pointless to me.

Evan usually enjoyed a beer with his meal on these days because he had a stop button. He knew his limit, but I couldn't have just one. I didn't know how to drink and not get drunk. I thought I was still eighteen at Colby and that the point of alcohol was to get blacked out.

Most Sundays after brunch, Evan sipped another beer while watching football, and I napped. We wouldn't drink again until the following Friday or Saturday night. I believed I had a healthy handle on my drinking. Getting drunk once or twice a week seemed safe, and all of my friends did the same thing.

Evan worked long hours at his law firm as a first-year associate, and I commuted to the suburbs every day to teach sixth grade at a private school in Wellesley. I enjoyed teaching and working with middle schoolers, but I never was passionate about my occupation. I felt as if I was biding my time, waiting to become a mother.

I was always waiting. Waiting for someone. Or something. Waiting for another jack-in-the-box. Expecting something big to happen with my life, good or bad, I wasn't sure. I had so many unresolved feelings about my past that it was difficult to live in the moment. Drinking on the weekends helped me escape the unsettledness.

We traveled all the time and skied up north and out west. We visited Napa Valley, Bermuda, and London, alcohol always playing a key role in our travels.

One winter, we took a trip out west to Lake Tahoe for a long weekend with some friends from Colby. We arrived in the middle of the night and slept very little for the duration of the three-day vacation.

Being around friends from college, we were immediately thrust back into the days of when we were all together on Mayflower Hill. We stayed up late playing drinking games and taking shots, skied all day on the slopes, and drank beers at lunchtime in the sunshine. I was either drunk, sick from the altitude, or working off my hangover during the entire seventy-two-hour trip.

I arrived home and headed to work to teach my sixth graders feeling completely depleted and exhausted. I was beginning to realize I couldn't binge drink around the clock like I used to when I was eighteen. Nonetheless, we always enjoyed those weekends away. I longed for the nostalgic reminder of my Colby days and did anything I could to feel like I was back in college.

Over Memorial Day weekend in May of 2008, Evan and I got married at the Wequassett Inn on Cape Cod. We were surrounded by close to a hundred and fifty friends and family. Most of the guests were friends from college, and it was a quintessential New England wedding weekend, complete with a lobster clambake rehearsal dinner on the ocean.

I had all of my close girlfriends there, which to me was what mattered most at the time. I had spent the year prior preparing for the wedding and planning every last detail. The majority of these efforts were done on my own. Mom played a very small part in the planning, rarely coming to the city for my dress fittings or down to the Cape for food tastings. My sisters were busy with their own lives as well.

I was a decisive yet easygoing bride. I knew what I wanted and executed the day quite seamlessly. It was a cloudless sunny day and nearly eighty degrees that afternoon in May. I made sure not to drink too much on my wedding day. I wanted to remember every moment.

Things were simpler during these years for me and Evan. Our lives revolved around work, travel, and each other. Although I dreamed of a future with children and a house in the suburbs with a nice yard, I was content. I was excited for what the years ahead looked like. I loved living in the city, and we were happy. But I was waiting for the other shoe to drop.

It wasn't until our first child, Brayden, was born in January of 2011 that life became a lot more complicated for us. All I ever wanted since I was a little girl and the days of playing dolls in the basement with my sisters on Winterset Road was to have a baby. The memories I have of creating our little houses in the woods and riding my bike up and down the driveway with my dolls strapped to my back were precious to me. I had readied myself for the role of motherhood for as long as I could remember. But nothing could prepare me for the level of challenges that I was met with when my firstborn arrived. Finally, the pain I had been storing away could no longer remain hidden.

Becoming A Mother (2011): Twenty-Eight Years Old

The truth can never stay buried. A week before Brayden was born, I had a moment that shaped my marriage and redefined my relationship with Evan forever.

After experiencing vivid, bizarrely lucid dreams for days, I woke suddenly and sat up, terrified by the images replaying in my brain.

It felt as if my mind was finally ready to uncover the truth from our senior year of college that I'd worked so hard to escape. Something I had been denying for a long time: a knowledge buried in my subconscious for years that could no longer stay hidden.

The jack-in-the-box had finally popped open.

Evan had secrets. Evan had betrayed me. The night he went to my field hockey coach's house was no longer concealed in the subconscious recesses of my brain. Out of nowhere, I was finally ready to confront him. It was as if the nine months of pregnancy and detox from alcohol had finally allowed my mind to clear. Or perhaps, days before giving birth, I knew I was on the precipice of a major milestone and needed to take care of this part of my past. What had happened in college, I saw it in my dream. It was finally time to confront Evan about it.

It was close to five o'clock in the morning. With a sickness in my stomach, I knew what I'd seen in my dreams to be true. Evan had cheated on me with my field hockey coach in college, and for some reason, I couldn't hide from it a moment longer. It was time to face the truth.

The images were all too realistic and the hurt was unbelievably intense, and in the depths of my soul, I had already known the truth for some time. In my dream, I was back in Colby confronting Evan about the infidelity he'd committed against me—something I never would have had the strength to do seven years prior.

How did I know the facts all along yet still choose to bury them in my mind? It was as if there were some sixth sense telling me something was off with him.

Maybe I'd caught wind of some rumor years ago, or sensed he'd been lying to me, and chose to ignore the signs. Maybe it was the fact that he'd taken a shower, something he never did at night.

Whatever it was, I could no longer ignore it. There was no more running from this secret anymore. I was finally ready to face the lies.

I shook Evan awake, shouting his name with rage in my voice and fury in my fists. I demanded to know what happened that night he went over to my coach's house for dinner.

Groggy with sleep and caught completely off guard, Evan stared at me with disbelief. "What?"

"Tell me the truth, right now!" I demanded.

He couldn't deny it, not when he stared into my crying eyes and down at my swollen nine-month pregnant belly.

"What? Why are you asking me this now? How did you know?" he whispered.

I pummeled his chest with closed fists and yelled his name loudly. Then the floodgates opened. I sobbed.

Evan admitted to other betrayals as well. There had been more than one girl.

"Tell me exactly what happened. With all of these girls!" I sobbed.

I needed to know about every transgression, every misstep, every tiny mistake he had made while we were dating for those three years at Colby. It poured out of him, and the relief of finally telling the truth was obvious. He had cheated on me a number of times throughout the years we dated back in college. And the substantial weight of his guilt was finally being shed. Was I opening the door to forgiveness? I didn't know. I was too hurt.

I felt lost. I was sick to my stomach. There was a hollowness to me. Even though I was nine months pregnant, I felt empty.

I was overwhelmed to learn that he'd cheated on me with more than just my coach but other friends of mine in college. He had betrayed me in so many ways. There were so many aspects of the story that broke me into a thousand pieces. I curled into a ball on our bathroom floor and cried. I locked myself in the bathroom for hours, alone with my baby and my destructive thoughts. I was broken. My marriage was a sham. My memories of Colby were destroyed. My heart was crushed.

I must have known the truth all along, but my subconscious had waited to deliver it to me at a time when I felt I should finally process it, days before I was about to become a mother. Something told me it was time for the secrets to come out. I needed to face the truth.

But I still couldn't process it. I wasn't strong enough. I had to bury it, pretend it was all okay. I couldn't talk about it or discuss it because we were about to have a baby together.

I was ashamed. As much as I wanted to walk away from Evan and never speak to him again for hurting me, I needed him. As he had deceived me all those years ago, he was in my life no matter what.

Still, I resented him. I hated him for hurting me and making me doubt my faith in him forever. I felt like he had betrayed me just like the men before him. As Jonathon had. As Dad had. And he was the one man who promised never to do that to me.

"You're a manipulative liar!" I told him. "You lied for so long! How could you!"

"I'm sorry," was all he could say.

I wavered between tears and anger for the next few days. I was so incredibly lost, and I didn't think I'd ever fully trust him again. Yet I knew I had no choice but to bury the pain and move on. Forge ahead. I focused on the new life inside me. My baby. My new purpose. But what else was lurking behind closed doors ready to jump out and ruin my happiness at any moment?

Evan made it his mission to fix things. He was determined to make it up to me, and he wanted to show me. "I'll spend the rest of my life proving to you how sorry I am," he told me day in and day out. "I was a stupid, immature college kid. I was selfish and young. I was dumb. I'm sorry. It was thoughtless college behavior."

"I don't even know what to say," I told him with sadness in my eyes. But we were connected. For so long, he was the one person that wouldn't let me fall, always catching me when I was struggling to keep my feet on the ground. He was the one who supported me and held me up.

I knew deep down that I would stand by him as he had always done for me. There was a special kind of forgiveness, love, and grace between us that can only come from two people who care for and understand each other on a cellular level. Even though it seemed like there was nobody to turn to, I knew at the end of the day, I still loved Evan.

I couldn't find it in my heart to forgive him like I wanted to in the beginning, but I knew I would try. It was an open wound, one that would take years to heal.

This was a secret he'd kept from me for too long. Unfortunately, it had ripped apart the trust I had for him, and I would eventually learn to cover up the pain in the only way I knew how, finding comfort in the one thing that made me feel safe. Alcohol.

Once I became a mother, I would learn to bury the sadness. I would find a way to forgive my husband, but only by masking the pain. Eventually, I would look to escape the memories. I would use booze to manage all of the hurt without even realizing that was what I was doing.

My First Baby (2011): Twenty-Eight Years Old

Deep down, there was so much that was broken already. I had buried so much pain that I wondered if there was room for any more hurt. I had no choice but to try. *Don't see. Don't tell. Don't feel.* I was slowly shattering inside from years of emotional instability.

Brayden was born a week later, after many hours of painful labor. The hurt caused by the revelations I discovered about my husband sat at the forefront of my mind. The celebration surrounding the birth of my firstborn was clouded. There was a sadness that existed and would remain for years. My husband had betrayed me. But I had to forge on.

Motherhood proved to be extremely challenging. Brayden was not an easy baby. For months, he wouldn't sleep for more than two hours at a time. In his first several days, he spit up constantly, making him fussy and uncomfortable. If he wasn't held nonstop, he screamed. I felt like I never got a break.

Breastfeeding was difficult. My nipples cracked and bled for days, and for the first eight weeks, I cried in agony every time he latched on. I experienced the exhaustion and stress many new moms undergo, and I constantly questioned if I was doing it all right.

I put a lot of pressure on myself to do things a certain way. I'd read all the how-to books on parenting and attended all the prenatal classes to ensure my baby was perfect in every way. I wanted him to sleep the right amount of hours, eat on a schedule, and follow what all the books said. At least this could be the one thing I could control, even if everything else in my world was spiraling. But motherhood became another piece of my life I was destined to be disappointed by.

Evan didn't help me during the nights with Brayden. His patience wore thin quickly when it came to getting the baby to take a bottle.

"I don't have the magic touch," he told me one night as he awkwardly held our baby out to me. "He doesn't like the bottle. He prefers the real thing."

"We need to try, I need a break sometimes," I pleaded. "Please."

"Fine," Evan said, frustrated and exhausted. "I got him. Go sleep."

But even then, I couldn't sleep for long. Either my breasts had to be pumped or my incessant worry would keep me awake. Sometimes, Evan dozed off while holding Brayden instead of placing him in the bassinet, and I woke to find them sleeping together in front of the TV at two in the morning. I was overwhelmed with fear that Evan was going to accidentally suffocate Brayden, and my anxiety gripped me like never before. I begged him to stay awake.

"You worry too much!" Evan replied. "Stop worrying. You just need to sleep. We're fine. Go to bed."

"He isn't supposed to sleep on you while you sleep!" I cried. My emotions were a wreck, and everything made me cry. "He's going to die of SIDS!"

"You sound crazy! You're creating irrational scenarios like your mother!" Evan shouted.

We screamed at each other in the middle of the night like this often, and I wondered what was happening to us. Where was the happy, blissful image of motherhood I had been promised?

I went to several new moms classes hoping to find the answer. I trudged through the mounds of slush and snow, pushing my stroller across the icy Boston sidewalks to the Prudential Center. Baby classes were often the only outings of the week for me.

Brayden and I also attended music hour, where we listened to a man strum a guitar in the middle of a windowless room. Brayden usually slept in my arms the entire time, but I felt understood and connected to the other moms in the class. I soon found myself a small group of new mothers to commiserate with over the sleepless nights, engorged breasts, and tiny humans we were responsible for.

Evan took some time off work to help me, but I felt distant and disconnected from him. I was still resentful over the revelations of his past infidelities. Despite trying to put them out of my mind, I couldn't help feeling angry. He didn't help me much during his time off, and ultimately he used his three-month paternity leave as a break to recharge from his own demanding associate's position at his law firm.

Evan and I had no family to rely on during this time in our lives, and I felt isolated during the early months of motherhood. Our parents both lived out of state, and no one visited us much. I didn't call Mom in the middle of the night for sleeping advice. That wasn't how our relationship was. When I did speak to her on the phone, she only peppered me with worrisome questions, and I found myself easing her mind instead of her easing mine. I figured it was simpler to just do it all on my own. That was how I'd been doing things anyway since I was eighteen.

I had no one to turn to about my issues concerning Evan. I thought often about what he'd done behind my back at Colby and the lies he'd told me for all those years after. I obsessed over it and wondered what else he'd lied about. I felt lost, alone, and afraid.

I had no problem not drinking for nine months because I enjoyed being pregnant. But once Brayden was born, I discovered a new relaxing ritual with a glass of red wine. It wasn't every single night, so it didn't seem to be a concern for me. But the wine always made me feel comforted. A little less alone. And this is what other moms did. They enjoyed a sophisticated glass of wine sometimes.

Having a drink in my system in those early days softened the edges and stopped my mind from racing. As a first-time mom, I questioned my every decision from the bedtime routine to my swaddle style. The wine stopped the constant cycling of my mind, turned down the incessant noise, and quieted the self-doubt.

Wine also helped me fall asleep. When the day was over and the baby was asleep, I was left alone with my thoughts. I fought a nonstop loop of images every night of my husband naked in bed with a long list of women I knew. I saw him sneaking around behind my back. But with half a bottle of wine, I could turn off that porno in my mind and fall asleep more easily.

I told myself that turning to alcohol occasionally wasn't a big deal. This was the only way to get through the day as a new mom: with a large goblet of cabernet as my reward at the end of a lonely afternoon. Sadly, my baby was not the gift; my wine was.

Middle of the Night (2011): Twenty-Eight Years Old

I stared down at his tiny round face. I didn't want to move him. My body was too tired. I was drained. I was still stitched and hemorrhaging from the delivery a week and a half ago. Why didn't anyone ever say it would be so hard?

He fit perfectly in my one arm, so I used my other hand and touched his soft, fuzzy blond hair. He lay there, milk still on his lips, squirming in my arms.

This was one of the only times he was truly content, when he was full and his diaper was changed. He was satisfied for the time being. For a moment, I could just enjoy him without him needing me to do anything else. Why did he need me so damn much? In a little bit, it would be time to get back up and begin the cycle again: change, nurse, burp, repeat.

I glanced at my iPhone and saw that it was after three o'clock in the morning. I was too tired to lay him down, and even if I did, he would probably spit up and cry. So I stayed put in the rocking chair with my newborn baby.

"Why don't you sleep more, little man?" I asked him.

It felt strange to be talking to this tiny human and to consider that he belonged to me. This precious being was my responsibility. This person that I already loved with my whole entire body. As Evan snored in the next room, I found myself feeling lost and alone.

"What am I doing? Why do I feel so sad?"

I started to cry. I knew it was the hormones causing me to do this, or the lack of sleep, so I just let the tears pour out. It was cathartic.

I leaned my head back against the chair and stared out of Brayden's bedroom window, gazing at the streetlight outside, tears clouding my vision. That was when I saw the snowflakes falling in the night sky, swirling in the yellow glow of the lamplights on Gray Street, and I smiled. I loved the coziness of watching the snow fall. It reminded me of catching the snowflakes on my tongue on the chairlift next to Dad and my sisters on Stratton Mountain when we were kids and singing "Scotland's Burning."

"How long has it been snowing?" I whispered to Brayden, kissing his forehead.

He was asleep. I leaned over and pulled one of the blankets Mom had knitted for Brayden up over my feet. Leaning back in the rocking chair, I watched the snowflakes flutter down from the sky. My baby was asleep in my arms, and watching the world outside, everything suddenly felt more manageable and safer. Underneath this blanket that Mom made, I relaxed, remembering the days of watching the snow as a little girl. I didn't feel so completely alone.

All at once, I felt a surge of strength and perhaps the belief that this small human in my arms was what would bring me back from the edge. I had been utterly broken and irreparably damaged by the things my husband had done to me. But there was a baby that relied on me now. He needed me, and he loved me. Looking down at the child in my arms, I experienced more love than I ever thought possible. I knew he could never break my heart. He would be the one to heal me.

Mommy Wine Time (2011): Twenty-Eight Years Old

When Brayden was a few months old, Evan went back to work. Feeling lonely, I forced myself one afternoon to meet up with friends from my mommy group. We had started to gather at each other's apartments for weekly playdates because we read that infants needed socialization. I think it was as much about the motherly connections as it was about forming friendships for our sleeping babies.

I showered and changed into my favorite black stretch pants. I bundled Brayden up in his thickest snow gear to brave the Boston winter. His pink face poked out from beneath the fuzzy sherpa blankets. Then I made my way over to my friend Hillary's apartment across town for that richly deserved glass of wine at four in the afternoon.

"I honestly don't know the difference between a size one or two nipple for the bottle. They look the same to me," my friend Liz said once we'd all settled the babies onto the carpet.

"I don't think it matters," Hillary said, sipping her drink. "Whichever one they take."

"When did you switch from the swaddle to the Magic Merlin Sleepsuit?" I asked, topping off my glass. "And what size should I start out with?"

Happy hour with these ladies was a bright light at the end of a dark tunnel on those cold, dreary days. It gave me an outlet to socialize, vent, and relax. But all of it involved alcohol. It broke up the repetitiveness of my days and gave me temporary relief from the monotony. Yet, at the same time, drinking at these gatherings unknowingly made me fall deeper into a dark abyss. In the past, I never drank during the week, let alone during the day. I would attend Friday afternoon happy hours after work occasionally, but day drinking was never my thing. This was uncharted territory. I was forcing myself to put on a show for these women. I pretended everything in my world was perfect when it wasn't.

Evan and I were still not talking about our issues from college. I was angry and in pain, but I never spoke about it with any of my friends. Just as I'd done with my parents, I shoved my resentment toward Evan into the recesses of my mind. Instead, every few days, I found myself at another playdate—a new group of mommies to laugh, chat, and drink with.

Heather lived in a full-service building in Back Bay, which was a short walk from our South End apartment. Her condo was an elaborate establishment with a doorman and elevator. The building was brand new, complete with a workout center, a kids' playroom, and a massive roof-deck.

Balancing Brayden on one hip and a diaper bag on the other, I pulled my bottle of wine out from inside the lower basket of the snow-covered stroller. I checked the time. It was three thirty, but I knew someone would have a drink with me.

The playdate was much the same as all the rest. Heather sat on the floor while her baby nursed from her bare breast. My friend Abby sat across from her on the couch as her daughter crawled across the hardwood floor in a determined fashion. Both ladies were already sipping wine.

I plopped Brayden down on the floor and immediately felt a sense of relief. Just seeing the other women made me feel comforted and less alone. I wasn't sure if it was their presence or the presence of alcohol that made me feel warm inside, but I was giddy with excitement for something different to break up the dull routine of my day.

"I brought some wine!" I announced.

"Thanks!" Heather said. "Grab a glass. Do you want some pinot?"

I came home a few hours later slightly tipsy, and I decided it was a good idea to clean the kitchen. After getting Brayden to bed, I was often faced with the internal dilemma of whether to have another drink.

I had begun to grow acutely aware of how good alcohol made me feel compared to nights I didn't drink. I observed how much I craved it and how much I thought about it. Quite often, I obsessed about that four o'clock drink: the first sip, the initial buzz, the warm sensation that encapsulated my body when the wine ran down my throat into my belly.

I thought about it far more than I should have, and I knew it wasn't a good sign, but I didn't acknowledge it to myself. When I sipped my wine in the evenings, I wasn't reminded of the things of the past I'd tried desperately to put out of my mind. The wine softened it all, numbed it away, and blurred the edges of my memory.

Evan was working at a new law firm, and his hours were worse than usual. Always a diligent and focused lawyer, he left for work early in the mornings and came home late at night. Brayden and I continued to spend our days attending Stroller Strides "mommy and me" classes, baby music lessons, and meeting friends at the end of the day. We often met Evan for a quick lunch when he could squeeze in the break.

It was around the time I stopped nursing Brayden when I found myself more and more tired at nine o'clock in the morning. I began to doze off on the couch when Brayden took his first nap of the day. I found it strange that I was so exhausted now that Brayden had finally started to sleep through the night. Then it occurred to me what might be going on.

I walked the three-mile trek through the Boston Public Garden and up to the financial district to see Evan during his lunch break that fall afternoon. I pushed Brayden in his red UPPAbaby stroller and touched the pregnancy stick in my pocket. I wasn't afraid; I was exhilarated. We would soon have two babies eighteen months apart. I'd always wanted children close in age.

As I hugged Evan on the street corner outside his office that afternoon, he checked his watch. "I have about thirty minutes for lunch," he said, bending over to give Brayden a kiss on the head.

When he stood back up, I handed him the pregnancy test.

"What is this?" he said, completely surprised, and began to laugh.

We hugged each other again and celebrated right there on the sidewalks of the financial district. We were truly excited. The painful secrets of our past had gone unmentioned for a long time, and it felt as if we were healing. We were learning to forge ahead, and I was beginning to trust him again. We were a growing family, and time would heal all wounds. Or so I believed.

We told Brayden he was going to be a big brother. Even though our marriage wasn't perfect, I believed our children would fix us and make me whole again.

I thought motherhood would be the magical cure for all the parts of my life that had become so misaligned. My parents had hurt me. Evan had betrayed me—the one person I trusted in this world. I was at my breaking point nine months before, but Brayden saved me. And now there would be another baby in my life. This was my chance to bring tiny people into this world that would love me unconditionally. I was elated.

Unbeknownst to me, the spackle holding all of these pieces together was the alcohol, and it was only a matter of time before it began to crack and fall apart.

Day 78: February 14, 2021

"Happy Valentine's Day!" Evan says.

"Cheers!" Brayden yells, bringing his milk to the center of the table.

"Cheers!" we all chime in. I bring my can of seltzer to my children's milk glasses and catch Evan's eye. He smiles at me, holding up his own water glass.

It's an unusual occurrence to have a night where everyone's home for dinner and not at dance, indoor soccer, or hockey practice, but we made it work. The kids begin to talk over one another, all trying to tell stories about how their school day went, not listening to a word anyone else is saying.

Normally, tonight would have given me license to get wasted. Before, I would have used the holiday as an open invitation to get after it. But after a few months of not drinking, I have enough sober experience now, and I can play the tape forward. I just have to fast-forward the evening a little and remind myself what would happen if I were to drink. I never did remember putting the kids to bed or spending time alone with Evan on those nights. I never enjoyed the actual food at dinner, and I was never really present for the conversations.

I was usually checked out, my mind elsewhere, always thinking about my next drink and not even concentrating on what we were celebrating in the first place. The next morning, I usually woke up feeling awful. My head would hurt so bad that I couldn't eat for half the day. None of that was ever very fun. I always hated myself a bit more every time it happened.

". . . and she didn't know she was unmuted on the call," Chase says. "And everyone could hear her talking!"

"People could hear what?" I ask, suddenly paying attention to the unfolding conversation.

"During the parents' Zoom call!" Chase says. "You were listening on your phone at my hockey practice. And apparently, you unmuted yourself. And while Mrs. Harris was talking, you interrupted her. You started talking to Jimmy's dad and everyone could hear you. Nathan, Annie, and Maddie's moms had to text you to let you know you were interrupting the call."

"Oh, Mom, that's bad!" Brayden says.

"I'm sorry," I say, laughing. "I had no idea I could even do that. I don't know how to use Zoom on my phone. I was just holding the phone in my hand. But yeah, I guess everyone could hear me talking about our vacation plans."

"Mom, you're so embarrassing!" Brayden adds.

"What else did you even say?" Parker asks.

"Oh, my God, I'm so embarrassed," Chase says.

The kids all start laughing at me and commiserating over the ridiculousness of my mistake.

"Woah, woah, woah!" Evan interrupts. "You should never be embarrassed by anything your mom does. You should be nothing but proud of her!" The kids stop laughing. They can tell he's being serious. "Everything your mom does—you should never laugh at her."

My children are taken aback by their father's sudden outburst. I smile, about to assure Evan that it's fine, but then Chase stands up. "You're right," he says. "I'm sorry." He hugs me.

"Your mom is amazing and you should never be ashamed of her, you guys know that, right?" Evan says, smiling at me with pride.

"It's fine, I don't care. It was awkward, actually," I laugh.

"No, Dad's right," Brayden says. "Sorry, Mom." He and Parker stand to give me a hug. I smile across the table at Evan. There is a shift in their demeanor, as if they understand what their father is saying. They seem to get it.

I sit back and sip my lime seltzer and consider my family. I guess moments like these never took place when I was drinking. It's a relief to know that when I make mistakes now, there's no shame anymore. I am their silly, somewhat flawed mother. I'm no longer the drunk mom they laugh at. They're proud of me. All of them. And just as I said the day I stopped drinking, these little ones are my reasons why. These kids continue to remind me every day of why I need to keep walking this road. These tiny people continue to save me.

Two Babies Under Two (2012): Thirty Years Old

I always enjoyed pregnancy. I also told myself that alcohol had no control over me because I was able to go nine months without drinking. How could I be addicted to alcohol if I could take almost a year off? I easily took those breaks. Despite the heartburn, back pain, and support bands needed for my extra-large belly, I loved being pregnant and marveled at what my body was doing.

At night, I cradled my belly and slept so well. By day, I waddled around happily in maternity clothes. Thinking about it now, this could have been because I was in a pseudo detox state and wasn't gulping down glasses of anxiety-inducing poison on a daily basis.

I focused my life and attention on my children. That was what it was all about. My parents seldom visited, so I relied on my small circle of mommy friends to get me through the days.

Chase was born on June 28, 2012, just shy of eighteen months from the day of his brother's birthday. Chase was the sweetest baby. He would turn out to be the most empathetic of our three children and a key component of our family unit.

He arrived on a hot summer's day on his own terms. I genuinely enjoyed the few days spent in the hospital. Nurses and doctors cared for me around the clock, and I felt loved and tended to nonstop. I had meals delivered whenever I wanted, could sleep when I needed, and it felt as if the staff was genuinely concerned for my well-being. I hadn't experienced that kind of care since I was a little girl. I didn't appreciate it the first time I was in the hospital with Brayden.

Days after Chase was born, I came home to our South End apartment and immediately drank a beer. I never would have done that after coming home from the hospital with my first child. By the second time around, my evening drink was already an established routine as part of my reward in parenting. I sipped the cold Sam's Summer Ale after nursing him to sleep in my arms. A feeling of relaxation and coziness settled me into the couch. My baby was in my arms. My toddler was playing quietly on the floor beside us. My husband was making dinner in the kitchen behind me. The sun beamed into our apartment on that ninety-degree summer afternoon, and I smiled to myself at the perfection that was my life.

Everything was what it should be. And the first few sips of alcohol that flowed into my system in those moments made me feel loose. Any fears and worries I had disappeared, and any stress or doubts softly melted away. For the next ten minutes, I contentedly sipped my beer and stared at the wall while Chase slept peacefully. In those few moments, everything was ideal. Easy. Simple. Until I tipped the bottle back and the last frothy sip of beer fell onto my tongue. The bottle was empty, and I soon felt deflated.

Chase began to stir and fuss. I began to panic. I had to get back to that feeling where everything felt happy and picture-perfect, but the moment was slipping away.

"Fuck!" Evan yelled.

"What?" I asked.

"I burned the chicken."

"Mamaaaaaaa!" Brayden whined. My head started to throb ever so slightly. I wanted to rewind it all and go back to the silence from ten minutes earlier. I closed my eyes, leaned my head back against the couch, and waited for it all to pass, wishing for the moment of quiet back. "Mamaaaa, look!"

I picked up my head and opened my eyes. I glanced over at my toddler and expected to see Brayden with a toy in hand. Instead, I saw him holding out both of his hands to me, covered in something brown. That was when I noticed his shorts were missing and his diaper was dangling around his ankles. He looked up at me expectantly, his blue eyes wide and curious, his pudgy baby hands reaching for me, coated in poop.

Chasing the buzz from the occasional glass of wine and zoning out at night a few times a week, all in the hopes of escaping the noise, chaos, and monotony of motherhood, became a regular occurrence. I craved the bliss-ful, idyllic image I'd envisioned as a little girl. I wanted the simplicity of what my sisters and I had created between the perfectly measured duct-taped lines in the basement of Winterset Road. And at the same time, I wanted to escape it because that idealism could never be achieved.

Once, when Chase was still an infant, Evan and I decided to go out on a date. I squeezed into my pre-pregnancy jeans and found the only top that fit my oversized, engorged breasts. We found a reservation nearby and left the kids with a friend. We immediately felt unleashed in the world, and there was an unexplained need to get wasted. We felt like we were back in college, so we ordered a bottle of wine and multiple vodka drinks.

We stumbled home drunk a few hours later after the boys were fast asleep. I had to pump my breasts, but the milk was so saturated with booze that it couldn't be salvaged. I felt frustrated because Evan had gone straight to bed. I was drunk, and I decided to wake him up and pick a fight with him.

We argued about the uneven balance in parenting duties, but we never actually addressed the elephant in the room. I was still bitter over Evan cheating on me in college. There was still a lot of pain and hurt that I was hanging onto and unable to unpack. We went to bed drunk and angry. The next day, we woke up and pretended the argument had never happened. That was our routine.

In the early months when both of the boys were under two, I would walk the streets of Boston all day long trying to get them to nap. Our condo was bursting at the seams, and it was easier to take their energy outside, meeting friends at different playgrounds. When it was raining, we walked in circles around the mall, looking in shop windows and running up and down the escalators. Chase, the easygoing infant, sat cozily in the baby carrier while his older brother ran circles around us at the park or wherever our path took us.

I remember staring at the train going by at one of our favorite parks off Berkeley Street, tired and dazed, thinking, *This is a lot of damn work. Is it bedtime yet? Can I have a drink?* It was only eleven o'clock in the morning.

The fall after Chase was born, we realized that our three-floor condo in the South End wasn't built for such young children. Maneuvering my double stroller through the cobblestone streets of Boston became a skill I no longer cared to master. Getting it down the flight of stairs multiple times a day with two kids into the garden-level entrance of our home was a workout in itself.

We still didn't have much family around to help, so we took the boys along with us and searched for places to live in the suburbs, focusing on towns close to the city so Evan could continue his long hours as an associate at the law firm downtown. We wanted an easy commute for him, which in hindsight was pointless since he was never around most mornings or evenings to help me anyway. During the week, I was very much on my own with the boys.

We eventually found a nice house in Newton, just outside of Boston. It was a good transition out of the city. Newton felt urban enough, with the T stopping through, and many of my mommy friends had also transplanted nearby there as well. It felt like a safe move for us.

Day 88: February 24, 2021

S itting on the quiet, sandy beach at the resort in Key West, Evan and I watch our three kids jump in and out of the waves. The hotel is small and private, away from friends or reminders of the past. We didn't choose the resort based on the number of swim-up pool bars or evening entertainment this time. We decided on a more low-key vibe and a place for the kids to be able to play safely. It's one of the first vacations where we can just sit back and let them hang out on their own on the beach. They're old enough now, and there's no constant, overwhelming fear of one of our babies being swept out to sea.

This is my first vacation without alcohol.

The sun sets behind us over the water and I take slow, deep, meditative breaths. The swirl of colors in the sky above feels like a blanket. I am content. I don't notice the agitation I used to experience at this time of day when having a drink in hand was all I could think about. It's gone.

I smile to myself. I would never have pictured myself happy like this, without alcohol. This has become our nightly routine this vacation. Ice cream on the beach after dinner followed by a walk and pictures in front of the sunset. We only have one vacation day left before we head back to Massachusetts—back to reality and back to the grind.

"When we get home, I think we should put our house on the market," I tell Evan, dipping my toes in the warm, salty water.

"For real?" he asks. "Why?"

"I think we could use a change."

"Okay. That's aggressive. There have been a lot of changes already."

"I just think it's time. We should stay in Needham but get out of that house. I've been thinking about it for a while. Those walls have seen too much. I think I need to start fresh. But in reality, the kids need a bigger yard and a safer street to play on. We've been saying this for years anyway. It's never felt like our forever home."

"I'm not saying you're wrong," Evan says, "but you've been going through a lot in the last two months, so maybe we should just slow this process down."

"Let's just start looking a bit more closely at the market when we get home, okay?"

"Sure," he concedes. "Okay, let's just see what's out there. I'm open to it."

I lay my head back on the chair and watch the children play. It's been a wonderful week. I drank early-morning coffee with Evan while we watched the sunrise over the ocean. I went paddleboarding with Brayden. I did a scavenger hunt with Chase and Parker on the beach, and I swam with the kids every day. I read my book and enjoyed some quality alone time. I saw a shark. I woke up in the night and stared out the window and listened to the tropical thunderstorm move in over the waters of Key West as lightning flashed across the dark sky. I was there for all of it, in the best way possible.

When we visited Bermuda as a child, Dad used to take me on a moped ride down to Castle Island beach at this time of day. We would bodysurf the waves together until it was time to go back to the house for dinner.

Sitting here now on the beach, I remember how on past vacations with my own kids, this would have been my favorite time to kick back and drink. Sunset is the best time of day to unwind. The golden hour. I would probably be polishing off a bottle of wine and looking for my next cocktail, forgetting entirely about the beautiful sight before me.

That's not me anymore. I no longer escape from these moments. Alcohol no longer has its claws in me, slowly crushing me. I am becoming whole again.

Our First House (2012): Thirty Years Old

When the boys were still little, we moved into our first home outside of the city. It was in an area called Newton Center, a renovated cape in a nice neighborhood. We were no longer within walking distance of the town or stores like before, but it was a transient stop on our way out of the city.

"We moved from the quietest street in the South End to the loudest, busiest road possible!" I told people jokingly.

"Why did you move, then?" my friends would ask.

"We needed space for these wild boys!" I explained. "I needed room to breathe."

The Newton house was a great investment. We had a lot more square footage and a great yard, and we could relax with the knowledge that our kids were in a great school system. But it never felt like home to us. Almost at once, I felt isolated and lost. The town seemed foreign, and I struggled to connect with the other moms I met. I never found people like me—people who liked to have wine at four in the afternoon during their kids' playdates.

My mornings were filled with baby classes and trips to the park, just like in the city. I went to the gym every day, bringing the boys to the kids' play space for their own exercise. My afternoons were sometimes followed with a glass of wine, but I drank alone instead of with other moms. I felt more alone than ever, and I missed my mommy friends from the city. Booze became my single comfort and ally in the suburbs. It became something I could rely on at times when Evan worked long hours back in Boston.

When we lived in the South End, it was easy to pick up a bottle of wine at any point in the day, as there were shops and liquor stores on practically every corner. When we moved to Newton, one of the biggest changes for me was not being able to drop into the liquor store on my walk home from the park. I now had to be strategic about my shopping. One evening after dinner, I loaded the boys up and headed to the liquor store to stock up on some wine. This was a particularly bad week full of extra tantrums and messy meals, and I'd gone a few days without any drinks at home. I decided I would have no more of that.

I pulled into the liquor store parking lot in our dented navy-blue Subaru well past the boys' scheduled bedtime. It took me five minutes to open up the double stroller and load up the boys in the parking lot. We walked inside the store, and I filled up the basket underneath with bottles and bottles of wine. As I was wheeling the stroller to the checkout, the metal bar that connected the tires together snapped in half. The boys and my wine went crashing to the floor, and the entire stroller frame shattered under the heavy load. Thankfully, no one was hurt—and miraculously, no wine was spilled.

"Oh, miss, let me help you! Are you okay?" the clerk said as he came running over to me.

"Mama, wha happen to da stwolla?" Brayden asked.

We made such a commotion and caused such a scene that the checkout line was held up as patrons stacked up behind us. It took several store clerks to help me carry my children, broken stroller, and booze to the car.

"Oh, my goodness! All this wine and alcohol for Daddy!" I lied. "Look at what it did to the stroller, boys! How silly! All this just for your dad!" My cheeks felt red hot and I stared at the ground, trying to laugh it off.

When I got home, I nearly tore the cork off with my teeth, devouring a full bottle of wine that evening. Back then, my drinking wasn't a nightly routine. I had some particularly bad days, waking up a little hungover after one too many. But I hadn't yet begun to hide the empty bottles from Evan.

The next morning after the liquor store incident, Evan pulled the empty from the garbage and turned to me. "Where did this wine come from?"

I sat at the island feeding Chase his breakfast, covered in mashed banana. Brayden yelled at me from his highchair for more Cheerios. "I had a few glasses at some point this week," I snapped. "Why?"

"You drank an entire bottle by yourself already this week?" he said, confused. "It's only Wednesday morning."

"Yes, it's been a long week already. It feels like it should be Friday."

He laughed. "Okay, fair enough. I gotta go to work now. I can't miss my train." He kissed each one of us on the head and was gone before I could process what had just happened or what I'd done.

Dishonesty always starts casually.

Round Three (2014): Thirty-Two Years Old

During the two short years we lived in Newton, our days blended together. On top of working long hours during the week, Evan devoted his weekends to continuing to prove himself to his colleagues by working on deals late into the night. Then he decided to run the Boston Marathon. He was running it for the One Fund, a charity set up to help the victims of the Boston Marathon bombing that occurred the year before. He was gone every evening for work. And he was then running early mornings on Saturdays, training for the big day in April. It was around this time that I discovered I was pregnant with our third baby. It occurred to us both that we were going to have three children under the age of four.

Again, I loved being pregnant, even with two rambunctious little boys beating each other up throughout my days. Naptime was a sacred time. I often took a long, heavy snooze in the afternoons as well, snuggled in beside the boys in my bed.

We had our routines back in the days of preschool, park playdates, and early bedtime. It was difficult and isolating when they were so young, but I enjoyed every minute of it. I was lonely at times, but I was content with a rigid schedule. And I never batted an eye at the idea of not being able to drink due to my pregnancies. It was a small sacrifice to make for my children, and I basked in the state of detox that I experienced for those few months. By the end when the nine months were over, I always looked forward to drinking again.

Parker was born on a hot afternoon on August 25, 2014. When she arrived, Mom came down and stayed with us for a week. She helped me with the boys while we were in the hospital. We needed assistance, and for the first time in many years, I truly turned to her for guidance.

Surprisingly and wonderfully, she said yes. In the past, she hadn't been able to come down to help, but for this baby, she stepped up. We finally had the space for her to stay with us, and she arrived ready to tackle the boys' big energy. It was comforting to know Mom was around to help with Brayden and Chase while I was in the hospital. Her being there gave us an extra set of eyes and hands. It provided a comfort I didn't know I was missing.

Mom folded laundry, read books to the boys, and made their meals. She comforted me and sat with me while I nursed Parker for what felt like hours on end once I got home from the hospital.

It was strange and nice all at once to have my mom there during some of the most vulnerable times of motherhood. I will forever be grateful to her for this time in our lives. It reminded me of the days when I was home sick from school, back when she used to sit with me on the couch knitting as I held my head over the trash can. Mom's presence was healing. Just knowing she was there was enough support. She brought me glasses of juice and plates of toast, and she placed folded up napkins on the tray just like she used to when I was a little girl.

Dealing with a newborn is an emotional, exhausting experience, and it can bring you to your knees. It can make you feel lost, isolated, and afraid. This was my third time feeling this way, and it wasn't any easier that time around. Even though I was supposed to be acting like a mother, I wanted to feel taken care of too. It was a reassuring feeling, something I was un-accustomed to experiencing from my mother.

During this brief time of seeing Mom, we enjoyed glasses of wine, laughing and reminiscing over our shared connection of motherhood. It was fun to be drinking with her like it was no big deal, and this grew into a regular occurrence over the coming years. Soon enough, sharing a bottle of wine together was comfortable for us, and gone were the days of me begging her to stop drinking.

When had the lines blurred together, and at what point did our drinking patterns become so similar? I had no idea when things had started to look so alike for us. But when had I stopped becoming concerned about her habits? Had I stopped feeling worried for her when I started to mimic her own behavior? Was this around the same time I began to lie to myself about my own alcohol consumption?

Once Evan was home on paternity leave, we questioned the amount of space we had as a family of five. We realized quickly we were outgrowing our first home in the suburbs of Newton. With Parker attached to my breast and the two boys in tow, we went house hunting.

We were always on the move, in search of something new. We toured one open house after another. Eventually, we decided to focus our sights on the town of Needham. We wanted a quaint, more family-friendly town. We also wanted to live somewhere less urban, and Needham was still on the commuter rail with great schools and a charming town center. It seemed like the perfect spot for us. We had friends who lived there, and it was filled with many young professionals with new families. Just like us.

We sold our house in Newton easily and moved to a larger, brand-new construction on the corner of a busy road in Needham. This home sat adjacent to a smaller, quieter street. It was part of a neighborhood, despite being on a main road. It was in a charming section of town with annual block parties, Easter Egg hunts, and an active Facebook group.

The house felt like an ideal spot for us to put down roots with three kids despite the trucks barreling past our kitchen window. The family across the street were friends from Colby, and they liked to drink and have a good time. I had a feeling we were going to have fun there, despite a faraway feeling that this might not be the perfect place for us.

The first evening in the new house, after the kids were asleep, we started to unpack the kitchen. There were boxes everywhere. We couldn't find the silverware or the plates, but I managed to find the wine opener right away. I uncorked a bottle of red and drank the entire thing myself that night. The next morning, I had trouble remembering where I'd unpacked things like the kids' cups and dishes.

One of the first activities in our new neighborhood was when we went trick-or-treating. I was excited to see that all the parents were carrying beers and cocktails around while walking their children from house to house. The best part about moving to Needham was that we immediately made friends with families that seemed similar to us. There were many young couples with three or four kids, all close in age. All were young professionals from similar backgrounds who knew a lot of the same people from our past. It felt comfortable. Familiar. Safe. The most common thread was that everyone also liked to drink just as much as we did.

We joined the country club near our house, assimilating seamlessly into the culture. Our boys joined town soccer teams and tried out for the hockey program, and I got involved with the YMCA and local mothers' groups.

I believed we were truly happy for the first time in a very long time, and it felt like the right fit. I took up a membership at a barre studio in town and began to meet new friends. Working out became part of my daily routine. I settled in and felt at home, taking the kids to their activities and preschool events. We walked to town, to the parks and grocery store, and enjoyed the brand-new home we were settling into.

At about this time, Evan left his position at the law firm in Boston and started a new job in-house at a biotech company. His half-hour commute north to the town of Lexington made his hours more manageable than ever before. He was sometimes home to help put the kids to bed and was even around in the mornings. For the first time in our marriage, he was present for me and the kids. And it was a relief to have his help a bit more on the weekends.

It was a learning curve for both of us as we figured out these new roles in our new home. All along, I believed that my ally, alcohol, kept me company. Drinking continued to be the one constant in my life, and it maintained a steady presence in my weekly routine. Truly, I thought I had it all.

Day 98: March 6, 2021

I stand in the hallway outside the kids' bathroom listening to Brayden and Chase as they brush their teeth before bedtime. I'm sleepy myself and ready to crawl into my cozy bed. Why does this process always take longer than usual? For some reason, they get slap-happy and more wound up now than at any other time of the day. Yet I listen in the doorway, smiling. I love their friendship. They make each other laugh constantly, and the brotherly banter fascinates me.

They stand at the mirror without their shirts on, and their matching Minecraft pajamas cling to their small nine- and ten-year-old bottoms. They lift their bare arms and compare their biceps, squeezing their fists and flexing like they've seen their dad do.

"My muscles are bigger than yours!" Chase says.

"No way, not true," Brayden declares.

They argue for a minute over these facts, as they always do, pointing out the variations in muscle size in each arm, even going so far as to use the floss to measure the circumference. Suddenly, Brayden lifts his arm and studies his armpits close to the mirror.

"Mom! Mom! Look!" he yells suddenly.

"What?" I say, shaken from my sleepy state.

"I got the puberty! Look!" He points to his armpit.

I walk into the bathroom and inspect the spot of skin he's pointing to. "Let me see," I say, smiling. "No, sorry, buddy. That's just a fuzz from the towel."

"Oh, man!" he says with disappointment. "I really thought that was a big old hair! Darn!"

"Soon, though, I promise. Any day now. And again, you don't catch 'the puberty.' It's not like it's some virus. It will be gradual. Slow, remember."

"When will I get the puberty?" Chase asks.

"You will *go through* puberty soon. Again, you don't 'get it,' but it seems like you both have some time."

"Awww," they say in unison, then laugh and take turns punching each other in the stomach.

I leave them alone in the bathroom. I'm too tired to keep telling them to stop. Eventually, they'll tire of this game and come find me to tuck them in. I return to my bedroom and sigh heavily at how old my children are getting. How is it that my boys are already looking for armpit and pubic hair? I smile, grateful that I'm here for it and not numbing myself with alcohol.

As soon as I plop down on the bed, I hear the boys laughing and talking loudly again. They come shuffling into my bedroom, Brayden pushing Chase in front of him.

"Mom, it's time," Brayden says with his hands on his brother's shoulders.

"Time for what?" I ask.

"Time for Chase to have 'the talk,' I think," he says, using air quotes while raising his eyebrows at me. "I'll be waiting outside for you, buddy, good luck. Mom, you got this."

As Brayden closes the door behind him, Chase stares at me expectantly. "What is 'the talk,' Mom? What's Brayden talking about?"

He has a goofy smile on his face, and he looks excited to be let in on this big secret. I chuckle to myself at the situation I've unexpectedly found myself in. One can never plan exactly how to tell their child about sex, but Brayden is a clever kid. He remembers having the chat almost a year ago and has been waiting for the day that Chase gets to join the inner circle. Brayden has been looking for his window, an opportunity to spring this on me.

I sit up and take a deep breath. Suddenly, I'm not so tired anymore, and

I'm thankful that I'm sober. "Okay," I begin, "so you know where babies come from, right?"

"Yes, they come out of the vagina," Chase says, very seriously. For some reason, he senses not to be silly about this important conversation.

"Well, do you know how they get in there?" I ask him. He shakes his head.

I begin my long, drawn-out, scientific explanation. After a while, it starts to make sense. Without warning, it's as if a lightbulb has gone off. His eyes get wide, and he looks at me with disbelief. The questions come at a rapid-fire pace.

"Do I have to do that? Did *you* do that? Did you do that with *Dad*? Is that where I came from?" he asks.

I slowly and calmly answer his questions.

I'm happy that there is no shame about sex in our house like there was when I was a child. I'm grateful that my children are comfortable enough to talk to me about the subject.

I think back to the conversations I tried to have with Mom when I was a child. The discussions were nonexistent.

Today, I can share and my kids can ask questions, and we can all speak about the topic without fear of being judged. We can discuss sex without being embarrassed. There are no secrets in this family. And sex is nothing to be ashamed of. This is a safe home with no lying or shameful privacies.

And through it all, I am clearheaded, sober, and confident these days in my ability to navigate my way through these awkward parent-child discussions. And I can calmly respond and appropriately deal with Brayden when I hear him unexpectedly giggling at the door.

Work Hard, Party Hard (2015): Thirty-Three Years Old

Having three kids under four during our first winter in Needham was difficult and isolating at times, but we managed to get through it. We received a record amount of snow in New England that year. We spent endless days playing trucks, Legos, and Hot

Wheels, interspersed with tantrums and tears. The afternoons at home felt long and tiring. There were some days when I counted down the minutes until bedtime when I could release the tension of motherhood with wine. I'd mindlessly scroll through Facebook on my phone at night with Bravo TV on in the background.

Springtime came fast, and before I knew it, it was summer. And with that, we were back at the country club down the road, outside with friends at the pool. As I continued to rely on alcohol as my release at the end of a long day, Evan also enjoyed his weekend imbibing. Neither of us questioned my behavior. Evan was sometimes the first to start day drinking on Saturday mornings at the pool, unintentionally enabling my habits. But it was okay because all the other moms and dads were doing it.

"Who wants a Corona? It's never too early at the club, ladies and gentlemen!" Evan would declare, unknowingly giving me the green light to start drinking.

It wasn't until Evan had his first drink that I was comfortable to start letting loose. Every time he would crack an early afternoon beer, I would open one too, reassuring myself that I didn't have a problem. Because it hadn't been my idea to start drinking.

Evan had a stop button, though. I didn't. Evan never got drunk. I did. Evan was the driver, and I didn't worry about those things. I never knew when enough was enough, and I always liked to keep the party going. I was the one who wanted to take the kids back to our friends' houses for more drinks and dinner after an afternoon of lounging by the pool. The kids wanted to keep playing with their friends, so why not? But Evan knew when to call it quits. I, on the other hand, didn't know when to be responsible and pull the ripcord. This sometimes led to arguments.

Even saw vacations as his time to kick back and not think about work. He wanted to relax, pop open a beer at eleven in the morning, and lay in the sun. I saw that as my license to drink heavily without fear or judgment. If Evan was letting loose, that was my time to get wild too.

Our views on drinking were always vastly different. I was drinking to escape and get drunk. Evan sometimes opened a beer because he was thirsty. He enjoyed the taste of Corona on the beach, but I craved the buzz. I needed to feel the release that alcohol provided. Sometimes he'd leave a few sips at the bottom of a bottle and I'd find them and finish them off.

I justified my drinking by comparing it to his. I rationalized my decision to order a drink because Evan was. He was getting another round? Fine, so could I. If he was drinking his second beer, I told myself that I could have a third. But I rarely thought about the difference in our body sizes. Two beers had a different effect on him than they did on me.

Unbeknownst to both of us, there was a deeply rooted anger that fueled my drinking. I had a pattern of turning to alcohol to cope when things got tough for me. I was looking to hide, to escape and numb myself. A part of me felt Evan wasn't allowed to judge my decisions because of the choices he'd made in the past. Deep down, I still held it over his head, but we never talked about it—and for this reason, he usually let it go when I got too drunk. There was a silent push and pull going on, and it was wearing us down.

Bermuda (2018): Thirty-Six Years Old

"Why did you need to bring that with you?" Evan asked, finally unable to hold back the interrogation a second longer.

"What do you mean?" I replied nonchalantly.

He gestured to the beer in my hand. "Did you really need that drink?" I sensed his aggravation in the way he was breathing, but was trying to act calm.

"Are you being serious?"

"Yeah," he said, "I am."

I'd already felt his irritation as we walked off the elevator. When he slammed the cab door behind me extra hard, I knew he wasn't pleased. But why the questions? Why was he starting this confrontation on our way out to dinner—on our last night of vacation? On my favorite island of Bermuda?

I felt his eyes on me but wouldn't look at him. I wouldn't give him that satisfaction. Keeping my focus on the turquoise water in front of me, I stared out the window of the cab. I tried to appreciate the setting sun on the horizon, but I had a hard time doing so. I was angry. He was ruining my buzz.

Evan had been the first to order early cocktails on the beach that day. The day before, he brought me a mimosa at my pool chair. We'd spent lazy afternoons in bed, wrapped up in each other's arms, with no children whining or crying. A haze of alcohol clouded our minds, feeling much like the early days of our relationship back in college. Now he was wondering about this one single drink?

The wind blew a salty curl of hair across my face, and I shook my head to move it out of my eyes. My sunglasses created a shield of privacy so I didn't have to look at my husband. I ignored him and took a long, drawn-out sip from the drink in my hand. I didn't understand why he always wanted to destroy these moments with this kind of conversation.

"It's vacation," I said, leaning my head back against the seat. "We go home tomorrow. Why do you suddenly care? You were just drinking with me, like, two seconds ago back on the beach."

"I thought we'd had enough," he sighed. "Why do you need a drink in the cab? On the way to dinner. It just seems . . . I don't know, excessive."

"It's our anniversary trip! We're celebrating. Why are you counting my drinks all of a sudden?"

Evan fell silent. We rode along the winding road, looking out at the terraced white roofs of the quintessential pink, blue, and yellow limestone homes dotting the hill above us. The gorgeous shoreline never ceased to amaze me, even after my countless visits to the island over the years. A moment later, Evan tried to take my hand, but I pushed him away.

"You're right," he said, smiling. "We should just enjoy this last night." Seemingly defeated, he added, "Let's find a fun bar in town for a cocktail before dinner since we'll be early."

I could tell he was trying to lure me back in, knowing he'd created a divide and wanting us to go back to the way it was only moments before.

Back to the laughter on the beach, the fun, the ease, and the happiness. He thought he'd shattered the moment, and he wanted to pretend what he said didn't actually happen.

I stared at the dazzling blue ocean out the window. I watched the horizon, feeling the ominous strength of the waves cresting far out in the distance. I felt a sadness and a longing as I spotted a Bermuda Longtail, the ethereal white bird native to the island, somersaulting through the sky.

I sipped my beer and wondered what the kids were doing. They were probably getting home from school about now. Walking off the bus and onto the front porch, being greeted by Mimi. This was the one time Evan's parents had come from Ohio to watch the kids, and I was determined to make it worth my while.

There was so much we both weren't saying. I knew Evan wasn't happy about my drinking, but there was so much pain buried beneath that alcohol. So much unforgiven shame and hurt. On that trip to Bermuda, we were trying to reclaim what we used to be, but we were lying to ourselves.

Almost too much was left unspoken that day, and deep down we knew it. It was easier to pretend everything was normal. Neither of us wanted to fight and ruin this anniversary trip away from the children. As I stared into my husband's disappointed eyes, perhaps part of me was beginning to unravel.

I was in one of my favorite places from my childhood, on an island that reminded me of my own parents, and I was behaving in a way that emulated the behavior they had taught me. Despite the years of resenting Evan, I had now developed my own secret without even realizing it. I was lying to my husband as well as to myself. Alcohol was becoming a problem for me, but I refused to see it.

Slow Spiral (2018): Thirty-Six Years Old

The more engaged we became with the community of Needham, the more we found ourselves socializing and hanging around with different friends. We also found ourselves drinking a lot more than usual. Without even realizing it, I decided who to have our kids play with based on whether or not they served wine at birthday parties and playdates. We unknowingly gravitated toward other adults that shared similar mind-sets as us.

For many months, neither Evan nor I spoke about the fact that we were drinking more than ever before. We got babysitters every weekend and met up with people for dinner at the club or in town. We drank with our neighbors across the street. We went to concerts, into Boston, or to friends' houses for late-night parties. The more people we met, the more fun we seemed to have.

Everyone drank this way, and no matter where we went, every couple showed up with wine in hand and enjoyed the party lifestyle as much as we did. We didn't think we were doing anything differently than anyone else. There was always a before-party and an after-party, and we reminisced the next day about the drunken debauchery that ensued among our group. It was hilarious and seemingly harmless fun. Everyone was doing it. We all commiserated together about our hangovers at the kids' early-morning soccer games every Saturday or Sunday.

I was back into the pattern of blacking out every time I went out on the weekend or every time we got a babysitter. When I left the house for a night out or had more than a few drinks, I couldn't control myself. I couldn't regulate my consumption and couldn't have only one drink in the evenings at home. I went hard and way too far every time, just like the Colby days and the days before kids.

"Let's try to go easy tonight, hm?" Evan said gently.

"Yeah, sure, whatever you say," I responded, shrugging as if I had no idea what he was referring to.

As far as I was concerned, I was drinking as much as the rest of my girlfriends, so I wasn't worried. I didn't like to talk about my drinking, though, and I made a point to move past it quickly whenever Evan men-tioned it.

I started out most Saturday nights by having some wine in the bathroom while I did my makeup and hair. I called these drinks "pregame personality drinks." I played music loudly from the Sonos speakers by myself. This nightly routine had the same ritualistic feel as pregaming back in the "virgin vault" freshman year at Colby.

When I was ready to head out for the night, I kissed the kids goodbye, giving the babysitter explicit instructions on the bedtime routine. We often came home way too late, and I inevitably was slurring my words.

Little did Evan know that I never remembered this part of the evening. It took many years for him to realize that I was, in fact, in a state of blackout. It also took a long time for him to catch onto the fact that I was drinking far more than he. I was sneaking drinks past him, smoking cigarettes when he wasn't looking, and lying about how much I consumed. He didn't realize for a long time how hungover I truly felt the next day, as I did a decent job of lying and hiding it from him. I popped Motrin and antacids and snuck off to throw up some mornings.

Eventually, I moved past drinking only on Fridays and Saturdays to doing so most nights. My intense alcohol consumption started to creep into the weekdays, and my heavy drinking habit became a daily occurrence. I found friends who invited me over for afternoon wine almost every day of the week. There was always someone looking to get drunk. I always had at least a few glasses of wine in the evening, often averting my eyes from Evan's when he walked in the door from work.

"Oh, no days off this week?" he asked me, eyeing up my wine glass.

"It's been a long day with the kids at home," I replied. "Yom Kippur, so no school."

"Oh, I see." Judgment oozed from his gaze.

Sundays always overwhelmed me. I used to feel an impending doom as my weekend was coming to an end because I would have to try to stop drinking for a few days. That always made me feel extra low for some reason, and I would endure a form of alcohol withdrawal. Sometimes, I needed to prove to Evan that I could stop, though, and at times I wanted to prove to myself that I didn't need to drink every day. Sunday implied the start of a new week, and in my mind, that indicated the need to reset my body. If my hangover was especially bad that day, I knew I needed a break.

Nights I didn't drink, I tossed and turned, unable to sleep without the booze coursing through my veins. Sleep was always a struggle since having children, and I dreaded going to bed without alcohol in my system. It was impossible to fall asleep without being drunk.

It took all of my strength to not drink for those few days a week, and more times than not, I failed. I tried using medicinal marijuana to help me escape, but it never worked. Sometimes I think I drank enough on Saturday night just to try to get me through to Tuesday. It was as if I wanted to consume enough alcohol so that maybe it would linger in my system for a few days. Or maybe if I purposefully gave myself a bad enough hangover on Sunday, I wouldn't want to drink for a while. It never worked.

I often woke up with "hangxiety." I was dehydrated and physically hungover, and on top of that, I felt depressed. The constant imbalance of dopamine and serotonin messed with my endorphin levels, sending me into a moody tailspin. This sometimes kept me from drinking for a day, but not always.

Many Sundays in the winter, we were invited to friends' houses for family dinner. We liked to call these "Sunday fundays." We watched football and ordered takeout, neglecting our parental responsibilities for a short time. I felt I was given a free license to drink along with everyone else. Evan rarely gave me a hard time for overindulging on those days, as he usually didn't monitor my drinks. He kicked back on the couch, let the kids play video games, and chatted with the other husbands. Meanwhile, in the kitchen, the wives gossiped over endless bottles of wine.

"Oh, my God, you know whose kid got kicked out of school last week?" Sarah said.

"No, who?" I asked.

"Oh, I heard about this from Diane at yoga," Kate said.

"No way!"

We discussed the latest Botox trends and allowed the kids to run around playing outside, no one worrying about the impending start of the week. I loved these days. It seemed everyone was on the same page as me. Until they weren't. For some reason, I was the only one waking up with a massive hangover the next day, forgetting what time we'd left or how we got the kids to bed. No one else was blacking out and forgetting if they even fed the kids dinner.

Sundays in the summertime were spent lounging around the pool at the country club. Instead of hanging out around the kitchen island at one another's houses, we laid out on the chairs in the sun. I ignored my swimming kids and let the lifeguards take care of them.

Evan was always great about jumping in and playing basketball in the pool with all the kids or going off the diving board, but I treated the weekend as my "time off." I cheered when he tossed the football to each child as they jumped into the pool, but that was the extent of my parental involvement. The moms and I took turns heading to the bar for rounds of rosé, focusing mostly on our tans and town gossip.

I hated being alone with the self-loathing, shameful thoughts on Monday mornings after the kids headed off for the day and Evan went to work. I used to sit alone, willing my hangover to pass, trying to forgive myself for the mistakes I'd made over the weekend. I hated the way I felt about myself after a long weekend of binge drinking.

"Why couldn't you make it until Wednesday without a drink? What the hell is wrong with you?" I would say to myself in the mirror.

In the mornings when I began to wake up covered in bruises and wondering where my phone was, I became angry and disappointed. I worried about myself. I wondered what exactly I did the night before, who I texted, or what I posted on social media. Once I located my phone, I scrolled feverishly through my texts searching for clues as to how the night ended and making sure I hadn't said anything stupid.

I gauged Evan's temperature toward me to see how badly I'd behaved if we were out, and nine times out of ten, he was annoyed with me. I then tried to take a few nights off to get back into his good graces—until one particularly bad Friday evening when everything got completely out of control and for the first time, I truly questioned where my drinking was headed.

Day 118: March 26, 2021

I have a lot of strange dreams in sobriety. I sometimes wake up after dreaming that I was drunk only to realize that it was all an extremely vivid nightmare. The relief I feel is palpable.

I wake in the early-morning hours after one particularly profound dream. It all feels so real and believable as I consider the images still fresh in my mind.

I stand at the window on a back porch looking in, watching my friends. The firepit is lit. A grill against the white clapboard house awaits. A Sunday funday. A bus-stop Friday. A late Saturday night at the bistro. The night sky is ominously dark.

It's a familiar spot, a house I've been to many times. But this time is different. I've packed my bags, I've put on my coat, and I'm about to head out. I'm leaving. On a trip, perhaps. It's a new journey. A vacation, alone. Into the night. The darkness. The unknown, it seems.

All there is to do now is get in the car. I must leave. It's time to go. I can't look back. But for some reason, I'm stuck here. Waiting. Watching them all.

I stare at my friends from the outside steps, peering at them from this side of the glass door—these people who always presented themselves as "my squad," the ones that had my back all these years. Now, my back stands alone against the dark of the night sky. I wait in the dimness of the streetlamp for a stranger to pick me up and take me away.

I wonder if anyone will notice me waiting. But no one sees me.

I am ready. I want to leave. I need to go. I've been readying myself for this next chapter of my life, and I want to go on this adventure. It's time.

My bags are packed and I'm ready, but something keeps me rooted here. What keeps me planted in this space? Why can't I move? When will I come back? I don't know. Maybe never. I can hear their faint laughter. I watch as they talk over one another. I see them gathered around the kitchen island, not listening to one another.

I'm leaving, but no one wants to say goodbye. Do they even notice that

I'm gone? Nope. The conversation is the same as it was last weekend. Stories. Whispers. Laughter. They retell the same tales over and over again. The same dialogue. The same unkind words. They tease one another and make fun of the people that aren't there. Empty conversations.

I listen and wait. Will someone notice me peering in? No one looks up. No one sees.

My car arrives, and I quietly place my bags in the trunk. It's time to leave this crew behind. I'm excited and grateful, but there is a small part of me that aches. The faces do not turn, and the laughter only increases. I can feel the hurt. The sadness envelops me, even though I know better things are waiting for me ahead.

The Uber ambles down the driveway, away from the faces behind the glass. The lamplight above me casts shadows across my face. We pull out into the night, leaving behind the warmth and familiarity of all I've ever known. But today, there is comfort in the unknown.

As I peel back the covers and open my eyes, I wake up feeling a welcomed loneliness that's hard to explain. But I force myself to breathe deeply, because I am grateful not to have a piercing headache like I would have if I were at that party in my dream. And I guess it's nice to remember how I got in bed last night, too. I must remind myself of all the goodness in each day.

Not all friendships are meant to last forever, Ronni tells me. Look for people that make you the best version of yourself, they say. Find those that stand by you and support you.

Saying goodbye is never easy.

The Garage (2018): Thirty-Six Years Old

It was a Friday, and the memories from that night are covered in a thick, gray haze. We had dinner with the neighbors like most Friday nights, and one bottle of wine turned into several. We sat around the island chatting about the upcoming kids' hockey season. Reminiscing about our college days. Gossiping about the neighbors. Talking about friends who weren't there.

We played country music way too loud and twirled around the kitchen, dragging our kids with us. I bounced three-year-old Parker on my hip. Her eyes were heavy with sleep, but she giggled anyway. We all laughed, singing along to the words of "Old Dominion," the children dancing at our feet.

It was after ten o'clock and well past the kids' bedtime when Evan pulled our car into the garage. Even though we lived only two minutes down the road, I managed to pass out in the passenger seat on the ride home. All three of the kids were crying, overtired, and in need of their beds. Evan had been smart to drive over in the first place because he knew how the night would end, even though we lived so close.

"Kim, get up! Wake up and take Parker to bed," Evan said, shaking me awake.

"Huh?" I opened one eye, looking around the dimly lit garage.

"Wake up! You need to get up and help me. Now!"

"Okay, I'm up!" I remember saying, irritated.

"I'll carry both boys to bed, but you need to help get Parker into her crib," he told me, frustrated. He was talking to me like I was a toddler.

"Okay, got it," I mumbled.

"Mama!" Parker screamed from the back of the minivan, strapped into her car seat, unable to move. Evan got the boys out of the car. Everyone continued to cry, and he walked inside the house.

"Kim, now!" Evan shouted to me over his shoulder from inside the mudroom.

"Yup, on it," I said, undoing my seatbelt. I went to open my car door but stopped, thinking I needed to rest for just a moment. That was the last thing I recall.

I woke up to Evan shaking me.

"Kim, what the fuck are you doing? Wake up! Get up!" he shouted.

It was perhaps twenty or thirty minutes later. I felt stiff. Frozen. Evan appeared in front of me. He had finished getting the boys to bed and found me and Parker still in the garage, which was now dark. He frantically shook me awake.

Parker was crying for me, kicking the back of my seat. I hadn't heard or felt her because I had passed out. I was too drunk to take care of my daughter. I reached for her hands and they were ice cold.

Evan opened my car door, and I rolled out onto the garage pavement. I was confused and unable to make sense of the situation. I began to realize what I'd done and struggled to get to my feet. Evan left me on the floor of the garage in the darkness and slammed the door, taking Parker to bed. I was barely able to make it to the mudroom. I passed out again in the entryway and slept there, slumped over on the cold, damp floor for most of the night. I woke up several hours later with a stiff neck and sore throat. I was completely disoriented. Evan hadn't come back for me, and I was sad he didn't.

I crawled into bed at around four o'clock in the morning. Evan didn't move to cuddle me like he normally did. He didn't talk to me, nor did he look me in the eye the next morning. He gave me the silent treatment the rest of the weekend, and it crushed me.

Evan and I never spoke about what happened that night in the garage. Instead, we went about our lives like normal. We plowed ahead, both of us hoping not to repeat those same choices. I secretly hoped I'd never get that drunk ever again. I promised myself that I would never hurt my children or endanger them in such a foolish way. But it would be a few more years and countless drunken mistakes before I would have the ability to admit to myself that I did, in fact, have a problem with alcohol.

Suburban Soirees (2019): Thirty-Seven Years Old

In Needham, my friends and I drank at the kids' baseball games on Tuesday nights. We brought our "mommy juice" mugs filled with beers and carried them to soccer practice on Thursday afternoons. I believed that everyone in Needham drank like this, so I was convinced my behavior was normal. I wasn't doing anything different from the majority of society.

"Cheers! It's the weekend, ladies!" I said, arriving at the neighbor's house at three o'clock on Friday afternoon. This was when we celebrated the end of the school week with a "bus-stop party," settling in with wine and cheese once the kids got off the bus. Later, we ordered pizza and let them watch movies while we popped one bottle after another. It was our reward as mothers. We were made to think this was the only way to kick back and relax. We were told to believe this was the only release. And our children witnessed this behavior, week after week, for months and months.

At times, I didn't see anything wrong with it because I walked the kids home to bed. I never drove them drunk. That was my reasoning. But deep down, I knew that subjecting my children to this behavior wasn't good for them. On top of that, there was the disappointed look on Evan's face when I walked through the front door on those afternoons. I was drunk, and he knew it. We both knew this wasn't a good way to parent our children.

After the incident in the garage, something began to feel more off-kilter, nudging me in the back of my mind. I had an unsettling feeling that was beginning to fester, but I ignored it. I believed my friends to drink just as much as me, so I didn't consider changing my ways. Besides, I didn't know anyone that didn't drink. I never considered sobriety as an option. Instead, I continued my behavior. I refused to believe that alcohol was creating an issue for me, so I was determined to keep juggling all the balls in the air.

On holidays or big events, it seemed that people condoned the excessive amount of drinking in our group of friends, so it was never strange that I partook so freely in it. It was a while, though, before Evan caught onto the fact that I didn't remember the end to my nights. It took many conversations between us that had me fishing for details on the way the evening concluded. The memories were always fuzzy.

"Kim," he would say, "we talked about this last night, don't you remember?"

I nodded and played along. "Oh, yes, I remember," I lied, pretending I'd simply forgotten. But there were times when Evan looked at me with sheer disappointment, aware that I was lying.

"You already told me that story, Kim. Remember? Last night at dinner," he said to me once, shaking his head. "We went over this already."

That was when Evan started to have less and less patience with me. We began to argue more. The judgment oozed from him, and I resented him for treating me like a child.

Eventually, I started to use my kids as pawns, making them ask their father questions for me so as not to incriminate myself. "Parker, go ask your dad what time we got home last night," I said to five-year-old Parker one morning.

There were moments when my drinking would progress, and I knew I needed to try to control my alcohol consumption again. In the spring of 2019, around Easter, after a particularly wild family gathering, I took a look in the mirror. I hadn't remembered filling the eggs with the neighbors for the neighborhood egg hunt the night before Easter. And I snuck out to the neighbors' for tequila shots when Evan fell asleep on the couch, stumbling home thirty minutes later after vomiting in our bushes. I also forgot to hide some of the Easter eggs around the house for the kids.

"I think I might be drinking a bit too much," I told my doctor later that following week at my yearly physical. I couldn't help but worry about my tequila shot fiasco and the recent run-in with our bushes.

"How much is too much?" she wondered.

I quickly backtracked because verbalizing it worried me even more. "Oh, I don't know, maybe just like four or five drinks, but only on the weekends," I told her, which was a huge understatement.

"Yes, that is a lot. You might want to think about cutting back to less than three a night, and try to drink only one night a week," she told me.

I nodded. Her suggestion blew my mind and seemed impossible to me. She didn't even know a fraction of the truth about my drinking.

After that visit with my doctor, I began lying to myself even more about my habits. I tried to moderate for a while. Instead of admitting that I had a problem with alcohol, I convinced myself I could drink normally, starting off with a few glasses during the week like my doctor recommended. But it always progressed further and further until I fell right back into the routine again. I drank even more that next cycle. My friends told me that everyone lied to their doctors about how much they drank. I was fine.

The setbacks were all part of the process of coming to terms with what was happening to me. I needed all of this to occur to see the picture fully. Every single shameful memory was a learning experience. Every single experience was another secret I held onto until it was time to come clean with myself. I was slowly building my own treasure trove of secrets.

Naples (2019): Thirty-Seven Years Old

The trip to Naples, Florida, was one of the last trips I took with my girlfriends from Needham before I realized I needed to stop drinking. I hardly remembered the flight home, only that I felt awful about what I did and wanted to come back early. It was supposed to be a wonderful vacation, but it ended so badly.

The weekend started out with mimosas in the limo on the way to the airport and with wine on the airplane.

"Cheers, ladies!" I said. "We've earned this escape!"

"Mama needs some sun!" Sarah said.

We all needed a break from everything our mundane lives required of us. It was a joyous, much-needed interruption from the carpools, sports practices, and school lunch preparations we were all so accustomed to dealing with on a daily basis. It was nice not to have our children yelling for us all day long.

We arrived in sunny Florida early on a Wednesday morning with so much eagerness. The long weekend began innocently enough, with dinner by the beach the first night. We made our way to the poolside tiki bar shortly after to sip fruity cocktails.

The plan was to take it easy those first few nights, hang out at the condo, and listen to live music by the pool. But like usual, I had no off switch. The specialty rum cocktail at the outdoor tiki bar had me drinking late into the evenings, which knocked me on my ass, forcing me to drink way too much.

The girls all ordered rum drinks after breakfast. I was still drunk from the night before, but I figured I had no choice but to join them. I was in a steady, constant state of drunkenness from there on out the entire time. We lay around drinking at the pool and drank our way through every meal.

On the third day, after much of the same, we decided to take tequila shots at dinner. I don't remember anything after calling an Uber to take us into downtown Naples for a late-night dance party at the bars.

I woke up the next morning still in my clothes. I rolled over and the right side of my face was extremely sore. I crawled out of bed, my body hunched over. I managed to make it to the bathroom practically bent in half, and I leaned my face onto the cool countertop. The tile felt amazing against my cheek. I turned the sink on and haphazardly splashed some water on my face, attempting to get some into my mouth. But even the droplets of water hurt my skin and my right eye. I felt so much pain. I was scared to look in the mirror, but I forced myself to stand up straight, slowly peeling open my eyes.

The image in the mirror startled me. The right side of my face next to my temple was cherry red and scraped up, and there were bits of gravel stuck to my hair. Little dots of dried, cracked blood lined my cheekbone. The skin around my right eye was purple and swollen.

My friends told me I had passed out when exiting the Uber after midnight. The memories started coming back to me in fragments. I remembered stepping out of the car and trying to talk to my friends and the driver. I recalled feeling incredibly tired and very drunk. I just wanted to lie down. The next thing I knew, I was flat out on the pavement and everyone was screaming my name. I had passed out.

I couldn't face another day of drunken regrets, and I was mortified and disgusted by the amount of booze I had consumed. I was acting like I was still in college. How was I still drinking to such excess?

After my friends told me what had happened, they stared at me with pity in their eyes.

"We almost called 911," Kate said.

"We almost couldn't wake you up," Trish added.

"But we didn't because we thought Evan would be mad at us. He doesn't like it when you drink too much," Sarah said. "And then you woke up."

No one said anything more. Everyone was worried about me that morning, but no one wanted to discuss it any further. I was alive. Barely. Just very battered. Physically and emotionally. So I called Evan.

"Hey, I'm so sorry," I said to him. "Please don't ask me to explain right now, but can you get me on the first flight home, please?"

"Now?" he asked, confused. "Today? You come home tomorrow. Can you just wait until then?"

"Please, I just want to get home."

"Are you sure you're okay? Did you ladies get in a fight?"

"No fight. I'm fine, I just want to come home early. I'll explain when I see you."

"Um, okay. I'll call the airline and change your flight to tonight," he said, only a minor sound of irritation in his voice. I knew it would cost money, but he also knew that I wouldn't do it if I didn't have to.

How had I let it get so far? My vacation was ruined. I had gone and destroyed this sacred time away with my friends. I'd blown it all up. Thankfully, Evan didn't press me any further that morning because I didn't know what to say. I couldn't explain it to myself, let alone to him. So I packed up, got in a taxi, and headed to the airport. Several hours later, I found myself sitting alone at the Naples airport bar.

"Flight 307 to Boston will begin boarding now. Please make your way to gate 32C."

"Oh, that's me! Excuse me, bartender, can I get one more glass of this pinot noir and the check, please?" I asked.

"You sure you want another glass?"

"Yes, can I get it in a to-go cup, please?"

"We aren't allowed to do that, ma'am, I'm sorry."

"Oh, okay, just a glass, then," I told him confidently.

The bartender brought me my wine and check, and as soon as he turned his back, I unscrewed a plastic Poland Spring water bottle and began to pour the glass of red wine into the mouth of the bottle. I could feel the older man next to me staring, but I ignored him.

"Are you sure that's a good idea?" he asked me. And as he said that, the wine splattered all over the bar top and my white shirt. By the time I got onto the plane, I cried myself to sleep with my sunglasses still on, a pink stain on my white cotton eyelet t-shirt, imagining what it would have been like for my friends to call my husband to tell him I was in the hospital. Or worse.

Evan hadn't asked any pertinent questions on the phone that morning. He saved the lecture for later when I got home and he saw my bruised face. He took one look at my black eye and wine-soaked clothing and couldn't hide his concern.

"What the hell happened?" he demanded.

"I don't know. I'm okay, though, it doesn't really hurt," I reassured him. "I'm fine, really."

After that trip, another tiny piece of me cracked. I was slowly shattering. It would be another year and a half before I'd be able to admit to myself that alcohol had a complete and total grip on me.

Day 141: April 17, 2021

Waiting at Logan airport in Boston, I scan the security line in front of me. I press both surgical masks tightly against my face, something I often do when I'm surrounded by too many people. I scurry quickly after Catherine, my wheelie suitcase bumping my heels.

"There are so many damn people here this early. Where are they all going?" I whisper.

"I know. It feels like half of Boston has decided to fly out this morning," Catherine replies flatly.

I realize it's not just the number of people around me that are making me feel uneasy. There's more to this unsettled feeling in my belly. When was the last time I went anywhere without Evan? Was it that trip to Naples? When was the last time I was on a girls' trip sober?

The last question sits at the forefront of my mind. Never. Quite the opposite. Lots of boozy memories filter through, one after another. A sober family vacation to Florida with the kids is one thing. But to be let loose in the airport with a friend is a whole other ballgame. I feel like a child sneaking out past curfew. I feel like I'm doing something wrong. Can I be trusted here?

The airport has always been one of my favorite drinking holes. This is one of the few places on earth where you can walk through the doors and it suddenly becomes socially acceptable, if not encouraged, to start drinking the moment you arrive. No matter the time of day or regardless of wherever the hell you might be, as long as planes are landing and taking off in the nearby vicinity, you can drink as much or as little as you damn well please. No one cares who you are or where you're going.

I used to especially love day drinking in a busy airport at the start of any vacation. Settling into the barstool, excitement took over as I shoved my suitcase underneath my feet, anticipating all the fun ahead of me. That first cocktail always had an exciting, celebratory feel, jumpstarting the party and opening the doors to relaxation.

On the flip side, I usually felt awful on my way home from vacation. Having consumed too much that day at the pool, I often needed to sip on something to work off a hangover. Or I was just sloppy and drunk, stumbling through security, dropping luggage, and desperate for a vacation from my vacation. Like that time coming home from Naples, bruised, drunk, and soaked in wine.

"Next!" the TSA agent calls out.

A moment later, I'm motioned through the metal detectors and work my way through the line of travelers, meeting Catherine on the other side of the gates.

As we slide our sneakers back on and grab our carry-on bags, we glance at each other with a knowing look. On either side of us are the glowing neon lights of a familiar sports bar. We start laughing because we both know we've stepped foot into the land of twenty-four-hour-a-day airport bars.

"What should we do now?" I ask.

"Hmm. Grab a coffee?" Catherine suggests.

"Check out the gift shop?"

"Do you need any magazines?"

"Nope, I'm all set. Do you need breakfast?"

"I'm not really hungry."

"Yeah, me neither. I already ate."

"Should we just find our gate?"

We giggle uncomfortably.

"I guess so. That's a good idea," I say.

We walk past another bustling bar, a smaller version of the popular Boston icon Legal Sea Foods, filled with a few happy patrons. I can't help but stare. Two ladies about our age sit side by side, legs facing one another, laughing boisterously. Between them sit two tall mimosas, the bubbles foaming at the top. Beside their glasses are another set of empty champagne flutes, indicating they're already on round two.

Catherine sees me looking and knows what I'm thinking. "Don't worry, they'll have a headache mid-flight," she says, reading my mind. I smile, and we keep walking.

Two hours later, our plane lands in Charleston, South Carolina, in the heaviest rain we've seen in months. We huddle together in our thin jackets, shivering under the awning outside the airport in the forty-nine-degree rain. I pull up the Uber app again. Four minutes until the car gets here.

I watch the dark, black clouds begin to drift closer, closing in above us through the palm trees. I open the text from Evan from earlier and look at the pictures of the kids in shorts and t-shirts in the sun back home. Massachusetts is experiencing an unseasonably warm string of weather, a heat wave during mid-April, while Catherine and I are facing record low temps down South. Typical.

Evan's text reads, "Enjoy this break. You deserve it."

I know he isn't worried about me on this girls' weekend, unlike all the other times that I've been away without him. Finally, he doesn't have to wonder if I'll make it back to the hotel at night. He doesn't have to worry about me falling out of an Uber and coming home with a black eye. For the first time in years, we can be apart from one another without me feeling guilty or him feeling frustrated.

"I knew it would be chilly here, but not a monsoon. What happened to our relaxing golf trip?" Catherine says.

"Maybe it's just a passing tropical storm. Isn't that what happens down in the South? Do these things blow through pretty fast?"

Suddenly, an alarm sounds on my phone, a blaring horn that makes us both jump, causing me to nearly drop my bags. All around us, people are looking down at their cell phones.

"What the hell is that?" Catherine asks.

Together, we read the bright-yellow banner that appears on the screen of my cell phone.

"Tornado warning in this area until 1:45 p.m. Take shelter now. Check local media," I read aloud.

We look at each other wide-eyed and then frantically start to gather our bags, the rain pelting us in the face. I notice that the other travelers don't seem as concerned just as our Uber driver pulls up and calls out my name.

"What do we do?" Catherine asks.

"We did just wait for this guy for almost a half hour, let's just go," I say, shivering.

I look around at the dozens of people now moving about their day, business as usual. I stare up at the sky and imagine a tornado sucking me up into its vortex, remembering what Mom used to tell me when I was little. She always said to hide in the basement.

"Fine. I guess you're right," Catherine says. "Let's do it."

I nod, ignoring Mom's voice in my head as we pile our bags into the trunk of the compact car. We throw ourselves into the back seat, happy for the relief from the wind and rain. Ronald, our Uber driver, zips out of the parking lot through the heavy rain. We can't even see out of the windows, it's pouring so hard, and all I can think is that I hope the kids are enjoying the sun back home. The tornado alerts beep on our phones again.

"Are there tornadoes around, or what?" Catherine asks Ronald.

"Listen, ladies, we've been getting these alerts all day. It's okay. Just do me a favor, will you? Just scan the horizon for funnel clouds, please. And hail. Hail means run like hell down in these parts."

Catherine giggles, assuming he's joking.

"I'm serious," he says, looking at us through the rearview mirror. "But now we're going over alligator alley, and there are no overpasses to hide under for miles."

"Oh, God," I say, the panic starting to rise.

"Breathe," Catherine whispers to me. "How long is this ride, Ronald?" she asks with as much calm in her voice as she can muster.

"It's just under an hour. Don't worry, I'll drive fast. And I'll buy you ladies a stiff drink when we get to the hotel," he says.

Catherine and I look at each other and have no other choice but to start giggling again.

"You cannot make this shit up," I whisper.

Ronald smiles, trying to get in on the joke, and the laughter takes over— the full-bellied kind I haven't experienced in years. The complete absurdity of our situation has brought tears to the edge of my eyes, and my jaw begins to ache. I'm terrified, but I'm having more fun than I have in years.

I'm suddenly taken aback by this sense of silliness and the fact that I'm laughing to cope with my anxiety. I'm surprised by this ability to feel everything all at once, but most of all to experience what I haven't felt in so long: pure, utter joy. And my mind isn't focused on alcohol. I'm acutely aware that there is no need for alcohol to feel the kind of giddiness I was only ever able to achieve after numerous glasses of wine. For so long, there was a need to drink just to feel anything at all.

All I ever wanted in my adult life was to have wine coursing through my veins to get me through a situation like this. I always thought I needed alcohol to make the flight better. To ease me through an awkward time. Alcohol was necessary to make all trips feel like a vacation. Alcohol provided relaxation. It eased the tension. I thought it made me happy. But I was so very wrong.

Finally, I'm feeling again, all on my own, without a drug or an artificial high. I feel a freedom that can be likened to the cold wind in my face on the ski slopes or of rowing a boat across the smooth surface of a lake at sunset or snuggling with my newborn baby in the middle of the night. Like the Bermuda Longtails that glide through the ocean sky, I feel free. Free to feel it all.

And it takes my breath away.

PART III

Confrontation (2019): Thirty-Seven Years Old

"Can we talk for a second?" Evan asked, closing our bedroom door.

I could tell the conversation was going to be serious, and a pit formed in my stomach. I hesitated and tried to read his expression. "Okay," I said.

He was quiet. His eyes were wider than usual, and he stared straight at me. There was no smile on his face. He folded his arms across his body and sat on the edge of the bed. I rolled onto my side, nursing my headache with a bottle of water.

"I think you're drinking too much," he said.

"Ugh, here we go," I moaned, irritation in my voice.

"I'm worried about you."

"Please, stop."

"Kim, listen."

"Where are the kids?" I asked.

"They're fine. They're watching TV downstairs."

Evan stood to shut the bedroom door. "Can we talk about last night? Do you remember what you did?"

"Why does it matter if I remember or not?" I couldn't look at him.

"It matters a lot."

My head throbbed, and I began to feel sick to my stomach over this confrontation. I hated these conversations. I recall the panic I felt at that moment, wondering what I'd done to bring us to that point again. I covered my face with my hands, feeling out of control. I wanted him to stop talking to me like a child. I felt so ashamed, so stupid. I knew he was right, but I didn't want to talk about it anymore. I hated these chats.

"Just go away. I know I fucked up. I won't do it again, you don't have to make me feel like a total lush," I said, still not looking in his direction. "I promise things will change. I'll do better. I won't drink like that again." It was a promise I genuinely wanted to keep.

"You said that the last time," Evan said.

"I know," I told him. "But this time will be different."

"Will it, though?"

"It will," I said. "I don't want to talk about it."

"We need to talk about it. You need to hear this."

"Go away, just please leave me alone."

"You fell down the stairs in front of the kids. Kim, you need to listen."

I was silent, absorbing his words. "Stop talking," I whispered.

"Brayden watched you. You hit your head. Do you really not remember any of this?" he asked me quietly.

That explained the throbbing on the left side of my head and my bruised backside. "Please stop," I whispered.

"You need to think about what's happening. We both know your family history with alcohol. Let's just say it like it is, okay? You need to be careful. You need to think about this."

I lay quietly beside him. As the silence stretched between us, I knew it warranted a response. But I felt conflicted. I was so annoyed that Evan had been drinking alongside me the night before but I was the one getting berated for letting it all get too out of control again. He had easily encouraged my drinking, but I ended up being the one with the hangover. I let it get too far. I fell down the stairs. And I didn't remember it all. He never got sloppy and did stupid things.

"Can't you just stop at two or three drinks? Why do you have to have so much every time?"

I was silent. I'm not sure what he wanted me to say because I didn't have an answer for him. He was frustrated that it was impossible for me not to want to get drunk.

"I know, you're right. I'll try harder," I said to him.

Again, more lies. Because I knew I could not control it. Evan didn't know what to do either. I felt that he was still enabling my drinking some days, encouraging me to participate alongside him, and then other days he wanted me to completely change. What I couldn't explain to him or myself was that I had no ability to do so. As much as he wanted his drinking buddy to get her shit together, I couldn't fix it. I couldn't have just one drink like he wanted me to. I was circling the drain.

Later that night, I tossed and turned in bed. I Googled the phrase "how to know if you are drinking too much." A variety of scary articles and words jumped off the screen, frightening me enough to turn off my phone momentarily: rehab, addiction, treatment, recovery. But I brought myself back to read more. I also impulsively purchased a book off Amazon and bookmarked a support group website.

I stopped drinking during the weekdays. I tried to change. After that confrontation in our bedroom, I worked hard to prove to both myself and my husband that everything would be fine. I really tried hard to drink less like Evan suggested.

It was often the same routine. After a while, I would go to dinner with my husband and order a glass of wine, asking his permission to get a second glass—like a child. I was resentful that he was making me feel this way and making me question my relationship with my buddy, my trusted friend. But I had no choice but to cooperate if I wanted to avoid having that shameful conversation again. I was determined to earn back my drinking privileges with good behavior.

Evan and I stopped going out with large groups of friends for a little while because we knew the temptation for me to get drunk was too great. We never really talked about the fact that many of my friends and their husbands drank the same way as me at times. So why was I being punished?

It wasn't fair. That was how it felt for so long. *This isn't fair.*

We continued with the charade. I had myself and Evan convinced for a long time that it would be okay. It was a cycle. I stopped for a bit and got it all under control. I showed him that I could be the kind of person who drinks one glass of wine at dinner, and then I spiraled again. But I eventually reined it in, telling myself I didn't have a problem. But there were early mornings lying awake in bed at four a.m. when I questioned it all. The shame cycle began again. I worried, and I cried.

Little did Evan know that during our quiet dinners out, I obsessed over every sip I took. I had a hard time concentrating on our conversations because I couldn't stop thinking about my next drink. Could I order another glass? Was I allowed another? Would he get angry? Could I steal a sip of his drink when he was in the bathroom? I watched what people at other tables ordered, and I kept my eye on the waitress. It consumed my every thought, and Evan never knew.

Nonetheless, as much as I tried not to, I always slipped back into the darkness. It happened the same way every time. After a month of good behavior, I started casually having a glass or two of wine during the week, having proved myself responsible. I thought that I could handle drinking alone again, little by little. That I could drink like my husband and enjoy one glass and not feel compelled to drink the entire bottle by myself.

It was a slippery slope. My one glass always turned into two. And that one day during the week when I was allowed to drink quickly morphed into a two-day rule. *Because staying at home with the kids is hard,* I told myself. Or if Evan and I had a fight, I felt I deserved it. Or it was vacation. A holiday. A family member was visiting. The sun was shining! There was always an excuse.

Within a few weeks, I was right back to drinking every single night of the week, often crushing a bottle of wine on the couch by myself. Evan would avert his eyes, huffing and puffing as he took out the recycling the next day. I popped Advil, chugged some water, and pretended nothing was wrong. Nothing to see here.

Evan would wait until I had another eventful Saturday night or did something stupid, which gave him allowance to approach me again about my consumption. Skipping the boys' hockey games because I hung around drinking with friends at brunch, blacking out on Thanksgiving, falling down the stairs drunk in front of the kids after a casual dinner out. I gave him endless opportunities to confront me.

"I think we need to talk about your drinking again," he would say, his comments stinging.

Sometimes, he was kind and loving; other times, not so much. Regardless, I always promised to do better. It was a vicious cycle. In every conversation we had, Evan was slowly cracking me open, and I didn't even realize it.

The Global Pandemic (February 2020): Thirty-Eight Years Old

The global pandemic was the beginning of the end for me. At the start of 2020, the world seemed to press pause on all things normal. When the pandemic began, my family was thrown into turmoil, and our seemingly pleasant existence was unexpectedly flipped upside down. Being a stay-at-home mom with three elementary-aged kids during quarantine for several months was the ultimate test of sanity and temptation. In the beginning, I homeschooled them under one roof. Also, all of their sports, activities, and social outlets were cut off. We were stuck indoors together twenty-four hours a day with no end in sight. We had never done this before. Nobody had. These were unprecedented times for our family and the entire world.

The fear of what was happening around us, the unknown, and the constant worrying overwhelmed us all. Life seemed canceled. The kids couldn't do any of the things they normally did or see any friends. I wondered how long we would all be stuck home. When would the kids go back to school? Would they ever have any other human interaction? When could we leave the house? When could we go to a grocery store? Would we all get sick? What would happen if we got Covid?

These questions sat heavily on me. I also had to pretend to be fearless for my kids and behave as if the world wasn't slowly imploding. It was a lot to handle. I had to stay strong, and I turned to my nightly glass of wine for that strength.

I obsessed over the news, and that didn't help me. Our one and only social outlet was visiting friends across the street to let the kids play together. We decided to "quaranteam" with these neighbors. We found ourselves walking over to their yard quite a bit, letting the kids play, and discussing the state of the world over beers and wine. We had a lot to talk about.

I also turned to socializing online whenever I could, most of which included alcohol. We had Zoom happy hours with signature cocktails. Zoom birthday parties with booze. Zoom family parties—always with alcohol. Whenever we could get out, we gathered in the driveways of others around fire pits and drank. Walking with friends? Bring your wine. All of these things included alcohol.

Monotonous daily routines were made entertaining and exciting by one thing only: booze. Life became terrifying, isolating, and unknown, and I didn't know how to manage any of it. It was always easier to numb out with a drink. I had always used alcohol to cope when I had a stressful day in normal times, and this was much worse. On top of that, I was constantly hungover and on edge, which didn't help my stress levels.

The mommy wine culture had always taught me that it was okay, encouraged even, to use wine to get through the day. To cope with a whiny child. To survive the teething phase. To get through the witching hours of the evening when they were babies. And I felt like I was back to the toddler days again, even though my kids were six, eight, and nine.

We had regressed. They had all reverted to tantrums and fighting, and my oldest was having the hardest time of all. He was managing his own stress, and little did I know that he was struggling more than any of us knew. And I was not there at all because I had turned to alcohol to get away from them. I was escaping to the bottom of a bottle every single afternoon, which I had been accustomed to doing in order to avoid dealing with the problems in my life, ever since I was a teenager.

The Secrets That Break You (2020): Thirty-Eight Years Old

Don't see. Don't speak. Don't feel.

These are the rules I was asked to follow for the majority of my life as a child, and even well into adulthood. I was required to keep my thoughts to myself. My parents might not have realized they expected this out of me, but that was how I learned to cope with my feelings within my complicated family dynamic. I took these lessons with me throughout my life. I decided the best way not to see, speak, or feel was to drink.

Many people in my life asked me to behave this way. When there were hard feelings or difficult emotions to discuss, it was easier to sweep them under the rug or do as was expected of me as a woman, as a daughter, and as a child. These were the steps I had to take for so long just to keep others in my family happy. To keep things working with my husband and my marriage. To make friends happy. To keep the world at bay. Alcohol aided me in doing all that.

I used alcohol to help keep me going when my parents got separated. I used it to help distract me from my traumas in college. I used it to give me confidence when I felt judged by others. I used wine to soothe me when I felt frustrated as a mother or when I was reminded of the mistakes my husband had made years ago before we got married. Anytime my mind went where I didn't want it to go, I numbed it with alcohol. I escaped to a place I didn't need to feel with the aid of this substance.

For so much of my life, I kept quiet. I did as I was told, behaved how I believed others wanted me to, and did what was expected of me. At times, that required not listening to what was hurting me or what was causing me pain. I ignored my needs in place of other people's. My cries often went unanswered. I learned not to feel anything at all. And for a very long time, I turned a blind eye to my emotions, holding all my secrets in, hiding in the shadows of my past. Drinking quieted the screaming inside my head.

I believe my parents did the best they could for me as a child. They unknowingly asked a lot of me once they set me loose in the world.

Alcohol was my one and only coping mechanism, but it slowly began to crush me. I drank to feel confident. I used it to tamp down the feelings. I drank it to stay hidden. But finally, it nearly brought me to the edge of shattering into a thousand tiny fragments.

My parents' secrets didn't break me. Evan's secret didn't destroy me. The many people in my world who lied and hurt me weren't the reasons for my slow decline. Keeping these things bottled up inside wasn't the ultimate problem. In the end, I learned to avoid all of this pain with the help of alcohol, and that was what nearly broke me.

But I was no longer going to be controlled by any of it. I would not let the booze crush me.

The last several months before I stopped drinking, I was keenly aware that I was consuming way too much. I poured large cocktails most nights only to suck them down before Evan arrived home from work. I checked the Find My iPhone app to see where he was on the highway. I located him to make sure he wasn't about to walk in on me chugging my drink. I hid empties under mac' and cheese boxes in the trash, strategically placing the bottles under other trash bags so Evan wouldn't hear the clinking sound.

In the last few weeks, I was waking up on the weekends and sneaking sips of vodka, hiding away the empties in the back of my closet. Knowing that Evan was driving us around in the car, I kept drinking through my Saturday. I often blacked out during the day without anyone realizing it, forgetting to eat meals or to feed my children.

By the end, alcohol had become a requirement for me to feel. To function. But it was all pointless.

Because I was numb. There was no feeling left in my body.

I couldn't feel pain.

I didn't know joy anymore.

I couldn't recognize guilt.

I couldn't experience worry.

I didn't understand sadness.

I just wanted to observe the physical sensation that alcohol provided. I needed to feel a buzz. The spinning inside my brain. The lightheadedness. The knowing that I was temporarily being released from my surroundings. The moment of being transported to another place, even if for a second or two. But the pleasure center in my brain was no longer functioning, unable to produce the release of dopamine or serotonin properly. I couldn't experience satisfaction from drinking, and it had been a very long time since I'd felt any kind of positive emotion.

I was constantly chasing the initial feeling that I got when the first drink hit my stomach. I wanted that brief, elated high. That sensation that I had been searching for since my first shot of Jack Daniels by my friend Jill's pool deck when we were fifteen years old. As soon as I felt the charge, my body became momentarily more powerful, and all the senseless decisions I continued to make were pushed from my mind. I was chasing it on a runaway speeding train. And I couldn't stop it.

Those last two weeks, I couldn't feel anything anymore. I was slowly drowning, slowly slipping away. Slowly falling into the darkness.

The Day Before the Last: November 27, 2020

The day before I quit drinking alcohol seemed like any other day to our family. Once I finished sneaking vodka alone in the house, I put Bunker in the crate and jumped into the car with my family to pick up our Christmas tree. Like always, Evan had no idea what I was doing to myself in private. We finally made it out of the house and to the Christmas tree lot before the morning rush, and it was fairly uneventful. For the most part, it felt pretty routine for the Friday after Thanksgiving. We got a gorgeous tree, came home, and set it up while listening to Christmas music.

Later that day, because it was so warm out, Evan and I spent the afternoon on the golf course, and the kids stayed home with their favorite babysitter. It seemed like a win-win situation for all of us. Evan and I enjoyed some cocktails while golfing in our brief time away from the kids. He had no idea I had been sneaking sips in the house all morning, though.

Walking into the mudroom at four o'clock in the afternoon, I bit my bottom lip, something I sometimes did to steady my voice when I found myself in that utterly familiar situation. I was drunk. I was gearing up, preparing to deal with the kids again. I had been drinking all day since the vodka I'd snuck early that morning while the kids waited in the car.

"We're home!" I shouted, overly excited. I tried to sound composed, telling myself to act normal.

Parker ran in and wrapped her small six-year-old arms around my legs. Her enthusiasm rattled me as I attempted to balance on one foot and untie my left golf shoe. I flung it. I wobbled as I sat down on the bench beneath the row of neatly organized jackets and backpacks. I pulled a rogue soccer shin guard out from beneath me.

Evan hastily pushed past me, and I could feel his annoyance at me. "I need to pay Erin. And we told her we'd be home over thirty minutes ago."

I hated that feeling, knowing he was irritated with me. I knew I was in trouble with him because I'd drunk too much on the golf course.

"Hi, Parker," I said. "How was the rest of your day? What did you do with Erin? Did you play outside?" I pulled Parker onto my lap and kissed the top of her head, holding her tightly. For a moment, I sat and breathed deeply, inhaling her soft blond curls and the faint smell of her lavender shampoo.

Evan spoke quietly with the babysitter, and I kept busy by rinsing some dishes in the sink, putting on my best sober performance. The boys wandered over to me, seemingly oblivious to my current state of inebriation.

"How did you hit 'em, Mom? What did you shoot?" asked Brayden.

I smiled down at them. I began to answer them but realized I hadn't even kept score. The last several holes on the golf course were a blur. I certainly hadn't needed that last drink I got at the gin shack.

"Oh, I played fine, just fine!" I said. "We had fun! Tell me about your day."

I hadn't meant to get that drunk. It started out so great. It was supposed to be a casual round with Evan on an unseasonably warm, quintessentially beautiful New England fall day. A nice daytime date, or a brief time out from the holiday chaos. An afternoon break from the kids to spend some quality time together and reconnect on an exhausting weekend filled with *so much* family time.

How had I gotten so drunk at the end? I consider Billy, the bartender at the turn, and his heavy hand. The drink he'd made was certainly stiffer than the last time. I was pretty sure he'd added a vodka floater to my John Daly. And then I had those two extra beers on top of that at the nineteenth hole. But then I thought about the vodka I'd snuck that morning, and I cringed.

It's hard to shake the look of disappointment on your husband's face at the end of the day. It felt like only moments before that we were singing along to Jason Derulo from the mini speaker on the eighth fairway, and I was laughing at my third shot out of the sand on the twelfth hole. Then things changed so drastically in such a short amount of time. He just suddenly got fed up with me. How did that happen?

I stood and stared at our Christmas tree in the family room, its white lights blurring before me. The sounds of the kids had become a sort of white noise, and it was almost as if I couldn't hear their joyful banter.

I couldn't believe we'd just got the tree that morning, before the spirited round of golf, before the beers, before the John Daly. I think back to my solo mission with the Tito's from early in the day at the hutch in the dining room and cringe at the fact I'd been secretly drinking for nearly seven hours. That's why I felt so drunk. And so tired.

We'd had a lovely time sifting through the ornaments as a family this morning. We laughed at finding Brayden's first baby handprint, and Chase's preschool picture pasted haphazardly to a pinecone. Parker danced around the room. So much joy on their faces. The mood was so different: Neil Diamond Christmas tunes on repeat, the kids arguing over who got to place the star at the end. But was I even a part of it? I felt so distracted. My mind was elsewhere, and I was focused on sneaking off for more vodka shots.

I kept telling myself I needed to be better. I promised myself I wouldn't do this anymore, but I had. Again.

I turned around and stumbled up the stairs drunk, but I had no idea that it would be for the very last time.

Up until that night, I felt a dullness in my life that pervaded every ounce of my being. Most days, I lived within a feeling of perpetual gloom, allowing alcohol to dictate my worth. On the outside, I appeared self-assured and at ease with myself, but on the inside, I was falling apart.

I felt as if I were existing at the bottom of a deep, shadowy cliff, staring up at the people around me, wondering how to climb up and out to the light above. The ocean existed far back. Miles of empty beaches stretched in every direction.

How could I reach my children? My husband? There were days that I was successful at clambering my way up the sides of the dark chasm, my fingernails digging into the crumbling earth as pieces of it fell away beneath me. Sometimes, I struggled up from the barren abyss and found my way to solid ground, emerging into the light, dazed and confused. At times, I tried to exist above that loneliness, but I often lost my strength. Eventually, I fell back even deeper, farther from the ones I loved, allowing the substance to take over once again. For a while, I felt placated within the safety of my lonely beach because I could avoid the looks of others. The problems of the real world up above were hidden for a bit, and I could silence the noise. It was easier to live within the shadows of my secrets.

But the dark loneliness began to wear on me. I began to sink farther from the light. My world was filled with a suffocating murkiness, and I was unable to climb to the surface as easily anymore. It was getting darker. The tide came in, and the waves began to pummel me.

My flailing and kicking only made it worse. I was sinking into quicksand. I could not see the light any longer. The space above me began to close in. Instead of the joyful, familiar faces of my loved ones, I saw only disappointment and shame looming above. The waves were crushing me. Discomfort was all I knew anymore.

I pleaded. I sobbed. Suddenly, I realized, I needed to get out. I needed to escape, for good.

And that next morning, hands pulled me up and away from the deep, angry darkness that was my life. Away from the crushing waves. Up away from the sharp rocks.

When I asked Evan for help to stop drinking, that was the day I found a lightness, a release from the dark. Away from the empty, desolate world. That was the day I found my freedom.

Day 190: June 5, 2021

The pain and pressure of the needle is sharp and burning, but it only lasts a brief moment. I exhale slowly, closing my eyes. The vibrations on my wrist are brief yet searing, so I try to distract myself with some of the display pictures on the wall. Faded illustrations of hearts. Dragons. A skull and crossbones. A naked mermaid with long hair and very large breasts.

Does it hurt more because it's directly on the bone? I look down at my arm and catch a brief glimpse of the black script across my wrist. Deirdre glances up at me and winks.

"You're doing great, lady," Deirdre says.

"Thanks," I say. "I mean, I did give birth to three rather large eight-pound babies, so this pain is sort of minimal compared to that, I guess."

"The women that come in here are always tougher than the men. Always."

"Ha! I believe it."

This is nothing compared to the awful, unforgiving, and always constant pain that alcohol has been over the past several years, I think. I look across the room at the fair-haired, freckle-faced girl lying on her stomach on the table opposite me. She's getting some sort of inscription tattooed on her neck. A poem or story across her back and shoulders. She appears to be asleep.

"Congrats on your sobriety, by the way," Deirdre says.

"Thank you," I say, smiling.

"How many days sober are you?"

"Just over six months," I say, sighing heavily.

She pauses and stares up at me from behind her mask. "That's incredible. I'm four years sober, actually, and my baby just turned two last week. So I know this road you're on all too well."

"Oh, wow. Yeah, we have stuff in common, I guess."

We sit in silence as she continues working on my tattoo.

"Almost done," she says.

I listen to the buzzing. The humming. I hear Evan's tentative voice in my head. "People are going to ask you why you got this, you know," he said to me last night while brushing our teeth, staring at my naked wrist. "People will constantly wonder. It'll be a conversation starter for the rest of your life."

His words echo in my mind. I wonder what the kids are doing back home as I lay here alone in this cold, sterile tattoo parlor in the middle of Boston. My three kids and husband are together in the comfort of our familiar house in the quiet suburbs playing in the yard, doing suburban family stuff, while I'm getting a tattoo, by myself, in the city. I never would have thought I'd be here in this position six months ago or a year ago.

"All done," Deirdre says.

I look down at my wrist and stare at the delicate black script across my arm.

"Thank you. It's perfect."

I smile, hop off the table, and walk to the full-length mirror on the wall on the other side of the room, past the sleeping girl. I gaze at myself. My light-brown hair hangs down past my shoulders, fuller and longer than ever. My cheekbones seem more pronounced, but I look and feel healthier. I stand a little bit taller. I think back to that morning six months ago when I watched Evan pour the wine down the kitchen sink. It feels like a lifetime ago. I look at my bony arms hanging down beside me, and I appear small. Young, all of a sudden. A little girl again.

The black writing is bold and prominent against my pale skin. I lift my arm and raise it to get a better look and read the letters once again, feeling a swell of pride and warmth. I read the word: *Free . . .*

I look up at the face in the mirror that stares back at me and smile at her. Thirty minutes later, I walk through my front door with the new ink on my wrist.

"Mom, let's see that tat!" Brayden yells as soon as I walk in the door.

I pull off the bandage and show it to them, and they all stare down at my arm smiling.

"Wow!" they say and begin to pepper me with questions.

"How much did it hurt?" Chase asks.

"Was it worse than a flu shot?" Brayden asks.

"Did it feel like a bee sting?" Parker asks.

After a small explanation to the kids last night about why I was getting this, they didn't question it much more. Now today, they are obviously only interested in the pain of it all. I told them I wanted a tattoo of the word *FREE* as a reminder to myself of how to live every day. I said I got four dots after the word that would always remind me of them and their father.

At this moment, I feel like it's a secret. A lie. There's so much more to this tattoo that's hard to explain to them. It's hard to encapsulate all that this single word represents. How do I explain it to my children?

This feeling of keeping a secret doesn't sit well. It feels familiar, and I'm racked with guilt. How do I explain it so they can appreciate its importance to me without scaring them? Without revealing too much?

A little while later, we're ready to head out to dinner as a family. On the way out the door, Brayden pulls me aside.

"Hey, Mom, can I ask you a question about your tattoo?" he says.

"Of course, bud, what's up?" I say, slipping my sandals on.

"What does it really mean?"

Brayden has always been intuitive and wise beyond his years. I hesitate and look up at my son. He swallows nervously, but I smile at his bravery.

"It's so cool of you to ask that. I love your curiosity . . . I'm happy to talk about it, actually."

"Really?"

"Yeah, you can ask me anything."

"Okay. So why did you get it? Why now?"

"Well. You know how I stopped drinking, and I've said that I always felt like I was sorta stuck?"

"Yeah. What does it mean, then?"

"Well, drinking made me feel like I was trapped. Alcohol made me feel that way. Like I couldn't get away from it, but when I finally made the choice to stop drinking, I felt so much better. When I decided to get sober, I didn't feel stuck anymore. Now, I feel free."

He stands quietly, contemplating my words. "I get it, I think," he says, smiling. He looks up at me, his big blue eyes wide and curious.

"I wanted to be a better mom, and I didn't think I could do that if I was drinking. It didn't make me feel good, it made me feel . . . well, stuck. When I was sad or mad or frustrated, I drank alcohol, hoping to feel better. But I learned pretty quickly that that wasn't the answer, and it was only making me feel worse. It made me more sad, more mad, more angry. More stuck."

"I understand. You were the opposite of free," he says quietly.

"And I was starting to rely on it in ways that I didn't like, because alcohol is addictive and not good for you. So to manage my pain, it ended up causing me more pain. So that's why I felt trapped. And that's when I realized I needed to stop."

"Okay. I get it. That's good, Mom. I think what you did is cool. Was it hard to stop?"

"Yes, buddy, it was. But I'm so happy now that I did. I'm so much better off."

"I can tell," he says. "Now that you're unstuck and now that you're free, you seem a lot happier."

Brayden sits for a while, picking at the skin around his fingernails. Then he looks up at me, hesitating for a moment. I can tell he has something more to say. "You've always said that our family doesn't have secrets. So I think it's unfair that you're keeping this secret from Chase and Parker," he says. "I think you should tell them what the tattoo means."

And with that, I'm nearly brought to tears. I think for a moment. "You're absolutely right," I tell him. "I will do that tonight at dinner."

Brayden has taught me so much in his ten years. Recently, he has brought me to realize an incredible amount about myself and this world. All of my children have done so much for me. Years ago, these little people taught me unconditional love at a time in my life when I didn't think it existed. They've shown me how to love harder than I ever imagined and have each taught me how to show compassion like I never knew I could.

We pile into the car and head to our country club for dinner. Meals out in the evenings are a bit different these days. Once we arrive, I eye up my usual spot on the outdoor sofa beside the fire pit on the bluestone patio overlooking the west lawn and the golf course. I am temporarily distracted by the exuberant group of ladies that have currently overtaken my former favorite seat. It has the best people-watching angle and view of the sunset. I used to post up here after a round of golf for drinks on Saturdays and stick around late into the evening, always overstaying my welcome. The waitstaff lingered, chatting by the bar, bored and anxiously ready to call it quits for the night.

"One more round, please, Nelson!" I would call, perched on my corner of the couch, the orange and red hues from the sunset lighting up the sky like a fireball. I always wanted to stick around, allowing that next drink to push me over the edge into oblivion. To the point of no return. Into blackness.

For a moment, I long for the silly, rowdy conversations of summers past—the wild banter that would ensue in my corner of the couch. Everything has shifted now, and I don't know where my place is with those people anymore. I no longer have a corner of a couch, and not all of my friends invite me out like they used to.

I smooth my white jeans, tuck my hair behind my ears, and take Evan's hand, following my children to our table. I'm grateful to be on this journey, though, and I feel an overwhelming joy for my completely different seat at this brand-new table across the patio.

As we settle into our table for five, I try to find the words to start the conversation Brayden so desperately wants me to have with the rest of the family. I begin to explain to my other children what I had just been discussing earlier at home—about my choice to stop drinking. Parker and Chase look at me with interest.

"I guess you don't drink wine at night anymore, now that I think about it," Parker says.

"I know you don't drink anymore, Mom. I also noticed you go to bed so much earlier. So what does the tattoo have to do with that?" Chase asks.

I smile and feel a heaviness recede. "I stopped drinking so I could be a better mother for you three. I wanted to do more for you. Be happier and healthier. I felt like I couldn't be a good mom *and* drink alcohol, but now I feel so awesome," I explain. "I'm doing this for you guys. All of you."

"She felt stuck, but now she's free," Brayden explains.

Chase comes around to my side of the table, wraps his arms around my waist, and looks up at me. "Mom, that must have been really hard for you to stop drinking. I'm really proud of you for doing this. I love you."

Evan looks at me across the table with pride. He smiles, tears in his eyes. I kiss the top of Chase's head as Parker and Brayden walk over and put their arms around my back. These children have truly helped me heal. From the beginning, they will always be the ones who rescued me.

Day 254: August 1, 2021

I stare across the lake at the house that holds so many memories: Spofford Lake in New Hampshire, the place I spent weekend after weekend visiting with my parents and sisters when I was a little girl. Where we listened to rainstorms on the porch and watched the Fourth of July parade from the dock every summer. The house that was my final home before I moved to Boston and started my own family.

I hang my legs off the edge of the mooring at the boat club where Jen and her husband Brian spend their days. This area is what they've come to call home now with their children, on Spofford Lake. They moved up here years ago and settled here with their family. Jen wanted a simpler life, she always said.

I visit the lake every so often to see my sisters and Mom. It's one of the only times during the year that we gather together for my kids to see their cousins, aunts, and grandmother. Every summer, Evan and I drive up for the day to celebrate Mom's birthday with my sisters. We come here to swim at the boat club for the day and take the kids out on the old ski boat that once belonged to Dad but now belongs to Jen. I watch the kids get dragged around the lake on the tube, just as Dad used to do to me when I was little.

My sisters and I don't visit one another all that often. We focus on our own lives these days. On our own tiny worlds, disconnected and apart from one another. Perhaps, especially for me, it's easier to live separately from them than to be reminded of the secrets from our past.

Every August, when we used to come to the lake, I usually drank myself silly at the campground, getting too drunk to care about my family or the fact that my kids were swimming off the same boat that I learned how to waterski on as a child. I used to let Evan deal with our kids while I drank large gulps of wine from red Solo cups like I was sixteen. Even though my kids loved coming up to Spofford, it used to make me sad. It was easier to just slide through the afternoon in a drunken haze than to be confronted with memories from my own childhood on the water.

Today, my toes skim the surface of the cool lake. I make out the tiny outline of our old lake house that once belonged to my family, in the distance, far across the water. The square frame of the house, the blue front, the shiny roof. I notice the bright-red house that sits directly to the right of it. Not much has changed on this beautiful lake.

I look down at the dark-blue water beneath me, wondering what creatures might lie below. The waves roll in, lapping against the wooden slats, splashing up against my bare legs. I stretch my arms behind me, leaning onto my elbows.

"Mommy!" Parker comes running down the dock and plops herself down beside me.

"Hi, where have you been?" I say, closing my eyes.

"I was watching Luke and Emma fishing over there," she tells me, pointing to her cousins. "What are you doing sitting here by yourself?"

"I'm just relaxing," I say, glancing over my shoulder at Jen, Laura, and Mom on the dock by the shore. I wave to them. Mom smiles merrily and waves back to me.

"Mom! Parker! Come in the lake!" I hear Chase call to us from the floating dock on the water. He begins to swim toward us.

"I'm just enjoying the sights and sounds of the lake!" I say.

"What does that mean?" he asks, puzzled, swimming up to me. He grabs my legs and hangs onto my feet.

"Do you see that blue house way over there across the water?" I point. "That tiny speck directly across from us? Well, that house used to belong to my family. I grew up going to that cottage as a little girl. This was my lake."

We look across the water, staring at the many houses that dot the shoreline. Abruptly, Brayden jumps into the water off the dock, splashing us all, and the moment of quiet is disrupted.

"Brayden!" everyone yells, and the fighting ensues.

Evan sits down with Parker and me and tosses the boys a football, and the boys begin to wrestle over it in the water, laughing.

"What do you mean this was your lake?" Parker asks me.

I contemplate my daughter's question. It's sad that so much from my childhood no longer exists. So much that my children don't know. Too many memories feel lost. I absorb the breeze on my skin, the calm of the air, and the peacefulness of the lake. The chaos of my children before me. I am reminded of how I used to play on the docks of this lake. Jumping off the float and splashing in the same velvety water like the kids. Rowing the boat into the pickleweeds.

I'm here for it all right now, watching my children do the same. The laughs. The fights. All of it. I am present. No longer numbing and escaping with a bottle of booze. I am sober, mindfully able to soak it all in. I am here. I feel a swell of joy inside my chest. Strong, powerful, and surging. Contentment, overwhelming and breathtaking. This is everything I ever wanted. Everything I pictured for myself when I was young.

It is beautiful.

For so long, I used alcohol to escape from my past. I drank to avoid the sadness that my parents made me feel. The anger that they caused. Finally, I can feel it all. I don't hide from these emotions anymore, and I can allow myself to be vulnerable again, like a child. I am no longer held back.

So at times, my parents, sisters, and I remain in an awkward space. I no longer hide in the shadows, concealing my truth, unable to live vulnerably. I have faced my fears on my own, and I've shown my mother and father what it's like to step outside the darkness and confront it. I know now there's a difference between being unable to do something and being fearful of the task before you. You can avoid the things that scare you for your entire life, or you can face them head-on.

Maybe we are always going to be wolves in people's skins. When we're together, we may never be able to speak the truth. My family may always be unwilling to peel back their disguises. When we're with one another, we're all still pretending, unable to move forward and forgive ourselves for our past mistakes. Perhaps we all still blame one another for the demise of our pack. I must do what I can and simply look ahead.

I believe Mom protected me as well as she could. She always did for me what she believed any mother should, and at times she was just trying to get through the day. She thought what she was doing was the best for her children, even though she lived a lot of her life in fear. Her fears devolved to me, and I learned to escape from the complex realities around me just as she had. In the end, we both needed to survive for our kids. We both needed to keep our heads above water. We both love our children and always wanted to be the best mothers we could be, never wanting to let them down.

I think my father did what he thought was going to serve me down the road. When he felt the time was right, he sent me off into the world to be on my own.

He gave me the nudge he believed I needed because he set me up for success. He thought that he had provided the necessary tools, and he let me go when he believed I could stand on my own two feet. He felt he had done everything he could for me, and it was time for him to follow his dreams finally. He loved his children, but he was ready to put himself first.

I may have stumbled along the way over the years, but I've finally discovered solid footing now too.

Both of my parents have allowed me to walk my own path and discover my freedom. I am living my truth, even if it took a while to find it. Even if it took me many years of shattering and breaking and building myself back up again. I am here. I am free.

The past is in the past. I must officially say goodbye to the house across the lake. To the pieces that once held me captive. To the secrets that trapped me.

The memories exist only as a ripple in the water—a microscopic break in the smooth, shiny surface of the lake. A flash of laughter across the reflection of my youth.

Day 304: September 28, 2021

We turn the corner and make a sharp left onto Gray Street in Boston. A night out in the city. I look up at the familiar brick buildings on both sides of me. I stretch my arms up in the air and spin around in the middle of the road.

"Oh, my God, it looks exactly the same!" I yell, laughing, letting go of Evan's hand.

"Yep, and people still park bumper to bumper," Evan says, pointing to the cars parked along the sidewalk.

"This place is a restaurant now, that's strange," I say, pointing to the old run-down building that used to reside at the end of the block. We continue down the middle of our old street in the heart of the South End of Boston, the leaves crunching beneath our feet.

The night is bustling, and people are headed out for the evening. A couple walks down the front steps of their apartment, hand in hand, laughing to one another. They scamper off down the street, deep in conversation. I look up at the empty apartment they just came from and think how that used to be us ten years ago.

"They're headed out to dinner, and we're already done!" I say, considering the delicious meal we just had around the corner at Coppa, one of our old favorite spots.

The moonlight creates a walkway for us down the middle of the quiet road. We walk and peer into the windows of the street-level apartments.

Looking at the cobblestone sidewalk beneath my feet, I remember pushing the double stroller over this uneven surface in a rainstorm. I think about my two small crying children tucked underneath the rain cover. How many times did I walk these streets just wishing the day away? Begging it all to fast-forward? Wanting it to get easier? Wondering when it would be five o'clock so I could have a drink?

We come upon the door to our beautiful old brick row house. It hasn't changed all that much. It still has the rounded entryway leading down the garden-level stairwell. The wrought iron gate looks the same, and the original rusted doorbell remains broken on the wall outside by the number 29A, hanging slightly crooked now on the old bricks.

We smile up at the building and the memories it holds, and Evan pulls me into his body. I lay my head on his shoulder. He knows I'm sad, as this is a part of our lives that we both cherished, but that chapter has been closed for so long. I brought my two babies home to this apartment. I stare up at the window off the street that was once their shared bedroom. I recall the night I sat below the lamplight watching the snowflakes flutter down, alone in the darkness with Brayden as a newborn, so many years ago.

I look at Evan and think about how broken I was back then, and how disconnected he and I were when we first became parents. All the trust and confidence I had in us was shattered at the time. How completely destroyed I felt ten years ago over the hurt Evan had caused me. I know now that I turned to alcohol as the only thing that brought me comfort during such a dark, frightening time in my life. As a new mother, I'd felt isolated from the moment my baby was born.

The memories of the beginning of our life together are cloaked in sadness, but I see so much light, too. Because I have learned from every experience. Evan has stood by me and supported me through the most difficult of times. We are connected on a cellular level, and for that, I am grateful.

I never could have seen the twists and turns my path would take. I didn't anticipate how much harder it would get. I didn't understand how far Evan and I would spiral as he watched me fall victim to the chains of addiction.

I wish I could sit beside myself in that cold nursery ten years ago, that new mother who sat crying, so scared, so alone with her infant in her arms, watching the snowflakes fall. I wish I could just whisper to her that it would all be okay someday—that she, her husband, and her family would all come out better in the end.

Evan and I continue down Gray Street, admiring the fall decorations on the doors.

"I'm going to start a podcast, I think," I tell Evan.

He stops walking and turns to me. "What do you mean?" he asks, confused.

"I'm going to do a podcast. I've been thinking about this, and I want to do it. I don't know how, but I'll learn. I want to talk to the world about everything I've been through this past year. Catherine and I have thought about doing it together. It's time people hear my story. I want to help others. I want to share my experience. I have nothing to hide, and I think I can help people. Other moms like me. Women like me. No secrets."

"I think that's amazing," Evan tells me.

We walk on, hand in hand, leaving behind the memories from our first home and closing a long overdue chapter from the past.

No secrets.

Day 365: November 28, 2021 (One Year Sober)

"Let's go, guys, who wants ice cream?" I call to the kids as I finish placing the last of the dirty dishes into the dishwasher. There is no complaining from anyone. All three kids come rushing around the corner through the kitchen and toward the back door. There's a mad dash to find sneakers and boots, and there's zero need to remind them to grab a jacket.

Everyone is excited about tonight's celebration.

"Let's go, Dad! Time to celebrate Mom's soberversary!" Chase yells.

"I bet Mom is getting a sundae!" Evan says with a smile on his face as he joins the kids at the back door with his jacket.

"I want a milkshake!" Parker says.

"Do they have root beer floats?" Brayden asks.

"Okay, I'm about ready now. Let me put this platter away and we can go," I tell them.

I finish cleaning up the kitchen from dinner and carry the clean casserole dish into the dining room to put back into the storage hutch, wiping it off with a rag as I walk into the dark room. I switch the light on with my elbow, listening to my children arguing over ice cream toppings and planning out their desserts.

I stand alone in the dining room and look at myself in the oversized mirror. I hesitate for a moment before the hutch that used to function as our bar top. The surface sits empty except for a round glass Simon Pearce bowl. There are no more handles of Tito's or Casamigos. We no longer have bottles of expensive wine lining the countertop. Gone are the shot glasses covered in a thin layer of alcohol residue that once crowded the grimy tray. A small layer of dust remains where the many bottles of half-drunk alcohol used to reside. I open the cabinet and put the casserole dish away.

"Kim, are you ready?" Evan asks.

"Yep, one second. Just putting this dish away. I'm coming right now."

"Okay, we'll be in the car waiting."

The mudroom door slams shut as Evan and the kids head outside to the car. I stand alone.

It's quiet. I contemplate the many times I paused in the silence of this house, just as I am now. How many times did I stand in this position, staring at this bar top, while my family waited for me in the car? How often did I precisely position the bathroom door just right? I hear the final whispers of a paralyzing memory that has only begun to fade.

I look at my reflection in the mirror above the hutch, reminding myself that I'll never be on the edge of shattering into a thousand tiny pieces ever again. I will never experience that darkness. I smile and walk out of the house to join my waiting family.

From an early age, I was taught to keep secrets. My parents were never able to acknowledge the challenges they faced, and they lived in the shadows for many years. They likely did this to protect my family from the town of Greenwich, the culture, and the times we lived in. I believe my parents did what they hoped was best for me at the time, but what was modeled for me was detrimental to my growth as a person. I learned to feel ashamed of the things that set me apart from others. I felt shame for the problems in my life. I learned to lie and cope with this discomfort in unhealthy ways. As I grew older, I began to conceal parts of myself to portray the image I wanted the world to see. My childhood was a good one, but it was built on deception, and I turned to alcohol to help me be who I wanted to be, to cope with unwanted emotions and to manage the world's expectations of me.

As an adult, I mastered the ability to deceive others and to hide my most dreaded flaws, refusing to acknowledge my past wounds, allowing very few to see the real me. Like other family members before me, I figured out that by not feeling certain emotions or by not acknowledging my truth, I could escape reality. I could hide from the people that harmed me but also could be who I wanted to be. Alcohol helped me do this.

Too scared to confront the realities that had come to define who I was, I spent the majority of my life focused on maintaining a faultless, perfect image. Alcohol helped me achieve that. I was often attempting to escape my wrongdoings before they could catch up with me. The people that hurt me would not destroy what I had built, so I buried the painful secrets and the traumas of my past under bottles of alcohol.

As a mother, I wanted to do everything right. I wanted to be the best I could be for my three children because things didn't end the way they were supposed to end for me when I was young. I was unknowingly taught to hide in the shadows. I was expected to shy away from the struggles before me. I was unaware that the examples laid out for me as a child would cause me such a hard time later in my life. So I stayed stuck. I began to drink more and more, denying myself a sense of understanding who I really was. I let the shame bury me.

For many years, I was too scared to feel vulnerable enough to face the reality of my past and what I was doing to my present and future self. Little did I know that these behaviors would cause me to avoid ever truly feeling. I avoided experiencing my children. My marriage. And my life. Until I had fallen deep enough into the darkness, and I had grown entirely weak.

Over the years, I've discovered how to be independent. To do things for myself, to parent differently from the way my parents did and to think in a manner other than how I was raised. I have learned from my past mistakes. But I didn't allow myself to be fully vulnerable, as I still was hiding behind alcohol for so very long. It wasn't until I nearly drowned in darkness that I realized something needed to change before all of my secrets destroyed me.

One year ago, on November 28, 2020, things shifted. That was the day that came to define me. I woke up, and everything about my life from that day forward was different. That was the day I decided to step out from the shadows. I had to start living each day differently, and living it for me. For my marriage. For my children. I needed to change it all or just slip away.

So I jumped off the runaway train that was my life, and somehow I managed to land on two feet, my unsteady legs wobbling beneath me. I decided to finally be seen. Face it all head-on and start feeling for the first time in a long time. From that day forward, there was no more hiding.

That was the day I fully embraced my vulnerability. I found the courage I needed to start living and feeling again.

That was the day I quit drinking alcohol.

That was the day I chose freedom.

EPILOGUE

In the early summer of my first year of sobriety, we moved away from the large modern home on the busy corner in Needham, leaving behind a house that contained years of darkness.

It's strange to look back on my life and all the homes I lived in. It was as if I'd always been running, searching for something I wasn't quite sure I'd ever find.

I was unhappy with how disconnected I felt with so many aspects of my life, and I blamed it on the physical spaces that I inhabited. It was always the houses that I resided in, the street, the town, or the neighborhood.

But in actuality it was a different part of me that needed mending. Internally and emotionally, I needed to be healed. It just so happened that we simultaneously found our dream home around the same time I decided to finally begin the process of fixing myself.

Alcohol had become a piece of my foundation and was so ingrained in who I was. The memories in our last home were clouded and darkened from the end of my drinking days. It was time to start fresh, with a clean slate in a new space.

We found a new home just down the road, and we still live in Needham at the end of a quiet neighborhood. It feels as if the final piece of our puzzle is complete.

The house we moved into is an older cape-style home. It is nestled on the banks of the Charles River yet still walking distance to town. Something about it felt perfectly right. It was time to move on from the newer, ostentatious home on the flashy corner of the fun party neighborhood. The house that held many memories from Parker's first Christmas through the dark, depressing months of quarantine when I was drinking too much. The walls that had seen an incredible amount and held too many secrets. The house that held so many lies.

I sat in that house one last morning surrounded by boxes in my favorite room—what I had come to call the blue room—on the morning that the movers arrived. The walls were covered in beautiful navy-blue grass cloth wallpaper, but since it was now filled with boxes, it no longer felt elegant or special. But I had always loved that room.

When designing the space, I pictured late-night gatherings around bottles of wine and plates of cheese. My vision came to fruition a few times, in fact. But I never remembered much from those nights, as they always ended in blurry blackouts.

It had been over a year since we'd hosted a party in that room. The walls that had seen many a drunken night laid witness to quieter days in recent weeks. That room came to be the space where Evan and I snuck off to have our coffee at six o'clock in the morning in the weeks prior to moving, planning out the next chapter of our lives. I never would have been able to wake up that early before because I was always too hungover.

Evan and I agreed it was time to find a different type of room to relax in. It was time to make new memories. To have coffee on a porch and stare at the river and enjoy many more early mornings in a brand-new, fresh space together with the kids.

When we first stepped foot in the new house down the road, it had a familiarity to it. I felt an energy instantly fill my soul with a warmth that I once knew. Our new property is vast, lush, and vibrantly full of grass, trees, and woods to explore. You don't hear traffic rushing by, only the sounds of birds chirping. The river is a private sanctuary right in our own backyard, a quiet place to fish, relax, or be alone. The neighborhood, filled with other young families with kids similar in ages to ours, is safe for children to bike around and explore. Brayden can finally roam.

The first time I saw this house, I imagined myself climbing the trees in the yard as a child. I envisioned Kimmy as a little girl creating a home in the clearing down by the river and playing make-believe in the woods out back. I pictured myself rowing a boat out on the river or fishing with the kids, just as I would have done thirty years ago. I knew this was the right spot for us. There was an undeniable calm and peacefulness at this home. A change we all so desperately needed.

Once we moved in, I found a room that gives me greater comfort than I ever knew. A room that faces the river, trees, birds, and expansive sky. The sun porch is filled with warmth and a new kind of energy. I feel a sense of safety and peacefulness, a feeling I never knew I needed from a home. This is where I spend my time writing.

I am grateful for the path that brought us here, the long meandering road through darkness that directed us to such a bright, beautiful spot. Our new house encompasses all of the things we need out of a home and everything I ever wanted for my children.

My dad came to visit our new house in the first few weeks, and I watched his body relax into the overstuffed chair as he absorbed the sounds of the sanctuary before him.

With the windows all around him, he looked out at the sky, the tall pine trees, the birds in the bushes, and the wide river before him. We sat in silence for a while, admiring the beauty before us.

"This is just magical, Kim, what a terrific spot," he said. "It's so quiet and peaceful! It reminds me of the Lake."

He looked around in wonder. And then he leaned his head back and closed his eyes. I imagined the memories of Winterset Road and Spofford Lake flooding his mind, as they do mine every day when I sit in these chairs. We relaxed in the sunroom together, allowing the images of our past to fill the space between us. Knowing that we still shared a love and appreciation for the simpler parts of life, I felt a connection to him that I hadn't felt in years.

I know my parents always wanted me to be happy. They gave me a childhood full of joy, wonder, and comfort on Winterset Road, at the lake, and in all of our special places throughout New England, as well as on our regular trips to Bermuda. But they had their own dark secrets they struggled to make sense of for so long.

My new home on the Charles River encapsulates so much of what is good from my childhood. I am able to call out from the deck to my children in the safety of our yard, just as my mother once did for me when I was a child.

As I prepare dinner in the kitchen in the evenings, I gaze out the windows and see my three kids running through the yard as I used to do. I'm grateful to be able to play the same role of loving mother for my children as my own mom did so well for me throughout my entire childhood. I'm present and here for all of it now, not hiding behind a haze of alcohol as I once was.

A type of euphoria and joy exists in all of us now, as I am reminded of what is pure in this life. There is a similar energy from my youth in this new home, a kind of solace and peace emanating from the walls. A simplicity. A vulnerability. At the same time, all the goodness that my parents taught me as a child has been rediscovered inside the fibers of my sober being, and for that, I am truly grateful. All the love they gave me, I carry it with me.

I know, within this home, this is where my kids are meant to grow up. In this space, I will flourish in my new state of joy and mindfulness. This is where we will find our strength.

As I walk around my house and move about my day, I feel the best parts of what I learned from my parents with me every day. I'm grateful for where I have ended up and all that I have learned.

Today, I am no longer falling and no longer drowning in darkness. The shadowy chasm has disappeared, and instead, there is nothing but wide-open, beautiful opportunities. Expansive, endless paths to search. I look around now and am no longer stuck. I'm not spending my days frantically crawling up and out, clawing at the earth, attempting to escape the enormous, crushing waves.

I have found quietude. I was lucky enough to get away. I was able to discover the light, as I escaped the darkness at last. My world is now brighter. It welcomes me with a colorful, calm, and fragrant feeling.

Today, alcohol no longer controls me.

Today, and every day, belongs to me.

Today, I am free.

AFTERWORD

Within the first week of quitting, I became addicted to my sobriety. I joined The Sober Mom Squad and The Luckiest Club, two online support groups, and I attended daily Zoom meetings.

I became obsessed with everything recovery. I read all the quit-lit books I could get my hands on, and I followed hundreds of accounts on Instagram, soon starting my own sobriety account (@asoberandstrongmom).

My voice had become so stifled as an adolescent and as an early adult because of all the secrets I had to keep. I finally found the power in my voice, and writing allowed me to express it. I created a blog (www.kimberlykearns.com) and began writing about my experiences almost daily and then weekly, and suddenly, for the first time in nearly twenty years, the words just came. They flowed freely and unapologetically. I found the best way to heal was to read about other people's stories and then write about my own experiences. I found the writing to be therapeutic. The words began to pour out of me as if they'd been stuck inside for over twenty years, hidden under bottles and bottles of booze.

I journaled every free morning, and I walked several miles every afternoon while listening to a variety of recovery podcasts. I rode the Peloton in the evening hours when Ursula, the wine witch, would start her chanting, and I went to bed early most nights after long, relaxing baths. I started therapy with an amazing woman named Ronni.

I did everything I was supposed to do in early recovery. I did all the self-care. I was slowly putting my life back together, and I was becoming a better, more present mom.

That was what kept me going. No secrets. No lies.

I worked hard on my blog. I made it public. People began to read it.

I started sharing my story with friends and proudly talking to the people I could at first trust. I realized, after putting myself out there, that there was freedom in the truth. Freedom in authenticity. Freedom in the journey. And through it all, I was finding joy and gratefulness for the experiences I had.

And I began to work on my relationships that needed mending. Many continue to be worked on still.

Day by day, I was becoming more present. I was feeling. By allowing a more authentic relationship with the world, I was slowly beginning to heal. I was writing about all these experiences, and people were listening. Friends were reaching out to me, telling me they were reading my blog, following my Instagram account, and reevaluating their own relationships with alcohol. People understood me. They were telling me they felt similar things. I was strong for putting it out there, they said.

I have a sobriety podcast now with my friend Catherine, and I'm the head writer for season three of the Webby Award-winning narrative podcast *F*cking Sober: The First 90 Days*.

Today, I continue to work on myself and repair the cracks in my life. At home, with regular meditation, I focus on the moments I am in each day, letting the memories of the past slip away. I have slowly stopped blaming myself for the mistakes I made over the many years with alcohol in my life. I've learned to find joy in the small moments. I've allowed myself to feel vulnerable again by reflecting on the traumas and events of my childhood and past. I stopped allowing the memories to control me. Now, I will continue to tell my story so others don't have to quietly suffer in silence.

Today, I continue to heal. And at thirty-nine years old, I feel like I'm finally comfortable being me.

ACKNOWLEDGMENTS

This book exists because of those who held my hand, pumped me up, wiped my tears, and listened to me talk endlessly. There are many people that experienced this adventure with me over the last couple of years, but there are a few specific individuals in particular who truly walked along beside me.

First, I want to thank my husband for his unwavering love, support, and understanding as I navigated my complicated relationship with alcohol for the last fourteen years of our marriage. As this story tells, he and I have seen each other through many different, turbulent times. Thank you, Evan, for encouraging me to tell my story my way. Thank you for letting me share my emotional truth. Thank you for showing me endless compassion. Thank you for remaining by me every step of the way. You have always been my strongest supporter, my biggest cheerleader, and the one person I know I can count on to give me the most honest advice. You read countless versions of this book, and you never complained once. Thank you for still getting excited to read my blog posts and liking all my Instagram reels. You cry more easily than I do, but you will always be better at loading the dishwasher than I will ever be. I love you for everything you do for this beautiful family of ours. You are my reason "why."

I want to acknowledge my three children: Brayden, Chase, and Parker. Thank you to my kids for being the other reason why I got sober. You three truly give me hope every day to keep moving forward in this sober life. I am grateful for each of you, and being your mom is a special gift. Because of you, I did one of the hardest things in the world, something I doubted for a long time that I had the strength to ever do. You three truly helped me find the courage to emerge from that darkness. So thank you for saving my life. Thank you for saving our family. Thank you for making me the happiest mom . . . Every day, you guide me toward being a better human. You have allowed me to discover how to be more compassionate and kinder to myself. You have taught me forgiveness. You remind me to practice empathy. You show me how to love without limits. You make me laugh. You sometimes frustrate me, but you teach me patience. You show me what it's like to want to fight. To live. To thrive. I have learned how to tie hockey skates so tight my fingers bleed, and I have taught myself to sew a bow onto a neoprene leopard-print leotard. Everything I do in this world, I do it for you guys. That's why I'm asleep by eight most nights. You have everything I can give and a bit more. I love you three. Thank you for saving me. I hope one day, when you are all grown up, you will truly understand my story.

I want to acknowledge the friends that have stood by me. There are some that read this book for me when it was in its varying stages of development. Thank you to those people that cheered me on and encouraged me to tell my story. Jen Bird, thank you for sitting with me on my porch that morning in November. I wouldn't be where I am today if it wasn't for your friendship. There are some friends that simply bring out the best in people, and that is you. Catherine, Francy, and Clair: You are the three greatest ducks I could hope for. I never need to perform, you hold space for me and you have always been truly happy for my success. I love you all. Kaitlin, you have been there to guide me, even in the beginning when I never could make it to a single history seminar at Colby. Thank you for having my back. Cate, you read that draft in record speed, so thank you, friend. Maura, you stumbled upon my Instagram account when I thought it was private and when I told no one about my sobriety, but you were one of my biggest and earliest supporters, and I appreciate that. Thank you to the rest of my Colby girls: Allison, Mandy, Meaghan, Ashley, Grace, Anker, and Amanda—thank you for your years of friendship. I don't know what I would do without the daily texts, laughter, and love from all of you. Trish and Sarah, thank you for taking walks, listening, and always checking in. Megan M., we have so much history and have walked such similar paths, and for that, we will always be connected.

Katie Bannon, I appreciate your incredible edits. Katie Mack, thank you for believing in my writing when I was less than a month sober. You took a chance on a fragile little human and have supported me since the beginning. EmJ and Dillon, y'all are brilliant and truly have helped develop me as a writer. Ronni—I wouldn't be who I am or where I am in this world without your guidance all these months. Vince, Glass Spider Publishing, and Judith, thank you for your roles in helping to bring this book to life.

Thank you to The Luckiest Club, The Sober Mom Squad, my blog readers and Instagram followers, and all my other friends—you know who you are. I am grateful for you, and I appreciate the support along the way. To Annie Grace, Laura McKowen, Glennon Doyle, Caroline Knapp, Clare Pooley, Catherine Gray, and all the other brave, sober women that came before me, thank you for having the courage to tell your story. Thank you for going first.

Finally, I would like to acknowledge Mom, Dad, and my sisters. I know this book may have been difficult for you to read at times, but I hope you will see that through it all I love you and appreciate everything I have learned from you. Please take my story as a gift of vulnerability and authenticity.

ABOUT THE AUTHOR

Kimberly Kearns is a wife to an incredible husband and a mother to three beautiful children. She currently lives in Needham, Massachusetts. She continues to tell her story of sobriety and inspire others every day on her blog at www.kimberlykearns.com, and through her Instagram account @asoberandstrongmom.

Kimberly co-hosts the podcast *The Weekend Sober* and is a writer for the Webby Award-winning narrative podcast *F*cking Sober: The First 90 Days.*

Writing has always been an escape for Kimberly, even as a little girl. Being able to express herself in words and getting lost in her imagination has served as a source of comfort to her as far back as she can remember.

CPSIA information can be obtained
at www.ICGtesting.com
Printed in the USA
JSHW011134011022
31125JS00001B/7